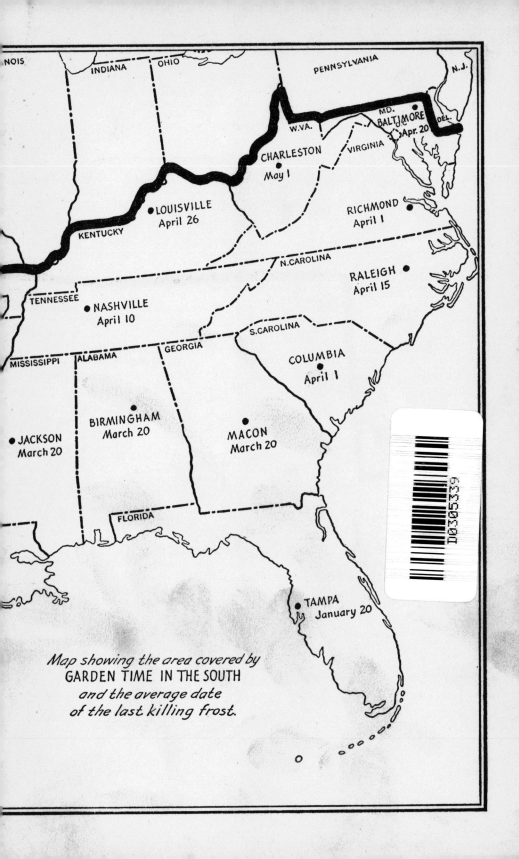

Map showing the area covered by
GARDEN TIME IN THE SOUTH
and the average date
of the last killing frost.

345 - 53

GARDEN TIME IN
THE SOUTH

Ancient boxwood sheltered by an ivy-draped brick wall.

GARDEN TIME IN THE SOUTH

BY
MATTIE ABNEY HARTZOG

1951

J. HORACE McFARLAND COMPANY
MOUNT PLEASANT PRESS
HARRISBURG, PA.

Completely Produced by

J. HORACE McFARLAND COMPANY
MOUNT PLEASANT PRESS
HARRISBURG, PA.

Dedicated

TO THE MEMORY OF
MY HUSBAND-COMPANION
ALBERT SIDNEY HARTZOG
TO WHOM I REFERRED AS
MY CRITIC

Preface

THE gardening information in this book is based on my own experience in planting in the Piedmont section of South Carolina and on scrapbooks about the South kept since 1930. With little change it applies to all the Southern States. And of course, many plants that grow in the South thrive in other parts of the country as well, the main difference being in the planting and flowering time. The directions given here may readily be adapted to other areas. Going north, the growing season is about a week later for each 100 miles of latitude and about the same for each 500 feet of elevation. If this book helps readers in their gardening or encourages them to make their home surroundings more beautiful, I shall feel repaid.

Each chapter is divided into a number of sections, each complete in itself. These subdivisions have been made for the convenience of garden clubs, although it is my hope that this will serve as a practical handbook for the individual as well. The central idea of each chapter and section is *time* in the garden.

I am indebted to the following for criticism on specific subjects: Mrs. Louie Blake, iris; Mrs. George W. Rush, flower arrangement; Dr. Sam C. Hodges, birds; Mrs. Cheney Meiere, gladioli; Mrs. J. P. Phillips, chrysanthemums; Mr. Dave C. Strother, camellias. I am grateful to *Flower Grower* for permission to use some diary material that I wrote for that magazine, and to my nephew, Henry K. Thayer, Jr., who gave suggestions on several sections. My appreciative thanks are given Mr. Harry L. Watson for the Introduction.

I shall always remember that the late Dr. J. Horace McFarland, horticulturist and author, gave me hope that my manuscript merited publication. My thanks also are extended to Miss Catherine E. Meikle for her interest and help, to Mrs. Albert D. Oliphant for her assistance and to the owners of gardens who so generously permitted me the use of illustrative material.

Without the understanding and encouragement of my husband, A. Sidney Hartzog, and his brother, Dr. Henry S. Hartzog, who read the entire manuscript, this book would never have been written.

MATTIE ABNEY HARTZOG

Contents

V For Bloom The Year Round

VI Emphasis On Color

VII Plants For Special Purposes

VIII Some Features Not To Be Overlooked

List of Illustrations

LIST OF ILLUSTRATIONS

xiv

Introduction

EVERYWHERE in the United States today there is a lively interest in garden cultivation. Especially active is this interest in flower gardens, but vegetable gardens are not overlooked, and fruits, both small and tree grown, are included. Enthusiastic gardeners of all types are found not only in the purely rural areas but even more so in the towns and cities. Almost every small community has a garden club, and in larger places such clubs may be counted almost by the dozen.

This revival of interest in the oldest occupation known to man is a most wholesome thing. But one great difficulty confronting the would-be cultivator of either flowers or vegetables, is the practical knowledge of how to do it and When. That "When" is capitalized because of its capital importance. Seeds planted at the wrong time will not produce flowers or fruit no matter how fertile the ground or how diligent the cultivation.

It is the purpose of this comprehensive and thoroughly practical book by Mrs. Mattie Abney Hartzog of Greenwood, S. C., to tell all garden lovers and workers in plain and understandable language just When things should be planted and how they should be worked.

Mrs. Hartzog has proved in her own state that she has the knowledge, supported by long and successful experience, to supply the needs of the amateur. To her through the years have come young and old gardeners, wanting to know what to plant and when to plant and what to do after the planting has been successful. In this book there are just the things they wanted to know. The matter of climate is properly given first place. All the other essentials, such as planning the garden, preparing the soil, location as to sun and shade, and how some of the South's most famous gardens have come into being, are set down so that both amateur and experienced gardeners will find pleasure and profit in reading.

Too many gardeners drop into the same class as certain flowers and fruits. That is to say, they work in their garden for only a certain part of the season and "let the garden go," as we say, for the rest of the year. Mrs. Hartzog shows that plants should never be neglected. Gardens can be, and should be, worked in spring, in summer, in autumn and in winter. One may have fresh flowers and vegetables on the table every month in the year.

Mrs. Hartzog's home is known and admired by flower lovers all over this part of the state. Some years ago the author began the work of reclaiming the flower garden, the vegetable garden and the orchard of the old home. She started then a program of landscaping and seasonal planting with the objective of having something coming, something going, and something blooming at its best every month of the year. Each year Mrs. Hartzog has worked out some new feature with the help of a few field hands from the farm. The results of this planning are now seen in one of the most attractive places in the city. The soils in all the planted areas around the home have been cultivated for well over a century, but today they are more fertile and productive than ever before, thanks to proper enrichment and expert cultivation. Here is an impressive example of the potential beauty of restoration in an old garden when modern knowledge is given an opportunity.

Mrs. Hartzog has kept a careful account of her work, much of it having been published in recent years in *The Flower Grower*. By reason of this day-by-day record of flower and vegetable growing, she has a really marvelous store of information and experience to draw upon. The present volume contains all this valuable and helpful data for the person who wants to start a garden but "does not know how," as well as for more skilled gardeners who still have some problems unsolved. The book is plain and practical; while it has a "southern exposure," it is adaptable to any and all sections of the country.

H. L. WATSON
Editor, The Greenwood (S.C.) *Index-Journal*

Visitors to the low South are sure to comment on the showy bloom of the bougainvillea. This vigorous climber blooms over a long period. (See page 57.)

A northern Florida garden makes generous use of greens to give a cool and restful effect. Situated as it is on different levels, it is easily viewed from this terrace where the shadows cast a checkerboard to match the flagstones.

Chapter I

Times Past And Present In Southern Gardens

OUR DEBT TO GARDENERS OF YESTERDAY

Among the first gardeners in the South who wrote of their experiences were Mrs. Lamboll, who grew flowers and vegetables before 1750, and Mrs. Martha Logan. Both lived in Charleston, S. C. Mrs. Logan kept a garden record and compiled it after she was seventy years old. It appeared in *The Gardener's Kalendar* after her death, in 1779.

After such pioneers as these came a host of nurserymen and plantsmen who found in the benign climate of the South the perfect setting for their experiments in cultural methods. Home gardeners are greatly indebted to these early growers, whose work was the basis for all the wonderful accomplishments of modern hybridizers.

Among the most famous horticulturists of the South was P. J. Berckmans, who was born in Belgium in 1830 and died at Fruitland Nurseries in Augusta, Ga., in 1910. He devoted his life to the advancement of southern horticulture. He founded the Georgia State Horticultural Society and served as its president from 1876 until his death.

Pliny Ford Reasoner collected and grew many semitropical and tropical plants. He was born in Illinois in 1863 and went to Florida in 1882. The plants tested in Royal Palm Nurseries, owned by Reasoner and a younger brother, are grown all over the lower South.

Henry Martin Stringfellow, who was born in Virginia in 1839 and died at Fayetteville, Ark., in 1912, spent most of his life in Texas opening the way for horticulture in waste lands by introducing new methods of drainage. He started the first pear orchard on the Gulf Coast. Texas is also indebted to him for the first Satsuma orange groves. His practice of pruning roots and tops of young fruit trees severely before transplanting is still referred to as the "Stringfellow method."

William Fletcher Heikes, born in Ohio in 1837, took over his father's nursery near Dayton and moved the business to Huntsville, Ala., in 1872. He was the first nurseryman to have nursery stock kept in cold storage during the shipping season and was the originator of the double root-grafting method of propagating. He died in 1911, having been president of the Alabama Horticultural Society from its beginning in 1903.

John S. Downer, of Culpeper County, Virginia, was a prominent pomologist early in the present century. He did a great deal toward improving fruit growing and for many years maintained a fruit experiment station at his nursery at Elkton, Ky.

These and many others helped to set high standards for gardening in the South. The present intense interest in plants and planting is a good omen for the future; it leads one to hope that our heritage of lovely gardens will be cherished, augmented by the large and small gardens being started every year.

A garden furnishes so much in the way of pleasure, seclusion, recreation and exercise that it seems almost impossible to live without one. Nowhere else can such peace of mind be achieved—and in these days, that means a lot!

SOME CELEBRATED SOUTHERN GARDENS

From earliest times the South has been noted for its gardens. Many of them have been preserved for us and are growing more and more beautiful with the passing years. Let us take a brief look at a few famous gardens in the upper, middle and lower areas of the South.

Mount Vernon is an excellent example of an eighteenth-century plantation. This estate has been restored and is maintained by the Mount Vernon Ladies' Association, founded by Miss Ann Pamela Cunningham of South Carolina and chartered by the state of Virginia. The garden today is practically as George Washington planned it before the Revolution. Some of the boxwood was planted as early as 1798, or before that time, and it is thought that a number of the large trees were set out in 1785. The restored kitchen garden follows the pattern of the times.

In Williamsburg, the colonial capital of the Old Dominion, where the gardens as well as the buildings have been reconstructed in the manner of the eighteenth century, one can readily visualize the past. Clipped holly hedges, boxwood, borders of violets and ground covers of ivy and honeysuckle are especially noticeable. In the spring the flowering bulbs are a joy to see. The green type of garden, with extensive use of trees and dwarf boxwood, gives Williamsburg a restful charm.

2

Only those trees, shrubs, flowers and vines known to have been used during the colonial period are growing in Williamsburg gardens; for example, magnolias, flowering dogwoods, oaks, red maple, sweet gum and pines; crape-myrtle, lilac, chaste-tree and pink-flowered bush honeysuckle; iris, rosemary, blue phlox and primroses. Old-fashioned roses are abundant, the beds bordered with greenery. In the fruit gardens are such trees as apple, peach, cherry, fig and pomegranate. Some are espaliered, to save space and add to the beauty of the garden.

In many historic gardens of Virginia, specimen tree boxwood, hedges of boxwood and borders of truedwarf boxwood are important features. Many of these plants are more than a century old. In some gardens are hedges of Virginia cedar, as well as terraces, sunken plantings, rose gardens and herb borders. Magnificent spreading trees and weeping willows often form accent points, while old-fashioned shrubs and other flowering plants are arranged in formal squares.

Thomas Jefferson not only designed his home at Monticello, Va., but did the landscape planning of the grounds. The Garden Club of Virginia is restoring the property.

A study of the plans of old-fashioned gardens enables one to reproduce some of their charming effects. It is interesting to note how old-time gardens seem to be an extension of the house, and how formal and informal plantings are blended. Gardens that are carefully planned and planted and properly tended show even more character as they are mellowed by age.

The gardens near Charleston, S. C., are world-famous. Thousands of tourists visit them annually, especially when camellias and azaleas are flowering. Middleton Gardens, one of these places near Charleston, comprising 45 areas, is believed to be the oldest landscaped garden in America. It is thought to have been laid out before 1740; at any rate, it was well planted in 1750. A hundred slaves are said to have labored nearly ten years to build the undulating terraces that stretch in the foreground to the lagoon called Butterfly Lake. There are balanced paths and lovely vistas, with wide lawns and terraces fronting the Ashley River. In the spring the garden is resplendent with the gorgeous colors of camellias and azaleas. Three of the original camellia plants brought to Middleton Place by the celebrated French botanist André Michaux are said to be among those that still bloom. One planted between 1783 and 1785 is 21 feet 9 inches high, with a spread of 33 feet and a circumference of 63 inches. Groups of crape-myrtles and cape-jasmine come into bloom later. The rose garden is shaped like a huge pie sliced with walks. Everywhere are venerable trees. One estimated at 900 years has a circumference of 37 feet and a diameter of more than 8 feet.

A few miles away are the Magnolia Gardens, belonging to an estate that has been in the Drayton family for 250 years. There had been a garden on the Drayton place from early colonial days, and about a century ago the grandfather of the present owner, in search of health in the open air, designed the gardens as they now are. Today there are 24 acres of informal wonderland. The winding paths are bordered with camellias and azaleas, some planted in 1843 and so large as to infringe on the walks. The tallest camellia in America is said to grow here. It is the variety John Harvard, 29 feet 6 inches high, with a spread of 21 feet and a circumference of 50 inches. Yellow jessamine, wisteria, Banksia and Cherokee roses swing from the trees. There are grand specimens of *Magnolia grandiflora*, numerous hollies, cedars, dogwoods and other trees and shrubs. The reflections in the lakes give back the enchanting coloring and make this a place loved by artists. Indeed, it is "an earthly paradise," as it has been called.

Cypress Gardens, 24 miles north of Charleston, were opened to the public for the first time in 1930. Originally this was a freshwater lake on a rice plantation. It was abandoned for more than a century to a wild growth of the subtropical vegetation of the Carolina coast. Now it is a fairyland of flowers where one may follow bright paths through the forest or paddle in a blue canoe through its waterways, the depth of which is little over 3 feet.

Here man has added such plants as *Daphne odora* to enhance what nature has already provided. The first plantings of these were made in 1930, and now these fragrant shrubs make a lovely display. The view is almost breath-taking as one glides under rustic cypress bridges covered with vines. In the spring there is the exquisite beauty of azaleas, bulbs and Spanish irises; wisterias hang in festoons from trees on the banks and islands, to which Banksia roses add their charms. As far as one can see is a background of large flowering dogwood and redbud. During summer and fall water-lilies and victorias are enticing in both leaf and flower.

Growing in the water are not only the old and new cypress trees with their tender green shoots but many black gums and pines. Numerous ferns thrive at the water's edge, and native marsh lilies (Zephyranthes) and wildflowers accompany the new large narcissi.

4

McKee's Jungle Gardens at Vero Beach, Fla., offer
plants from various parts of the world in addition to the
tropical specimens native to the region.   (See page 6.)

Azaleas at Bellingrath Gardens, near Mobile, Ala., are admired for their blending of color.

In the low-country gardens of South Carolina nothing is so surpassingly beautiful as the flaming colors of azaleas reflected in the onyx water. (Tannic acid from the roots of trees makes the clear water look dark.) Giant live oaks and bald cypresses draped with great veils of Spanish moss give a weird aspect to the scene. The combination of blending colors, bird songs and whiffs of fragrance makes one feel he is in another world.

Azaleas of China, imported from France, have been notable in Mobile, Ala., for almost 200 years. Some of the bushes are between 15 and 20 feet high. Only in recent years has an effort been made to let the public know of them. Now there is a drive of many miles through the city and its suburbs, lined with plantings. Along Mobile's Azalea Trail, so showy in spring, are guideposts to many interesting places.

Bellingrath Gardens is a remarkable place, appropriately called a "Charm Spot of the Deep South." Here 60 acres have been landscaped where originally grew wild magnolias, holly, dogwoods, pines, bays, live and water oaks entangled with gray moss. The natural beauty has been preserved and increased by the use of numerous camellias of both Sasanqua and Japonica types, azaleas in variety and other shrubs. Many azaleas are naturalized and show to advantage among the trees.

The development of Bellingrath Gardens was begun about 1928 under the supervision of the owners, Mr. and Mrs. Walter D. Bellingrath, whose dream of having gardens charming every month in the year has come true. Among the many plants that change the coloring of the place as the seasons pass are allamanda, double-flowered white spirea, mountain-laurel, cape-jasmine, oleander, hibiscus and crape-myrtle. Venerable oaks and tall pines hung with Spanish moss frame vistas of beauty. There are fountains and natural streams to reflect the various ranges of color. The gardens are located on a bluff overlooking the junction of three rivers. As one views an expanse of green lawns, with flagstone walks leading to beauty spots, and hears the trickling of water and the singing of mockingbirds, while inhaling the sweet perfume of flowers such as the sweet olive (*Osmanthus fragrans*), he wonders how any garden could be more marvelous.

In Natchez, Miss., on bluffs above the Mississippi River, magnificent houses of the colonial and ante-bellum period stand today, emblems of old-time southern hospitality. Each spring pilgrimages to Natchez, where the old South still lives, are sponsored by local

5

garden clubs. Their purpose is to preserve the traditions of this area and to restore gardens and buildings to the glory of their former days. The houses with their original furniture and heirlooms and the gardens with their ancient trees, boxwoods, camellias, azaleas and cape-jasmine are intensely interesting. Live oak avenues lead to some of the places. A visitor to Natchez, surrounded by stately homes of bygone days and charming old gardens, can learn much about gardening. Old plants that have grown more beautiful with time help us to realize the possibilities of a modern garden.

At Vero Beach on the Indian River in Florida, are located McKee's Jungle Gardens. Tropical trees and many semitropical plants grow here. The wide collection of plants from various parts of the world makes these gardens of particular botanical interest. It is said that the largest group of water-lilies growing out-of-doors the year around in America may be seen in these gardens. Here too, orchids are naturalized upon trees. Cow-horn orchids (*Cyrtopodium punctatum*), native to southern Florida, are quite striking with their variegated tones of greenish yellow and reddish brown. Great masses of them form on trees, and each plant bears a multitude of flowers.

Historic Garden Week in Virginia, the Maryland House and Garden Pilgrimage, Open House Week in Kentucky, the New Orleans Spring Fiesta and various other special tours are bringing appreciative visitors to old southern mansions and gardens in growing numbers.

Chapter II

It's Time To Learn The Fundamentals

CLIMATIC ZONES IN THE SOUTH

In the South, taken as a whole, there is a Coastal zone, the Piedmont plains at the foot of the mountains, and the Mountain section. What is known as the Fall line runs approximately through Holly Springs and Columbus, Miss.; Montgomery, Ala.; Columbus, Macon and Augusta, Ga.; Camden and Columbia, S. C.; and Raleigh and Weldon, N. C. The Coastal zone extends from this Fall line to the Atlantic Ocean and the Gulf of Mexico. The Piedmont plains lie between the Coastal zone and the mountains. The upper or Mountain zone runs near the Kentucky line and includes Maryland, parts of North Carolina, Tennessee, Georgia, Alabama, Virginia and South Carolina. Formerly the "Deep South" included the lower and part of the western section of Alabama, Louisiana, parts of Texas and even Arkansas; sometimes Georgia and South Carolina are now included in the term, although they used to be considered a part of the "Upper South."

From a gardener's point of view the Southern States include Virginia, Tennessee, North Carolina, South Carolina, Georgia, Florida, Alabama, Mississippi, Louisiana, Texas, Arkansas, Maryland, West Virginia, Kentucky, lower Missouri and Oklahoma.

Southern Texas and the Gulf Coast are subtropical and the southern part of Florida is tropical. It would be difficult to make an exact map of the subtropical area and the lower and upper austral regions, for the boundary lines are indefinite in most of the states. Arkansas, lower Missouri, Kentucky, West Virginia, Virginia and Tennessee belong to the border region, others to the southern region, and Maryland also by tradition to the southern region. All of these have the "southern atmosphere."

The Southern States differ in climate, soil and elevation. A few hundred feet of altitude makes a considerable difference in the seasons. Although the four seasons bring changes in the temperature, it is pleasant to work outdoors in the South some days of every month in the year.

Occasionally early-blooming flowers are killed by a freeze even

7

in the warmer areas. Frost occurs as late as March in the lower South, April in the middle section and May in the mountain area. In the upper sections there is apt to be frost early in October; usually a killing frost does not come in the middle section until November.

As in other parts of the United States, the South has very dry and then again quite wet periods. A sudden change of weather is likely to occur, possibly of short duration. But even with the disappointments and mistakes that are sure to accompany our unpredictable weather, gardening is a fascinating adventure.

PLAN BEFORE PLANTING

Originally a garden was an inclosed area where plants were cultivated. Today the word has broadened to include the complete surroundings about the house. The individual trees, shrubs, flowering plants and lawn areas are not so important as the way they are arranged. One should have a plan for enhancing the beauty of the setting around the home; without it there is danger of overplanting. Thoughtful planning saves both material and labor, for plants can readily be moved on paper. A good plan indicates where immediate planting is to be done and also how future additions may be incorporated.

The intelligent garden planner takes into consideration the size of the grounds, the way the land lies, the architecture, the size and placing of the house and outbuildings, color harmony of house and plantings, and the type of garden desired. All of this goes on paper first. Every situation calls for different plans. Landscaping, after all, is simply planning an improvement of the landscape to obtain harmony and balance. The important thing is to have a plan and work toward it. Then one enjoys the garden as it grows, for a gardener lives in the future as well as the present, and a garden is to be lived with and in for a long time. In the South people live out-of-doors at least nine months of the year, so why not plan for this?

The plan may aim for either a naturalistic or a formal effect. The natural style, which imitates nature, requires least care when completed and is easier to keep in condition. The formal type is best for very small grounds. Care and attention are required to keep each part balanced and the hedges uniformly trimmed. The modern tendency is to blend the two types.

When doing over grounds that already have plantings, natural or otherwise, do not take out existing material until a plan has been

8

decided on. Some plants will look better in a different location. Trees and other factors may influence the design. Choose plants that suit the spot rather than make over the garden to fit new plants. It does not matter if the garden is quite small; it can have good design and may contain choice varieties of plants. A small garden looks less spotty with just a few varieties but enough plants of each kind to make a telling display.

Usually it is best to use plant material that is indigenous to the region. Consider the form of plants, foliage color and texture, season and color of bloom and ultimate size. Choose plants that are attractive for more than one season, not forgetting evergreens and berries for the autumn and winter landscape. Shrubs are used sometimes as specimens but mostly in masses; the form, flowers, foliage and fruits are to be considered. Trees are needed on a well-planned place for shade and for shadows, and a good lawn is very important in providing a setting for the house and plants.

A tall house can have a heavier foundation planting than a one-story house. A low building needs to have some of the base showing so that it will not look smothered. Foundation plantings must be in harmony with the house, and the base of the dwelling must not be so well hidden that the building seems to be resting on the planting.

At least some of the plants should be slow growing. One of the best border plants in the South is truedwarf boxwood (*Buxus sempervirens suffruticosa*). A colonial type house, in particular, should have this most desirable evergreen.

Keep the lawn open and the margins planted at different heights, bearing in mind the texture, color and airiness of all the plants. Provide accents to avoid monotony. Variegated foliage plants are good among evergreens.

Walks and driveways should be in keeping with the garden plan; these lead the eye as well as the foot. The necessary curves should be pleasing. Steps can be made interesting when walks go from one level to another, with the slopes, terraces or rock walls planted effectively.

In planning a garden the background must not be forgotten. For beauty and privacy, unsightly places must be screened with plantings. For this purpose Carolina cherry-laurel (*Prunus (Laurocerasus) caroliniana*), sometimes called mock-orange, is an excellent evergreen in the South; so is *Photinia serrulata* and the more rapid-growing, larger-leaved types of ligustrum. A windbreak may have to be planted, and there should be vistas to desirable scenes. A tree well placed can

9

bring out a lovely view. Matched columnar conifers are often used to frame an attraction.

Be sure to provide a play-place for the children; they will have memories of their happy childhood as long as they live. Views from windows and entrances ought to be interesting, and the service yard and plantings about the garage should not be overlooked. Remember that surprises and seclusion make a garden enchanting.

After the garden is planned, it is important for the ground to be put into condition. One wants the planting and upkeep to be as easy as possible. A good idea is to make the lawn first and set out the trees, then the foundation planting and the background. After this make a border of shrubs or a hedge. Later set out the perennials and other flowering plants. Finally the outdoor living room, lily pool and other units may be added, with the vegetable garden and orchard if there is room. Long-time planning is well worth while.

SOIL

Before any planting is attempted, the soil should be thoroughly prepared. Deep digging gives feeding roots a chance to go deep for moisture and food. Below the topsoil, which is only a few inches thick, the subsoil is often different in composition and texture. Working the soil and adding humus to it gradually conditions this subsoil and gives better results than using commercial fertilizers.

Humus is partially decayed vegetable matter, which holds water and helps plants to withstand drought. When there is plenty of it in the ground, it is unnecessary to add clinkers and stones for drainage. Good drainage is very important, for plant roots decay where water stagnates. Humus binds the soil and keeps it from washing during rains. A good soil is open and porous and allows air to enter; humus keeps it in that state. (This does not mean that air pockets should be left about roots, which must be firm in the soil.)

To maintain a source of humus close at hand, it is well to have a compost heap made of leaves, rakings from the yard, grass clippings, vegetable refuse or any matter that will rot and make a rich soil. Keep out diseased plants and seed-bearing weeds, and leave a depression in the top of the heap for rains to enter and dampen the compost. It should be forked over occasionally to hasten decomposition. Leaf mold can be made quickly by sprinkling thoroughly mixed chemicals among the piled leaves: ammonium sulphate or nitrate of soda, lime, superphosphate, and muriate of potash.

10

Starting with good soil is very important, but fresh supplies of humus should be added from time to time.

From a physical standpoint all good soil should be composed of humus, sand, clay and silt. Much sand in the garden loam makes a warm soil but does not hold moisture or plant food well. Humus is needed to bind it together. On the other hand, a large amount of clay produces a wet or cold soil, hard when dry and sticky when wet. This should be loosened with humus; the addition of lime will make an excellent clay loam. Silt is a deposit of earth from standing or running water.

Well-decayed manure, which has passed the fermenting stage, is high in humus and is a valuable food when dug under. This improves the texture of the soil and helps it to hold moisture. Peat, a partially decayed swamp material, also improves the soil texture but supplies no food except a little nitrogen. Coal ashes will lighten soil, keep it from baking and improve drainage. The ashes contain lime and a small amount of iron and potash.

Soil ought to be good both physically and chemically—light and loose, able to retain moisture and yet not sour. Chemicals can easily be added. After the soil has been prepared you will want to know just what the chemical reaction is, whether acid (sour) or alkaline (sweet), or a neutral blending of the two.

The majority of plants thrive in a neutral soil, but some are more particular. Many, such as azaleas, need one that has high acid content. It is well to have the soil analyzed, not to test its fertility but to ascertain the acidity. The conditions then can be corrected to suit the plants.

If a special soil is wanted, the tests should be made at intervals, for chemical changes may occur in it. One way to test it is to use organic dyes, or litmus paper; the dyes change color with the variation of acidity. Soil-testing kits, obtainable at seed stores, provide a chart of colors with which to compare colors developed when testing and thus determine the degree of acidity.

The best way to have garden soil tested is to send samples of it to state colleges and experiment stations. The sample should be about 6 inches deep, taken out in as even a slice as possible from the top to the bottom. It is better to take samples from more than one spot. Mix the soil thoroughly; ½ pint will be enough to test.

To indicate how much acid is in the soil the symbol pH, an abbreviation for the "hydrogen ion concentration," is used. The term pH7 represents a neutral soil, a balance of acidity and alkalinity.

As the soil becomes more acid or sour, the pH number will be smaller: pH6, pH5. The symbol pH4 represents a strongly acid soil, while figures below that mean extremely acid soil. As it becomes more alkaline or sweeter, the pH number will be higher; pH8 and figures above this signify strongly alkaline. If we learn that certain plants thrive best in a soil with a pH5, we know they require a medium strong acid soil. When the recommendation is for pH8, we know the plant needs a very alkaline soil.

Acidity may be increased by digging peat moss, crumbling tree bark, rotted wood, old sawdust, fresh oak leaves or pine needles into the soil. Aluminum sulphate sprinkled on the ground, ½ pound to the square yard, or powdered sulphur or superphosphate will keep the soil acid. Cottonseed meal or a continued use of ammonium sulphate also will raise the acidity. Or coffee grounds may be scattered around acid-loving plants. These plants thrive on the iron that becomes available as the acidity of the soil becomes greater.

To increase the alkalinity or sweetness of the soil, use lime, which also gives the calcium that is so necessary to some plants and is often washed away. Ground shell, gypsum or old plaster are often put on sour soils to sweeten them; constant application of sodium nitrate also will reduce acidity. Eggshells, which contain some lime, may be placed about tall bearded iris. A sour soil that has not been worked can be put in good condition with a cover crop and lime. Do not use builder's lime, but agricultural lime, which is ground limestone (calcium carbonate). Too much of it may kill plants or cause the foliage to turn yellow. Manganese sulphate will correct this trouble, but before using it, one should seek advice from a soil expert.

Moss is not an indication of an acid or sour soil. Moss or green algæ will thrive in almost any damp spot, especially in the shade. It will grow on moist soil that is alkaline if there are not plants to keep it off; but when soil becomes acid and plants die, moss will still grow. Its presence indicates too much shade, poor drainage or need of fertilizer.

Vigorously growing plants show that the soil is right, and under such conditions there is no need to bother with an analysis. Before attempting to change a soil, be sure that what you are about to do will meet the requirements of the plants to be grown there. Knowledge of the kind of soil needed to grow practically all plants can be easily ascertained from nurserymen, catalogs and garden literature.

At Magnolia Gardens, near Charleston, S. C., lakes give back enchanting colors. (See page 4.)

These pads of *Victoria regia*, the royal water-lily, at Cypress Gardens, north of Charleston, S. C., are over 6 feet in diameter. The flowers bloom from mid-August to October. (See page 4.)

PLANT FOOD

If food is not found naturally in the soil, it must be applied and made available to plants. A soil is "alive" or "dead" according to the food present in it.

Organic fertilizer, which builds up and enriches land, is produced by animals or decayed plants. Barnyard manure is such a fertilizer; it furnishes plant food and also improves the texture of the soil. Usually gardeners speak of organic fertilizer as "natural manure" or just "manure." This is good food for plants when it is well decayed and mixed thoroughly with the soil. It makes a satisfactory loam for practically all vegetation. Manure, especially when unfermented, contains some seed of grasses and weeds that are troublesome when they germinate, but cultivation to get rid of them helps the soil. Manures and natural composts are deficient in phosphoric acid; for that reason it is good practice to use superphosphate in conjunction with manure.

Inorganic fertilizer is made up of minerals, such as nitrogen, phosphoric acid and potash. In a fertilizer formula these elements are indicated by numbers. The first number represents the nitrogen content, the second number phosphoric acid and the third number potash. For example, the numbers 4-12-4 applied to fertilizer mean there are four parts of nitrogen, twelve parts of phosphorus and four parts of potash. They are primary foods. When these are in proportion to make good growth, the fertilizer is called a balanced food. Other plant foods lacking in many soils are calcium oxide, sulphur and magnesium oxide, and the minor elements such as iron, copper, zinc, boron and manganese.

Commercial fertilizers are stimulants that give food necessary for at least a season but do not improve the texture of the soil. Gardeners speak of them as "artificial manure." It is usually better to make use of a complete balanced food rather than the separate elements; there are different mixtures for particular plants.

Nitrogen gives stature to plants, enlivens color and stimulates growth of leaves and stems. Too much of it makes plants grow spindly and possibly without blooms. Nitrate of soda is the fastest-acting form of nitrogen and should be used early in the growing season. Phosphorus is generally needed to produce stronger flowers, fruits and seeds. Bonemeal and superphosphate are the common forms in which it is carried; these are slow acting. Potassium is the element that makes good roots, stiffens the plant, heightens

13

the color and builds up resistance to disease. The common carrier is muriate of potash.

Lime and wood ashes should not be mixed with manure, for chemical action will take place at once and nitrogen in the manure will escape in the form of ammonia. Apply the manure to the ground first, so that the ammonia may be absorbed by the soil. Ammonia, though not a fertilizer, is a stimulant that gives vegetation an "appetite" to take in food. Calcium, essential to most plants, is supplied by lime, which also corrects soil acidity and makes plant food available.

Hardwood ashes may be applied like lime, by spreading on the ground and raking in. Unleached hardwood ashes contain potash, lime and a little phosphoric acid and are a help if the soil is not already too alkaline. Soot is a chemical fertilizer that will give good color to foliage and flowers when dug about plants. Cottonseed meal, much used in the South, is an ideal food if the soil needs to be kept acid.

Fertilizer is spaded into the ground when it is prepared for planting; or any of the fertilizers may be spread on top of the ground in dry form, dug in lightly and then washed in with water. If the soil is already wet, the fertilizers will dissolve in the damp earth without more watering. One must be careful not to burn the leaves and stems of plants when applying any plant food. The food is meant for the roots, not the foliage.

Feeding with liquid manure is a good way to increase plant growth and improve vegetables and flowers. This solution can be made by soaking stable manure in water. When the liquid is the color of weak tea, it is applied once or twice a week to plants before they flower. If one hasn't the manure, a liquid food can be made with dried blood, sodium nitrate, ammonium sulphate or potassium sulphate. Use about an ounce to 2 gallons of water. Pour the liquid manure around plants after the ground has been watered. Do not let it get on the foliage. You will soon see the effect of such quick-acting food in vigorous growth and larger flowers of better color.

Astonishing results are obtained in plant growth by using a solution of vitamin B_1. This is not a fertilizer but is a stimulant that causes roots to grow and use the plant food and moisture in the soil. It is particularly useful in moving plants that are not easily transplanted.

In order to thrive, plants must have adequate food in the soil along with a supply of air and moisture.

14

SOWING THE SEED

Be sure to buy good seeds. Patronize your local dealer if he carries them. The seeds that you have saved from your garden will make good plants but they may not come true to color, especially if the flowers are the kind that bees like to visit. Seedlings are not always like parents. When buying, it is better to get a few "best" rather than quantities of cheaper seed. Inferior plants take up as much space as good ones and require as much care, but the results are generally far from satisfactory.

Catalogs are full of information about the reaction of plants to certain soils, the kinds of plant food needed and the preferred location. Directions on seed packages explain the culture required and sometimes indicate the number of days it takes the seed to germinate. The catalogs list many rare plants, but some of our so-called common or familiar kinds are as ornamental as the rare varieties. A few novelties added each year, however, bring a zest to gardening.

You may like to save seeds from your own plants. Be sure they are mature and dry when gathered. The first flowers on a plant generally develop best. Keep all withered blooms removed from the plants except those left to mature for seed. Some seeds lose their viability in a few weeks or months; others will germinate even when kept for several years. If your seeds are not planted at once, label them and keep them in a dry place.

Seeds can be tested for germination. A good way is to use a dampened blotter fitted in a plate. Shake the seed on the blotter and fit an inverted plate over the first one. Put this in a warm place (60 to 70 degrees) and keep the blotter moist. Some seeds sprout in a few days, while others take longer. Those that fail to sprout in a month are probably defective.

Seeds can be sown in any seed flat with good drainage, in hotbeds, or in the open ground according to the plants and season. Sifted loam, sand and leaf mold make a good soil for a seed bed and should be watered a day before the planting is done. If seed flats are used, they should not be in direct sunlight until the plants are up; they can be covered with damp burlap until then. Do not let them dry out; keep the soil moist but not wet.

Seeds of hardy annuals sown in the open in autumn will flower the following spring. Many seeds germinate better after being frozen in the ground over winter, such as alpine plants that are native to colder regions. Seeds of half-hardy annuals sown in good mellow soil in spring as soon as frosts are over, will bloom the same summer and fall. Tender annual seeds should not be planted in the open until the ground is warm.

Some plants, like poppies, on account of the formation of their roots, resent transplanting. The seeds must be sown where they are to stay, but the plants need to be thinned out.

In most parts of the South hotbeds are planted in January and February. It is a pleasure to observe how fast the seeds sprout and plants grow. Hotbeds do not have to be electrically heated, but they do need heat from the bottom. Select a location on the south or sunny side in order to have the benefit of the sun. The frame should be higher on the northern side, as protection from the wind. Make the frame about 12 to 16 inches high in the back and 10 to 12 inches high in front. Spade out the soil a few feet, place clinkers in the bottom for drainage, add fresh manure mixed with litter for bottom heat, place a little loam over this, wet it, and close the glass sash to let the mixture heat. (Standard size sash are 3 by 6 feet, so the bed can be 3 or 6 feet wide or the length of any multiple of three.) In a few days open the sash and add some well-rotted manure. If the roots should reach the fresh manure in the bottom, they would be burnt. Cover this decomposed manure with a few inches of good garden soil. Smooth it and cover again with glass sash to heat, then cool to about 70 degrees before planting.

Seeds are usually planted twice their depth. The germination of hard seed can be hastened by clipping the outside covering. Dusting with hormone powder also promotes germination. When the soil dries in the bed, water carefully with a sprinkler to keep from washing up the seeds; for though larger seeds are planted twice their thickness, fine ones are merely pressed into the soil. The soil must be firm about the seed to provide a close contact for the sprouts. Shade the glass from the sun with canvas or paper until growth starts, and then gradually take off the covering. When moisture shows under the glass, the soil is too wet and the sash should be raised. When the temperature under the glass reaches about 75 degrees, the sash should be raised an inch or two. As the plants grow, they will need light and air. On sunny days raise the sash for at least half an hour to allow air to enter. As the weather gets warmer, the sash can be left off to permit the plants to harden.

Coldframes depend only on the sun and do not have any heating material. They can be made on the surface of the ground, but a trench is usually dug. The coldframes may be covered with glass,

16

Rhododendron carolinianum

In mountainous regions of the upper South rhododendrons are among the most commanding of the evergreen shrubs. West Virginia has chosen *Rhododendron maximum* as her state flower.

Paul's Scarlet Climber has been called the most widely planted rose in the whole country, and one can well believe that to be true. It is hard to imagine a better location for it than against a snowy white fence, arbor or lattice. (See page 122.)

and as the weather gets warmer they may be shaded with laths as a protection from the sun. They are very useful in growing plants in the summer as well as for hardening those that have been transplanted from hotbeds.

The soil where seedlings are grown can be sterilized by heating or by pouring boiling water or a sterilizing solution over it. Prepared sterilizing powders are also obtainable.

Sometimes after the plants come up, a fungus covers the soil and attacks tender stems. This is called "damping off." To get rid of it, scrape between the plants with a small instrument and do not water much. Lime-sulphur or coal dust sprinkled between the plants is helpful. As soon as the seedlings are large enough, transplant them so that they will have more room. A pinch of Semesan shaken over seeds before planting will help prevent damping off.

A simple way to destroy harmful organisms in soil is to treat the soil with formaldehyde before planting. Use a tablespoonful of 40 percent formaldehyde diluted with three or four parts water, sprinkle over soil and mix in. After twenty-four hours seeds can be planted. Or seeds can be treated with chemicals after sowing, using an ounce of copper carbonate mixed with 6 quarts of water. Sprinkle this over the bed, a quart to a square foot of soil, after the seeds are planted. Or stir ¾ ounce of copper oxide in 5 gallons of water and sprinkle it on the bed when the seeds are sown, again as they begin to come up, and finally when seedlings are an inch high.

When transplanting seedlings, care must be taken not to break off the tender roots. The soil must be made firm around them. Roots must have moisture, air and food, with the right amount of sun and shade for the plants.

"Pelletized" seeds, which are seeds coated with fertilizer, fungicide, insecticide and hormones, are now being put on the market. They are more sure to grow and are protected from disease and insects. The coating makes it possible for these seeds to resist extremes of weather, and they can, therefore, be planted earlier and will produce sooner than untreated seeds. They are, of course, somewhat higher in price. The smallest seeds when coated are about pea size and can be planted separately, thus saving the work of transplanting. Many pelletized seeds, such as petunias and zinnias, can now be obtained with a coating of the same color as the flowers. This may be helpful in planting for color harmony. Progressive gardeners are ever on the lookout for such evidences of progress in the field of horticultural chemistry.

LOCATION OF PLANTS

For best results you must see that plants have what they require. One essential is a suitable location. You cannot expect sun-loving plants to thrive in the shade nor moisture-loving plants in a dry spot.

A plant that requires full sun should be exposed to the direct rays of the sun. Partial shade means part sunshine and part shade, while light shade signifies the shade under low-growing or light-growing plants or under trees that have high branches. Deep shade is made by the heavy growth of leaves on deciduous trees, and full shade is all-time shade cast by buildings or evergreens.

Full sun is necessary in the vegetable garden and orchard. Most annuals require full sun to flower well, though a few, like alyssum, petunias and pansies, will stand some shade. There are perennials, shrubs and vines that require shade and others that will put up with it. Many plants thrive in either sun or partial shade.

Some well-known shrubs that will do well in the South in partial shade include azaleas, beauty-bush (Kolkwitzia), breath-of-spring (*Lonicera fragrantissima*), camellias in middle and lower sections, golden-bells (*Forsythia suspensa*), kerria, maple-leaf viburnum (*Viburnum acerifolium*) in middle and upper areas and *Spiræa Vanhouttei*.

Some perennials prefer or thrive in light shade. Examples are bleeding-heart (*Dicentra spectabilis*), early-blooming bulbs, coral-bells (Heuchera), day-lilies (Hemerocallis), lily-of-the-valley (*Convallaria majalis*), madonna, tiger and speciosum lilies, *Phlox divaricata*, plantain-lily (Hosta), primrose (*Primula vulgaris*) and Virginia bluebells (Mertensia). (For others, see Chapter VI.) *Vinca minor*, English ivy (*Hedera Helix*) and spurge (Pachysandra) are ground covers that grow well in shade under trees, as well as wildflowers and wood ferns. (See also Chapter VIII.)

The heat of the sun can scald in winter as well as in summer. Plants wither through transpiration, when the sun draws moisture from the leaves just as it does from the soil. The gardener utilizes this knowledge as he cuts out trees to admit the sunshine or plants them for shade and coolness.

One who has a garden should know that plants on the south or sunny side bloom earliest; so early-flowering plants, when grown on the north side, are not so likely to have their early flowers turn brown over night from a cold snap. Their flowering time will be later, however, than if grown on the south side. Tender growth does better on the north side in our Southern States.

The graceful beauty-bush is a shrub that can stand a partly shaded location in the South. Its long, arched branches are a mass of bell-shaped, pink flowers in April, and after the blooms have disappeared silky seed pods come. This is a very fast grower and often needs to be pruned back after its blooming season. It is one of the most charming of all the valuable plants that have been brought to us from China, its native home.

A perennial border like this is not the work of a few moments or even days. It takes care and patience to combine colors, heights and flower forms to make a succession of garden pictures.

Chapter III
Time For The Main Operations

CULTIVATING AND EXTERMINATING WEEDS

Cultivation of the soil accomplishes a variety of results. It admits air to the soil, mixes plant food in the ground, conserves moisture, destroys insect pests, eradicates weeds and adds to the appearance of the garden.

Plants need air both in the ground and above it. Digging conditions the soil for the plants, making the ground soft and the top loose so that air can enter. It acts as a stimulant and is more important than watering. When there is constant cultivation, moisture is conserved to such an extent that watering is not needed except during a very dry spell. If soil is not worked, moisture evaporates quickly. Cultivating plants is just as necessary as fertilizing them, for unless plant food gets down into the earth where the roots can absorb it, it is useless.

When the ground is kept cultivated, many insects and insect eggs are turned up and destroyed, and the growth of weeds and grasses is checked. As early as possible in spring, the routine should be started in order to keep down weeds and to prevent the soil from packing. It should be dry enough not to ball but should fall apart when a sample is squeezed in the hand. Working the ground when it is too wet does more harm than good, for that creates a hardpan soil that will take a long time to get in proper condition.

During the growing season it is well to cultivate after every rain, as soon as the soil is dry enough. After the plants start growth, the surface should be loosened only slightly, about an inch deep, to keep moisture near the roots. Deep digging will injure the roots. In late fall, the job can be stopped to allow plants to harden for winter. After frosts, if the ground is roughened, frost action will pulverize the soil and the rains will soak in.

Weeds often have to be pulled up by hand, especially in rock gardens. Just after rains they come out easily. When manure is not well rotted, it may carry weed seed and cause a lot of trouble. Each weed that matures produces numberless seeds that are scattered far and wide by birds or winds. Some weed seeds retain their vitality in the soil for years; all they require is warmth to bring them to life. Cockleburs have two seeds in each bur; one may germinate right away, and the other take two or more years. It is said that the seeds of mullein and smartweed will grow after being fifty years in the soil.

Chickweed, one of the worst weeds in the South, comes during the fall and lasts through the winter. It is killed by the hot sun in spring, but in the meantime it has spread and choked many plants. Constant cultivation will keep it down. It can be killed by applications of a solution of a pound of iron sulphate in a gallon of water. It does not like acid soil.

Those who are susceptible to poison ivy (*Rhus radicans*) should watch out for this root-climbing vine that thrives in untilled land. Each leaf has three leaflets, and the berries are grayish white. It is sometimes confused with the harmless Virginia creeper with five leaflets and bluish black berries. Poison ivy spreads by suckers, and pieces of root left in the ground will sprout again. Poison oak (*Rhus Toxicodendron*) is a form of poison ivy that is more shrubby. Its berries are whitish, and sometimes there are five leaflets. A strong brine solution may be used to get rid of poison ivy, or it can be eradicated by applying second-hand crankcase oil. The oil and brine solutions are more effective when the soil is dry, and they may have to be used more than once to kill the underground stems. To check the rootlets, kerosene may be sprinkled on the ground. This, however, will make the soil unfit for other vegetation. Ammonium sulfamate spray, ¾ pound to a gallon of water, will get rid of poison ivy. Borax put on the ground will also eradicate poison ivy but may kill other plants; Virginia creeper is one that does not mind borax in the soil.

If grubbing out roots of dandelions and plantains proves too tedious, gasoline or kerosene may be applied to the tops. (When pieces of roots are left, several new crowns will form.) Some prefer to use a chemical compound of a pound of copperas or iron sulphate to 1½ gallons of water. This will burn weeds and not hurt the grass to any extent. The applications may have to be made several times. There are also instruments for dropping chemicals in the crowns of weeds to destroy them, and new preparations for eradicating weeds are constantly appearing on the market. It may simplify matters to use them, but in all cases the directions must be followed carefully.

Annual crabgrass, germinating in spring and early summer,

and perennial quackgrass can be rooted out or smothered out. To keep them from reseeding in lawns, rake to raise the seed heads before mowing the grass; then the heads can be cut and raked off. The quackgrass has roots that spread by creeping. To exterminate it, the roots must be torn out. If the roots are turned under 6 inches or more, they will die.

WATERING

Like human beings, plants need both food and water. And if they do not get water, plant roots are unable to assimilate the nutrients in the soil. Moisture *must* reach feeding roots. Thorough watering causes roots to go down, which helps the plants to stand droughts. Water must be added when the top 2 inches of the ground is rather dry, or if small buds and tips of growth begin to wilt. When water is needed, soak the ground thoroughly. If a spray is used, keep it running for several hours. A mere sprinkling encourages topsurface roots that can be killed easily by dry weather.

When the soil dries enough to be workable, cultivate to conserve moisture and to prevent baking. Moisture means much to vegetation, but plants do not do well in a soil that is continually wet. Heavy clay soils do not dry out so quickly as warm sandy ones. Hardwood plants, like camellias and azaleas, suffer more from lack of water than plants that have soft stems which revive quickly even when their stems have wilted. Growing plants require more water than dormant ones.

Water plants well when they are first set out, and for a season or two after that until they become established, especially if the branches were not cut back to balance the loss of roots from digging. If a depression is left around shrubs and trees, water can go to the roots. If earth is mounded around them, the needed water is drained away.

Evening is usually the best time for watering, because the moisture can soak down during the night. But in the rose garden, and about perennials and annuals subject to mildew, it is better to water in the morning so that the plants will not go into the night with wet foliage. When they are watered in the morning, the sun will dry any moisture on the leaves.

Underground or overhead irrigation is convenient but expensive, and most of us must depend on the hose or watering pots. A good way to soak the ground in the garden is to take the nozzle from the hose, put the end of the hose on a stone or board to prevent washing away of the soil, and let water run around the plants. The best

21

time for surface sprinkling is in the evening. If grass or other plantings are watered in the heat of the day, the foliage is likely to burn.

It is cheaper to save plants by watering during a drought than
to grow new plants. Bucketfuls of water poured around them will
save them until rain comes. One old method of watering is to place
a tin can with holes in it in the ground near the roots of a plant and
fill the can with water.

After light frosts annuals or any flowering plants will thaw more
slowly if they are sprinkled with water early in the morning. This
will keep them from being injured.

Unless there have been heavy rains, evergreens should be soaked
well before the ground freezes. All plants with leaves constantly
transpire water; evergreens do this slowly in winter and need water
at their roots to make up for it. If conifers do not have enough water,
the evergreen leaves or needles are harmed. Newly planted specimens particularly need to be soaked so that the whole plant will be
supplied with water until weather gets to the freezing point.

MULCHING

The purpose of a mulch is to protect roots from heat, cold or
drought. A summer mulch keeps down weeds, conserves moisture
and prevents the sun from drying out the ground. A dust mulch is
made by stirring up the surface, to keep the underneath soil moist.

The best time to apply summer mulch is after plants have been
watered several times and are established, or just after a rain. A
mulch about 2 inches thick saves cultivation. Leaf mold or peat moss,
strawy leaves, rice hulls or shredded sugar cane may be used. Dry
grass clippings also make a good mulch; if they are green, only a thin
layer should be put on, for they may ferment and sour the soil.

Leaves and peat moss act as a mulch and also as a soil builder.
Where there have been swamps or bogs for a long time, the surface
is usually peat moss. This is a vegetable matter free from weeds, which
absorbs water freely. Besides being a fine mulch, it supplies excellent
humus to work into the soil. Shrubs and trees can be kept free of
weeds by a mulch similar to woodland ground cover.

The purpose of a winter mulch is to protect plants not from
freezing but from the effects of alternate freezing and thawing of
the soil about their roots. Freezing and thawing of the ground makes
the soil expand, and shallow-rooted plants are damaged by being
heaved out. A winter mulch holds the cold, keeps the soil at an even

Photo by Carl Julien

The author in her garden in Greenwood, S. C.

Photo by Carl Julien

The author's home in Greenwood, S. C.

temperature and protects it from high winds. The material used is determined by the region and what is available. Most perennials do not need extra covering in the South. In fact, many die from being protected, for anything that mats down may smother the plants or cause them to rot. If a mulch is used, wait until the ground has frozen somewhat before applying it.

In the South a winter mulch is raked off or dug into the soil in early spring. It is best to do this on cloudy days, giving the plants a chance to harden. Plants like azaleas that root close to the surface require a mulch in both summer and winter. It should not be a dust mulch, for digging will damage the roots.

It is advisable to spray the ground around plants, as well as their tops, with some good fungicide before putting on a winter mulch. This helps prevent the spread of diseases, such as blackspot on roses, which will remain during the winter on fallen leaves. In most of the South, roses come through winter better without mulch. In the colder sections, earth can be mounded about them to a height of 6 inches. Soil for hilling should be obtained elsewhere, for if it is taken out between the plants the roots will not be covered enough. Bulbs do not need to be mulched. A mulch about peonies and certain lilies will keep the roots cool, and warm weather and thawing will not make the plants sprout too soon.

The same mulch is not suited to all plants. For herbaceous perennials a thick coating of manure and leaves can be used, but on plants that have a winter top this mulch would get wet and soggy and could cause the plants to decay. If a covering is used over plants with top growth, let it be light, like straw or pieces of evergreens fastened down. It is a doubtful practice to let leaves lie as they fall. A wind may blow them off just when they are needed, or they may gather too thickly. Leaves are suitable for use in shrubbery borders, for they can be dug in when spring comes or left to decay.

PRUNING

Plants are pruned to preserve their health, to keep them in shape and to make finer blooms and fruits. Cutting out dead and diseased parts stimulates new growth. Many shrubs need to have some of the old canes cut to the ground at least every other year. When shrubs grow too high or get too open, new growth with softer and finer foliage will develop if main branches and stems are cut back.

Root pruning increases flowers and fruit on some plants, for it induces numerous feeding roots to grow close to the main stem, which make it possible for the plant to take more nourishment. Often wisteria is made to bloom by root pruning. To do this, cut down through the roots with a sharp spade, about 2 feet from the main trunk. If runners of wisteria are cut off from time to time in summer, the vines will bloom better.

Pruning saws, as well as different size shears, are needed and should always be kept sharp.

The proper time to prune is important. A safe general rule is to prune flowering shrubs just after they bloom. Deciduous shrubs that bloom from late winter to about mid-June are pruned in early summer, not later than July, so that those that bloom on new wood can make growth for the next spring's flowers. Summer and fall bloomers are pruned in autumn and winter. If early-flowering shrubs are cut back in winter, most of the flower buds will be clipped off. Only those that bloom in late summer and fall should be pruned in late winter; they produce flowers on the current season's growth.

In pruning shrubs, be sure to shorten side branches as well as top ones. Study the plants, and thin them in order to admit light and air. Take out weak growth and some of the oldest branches to the ground. New growth will appear, and the size and quality of the flowers will be improved. Design the trimming to produce a natural-looking shape. Avoid leaving stubs to die and form a breeding place for insects and diseases. Cut just above a bud, preferably an outside one, to encourage open growth. Shrubs are usually cut back about one-third.

Flowering quinces bloom on old wood, and cutting long sprays of blossoms will take care of pruning until thinning is needed. If flowers of lilacs (Syringa) are cut carefully, with the shape of the shrub in mind, the bushes will not require other trimming for years. Some shrubs, like butterfly-bushes, are better if pruned severely. Many plants are valuable in the landscape for highly colored twigs, such as the red-branched, yellow and gray dogwoods. These should be pruned hard even if some of the flowers are lost, for the brightest-colored twigs are on the current season's growth.

To prune broadleaf evergreens, wait until growth starts in the spring. Evergreens should be kept shapely. Conifers are usually sheared twice a year, about February and again the last of August when growth has finished. Clipping off ends of new growth several times a season contributes to their growth and proper shape. Formal hedges should be trimmed about four times a year to keep them dense. Trim privet and cherry-laurel hedges before the stems of the new growth become hardened. The clipping should be done several times during the growing season. If the sides are slightly wider at the bottom, sun and air can reach the lower part, which otherwise might become leggy.

To prune trees, saw limbs upward a few inches from the trunk, about one-third through, to keep from stripping the bark; then saw from the top. The stub can be taken off smooth, as close to the tree as possible, by sawing downward. Winter or very early spring is the best time to prune most trees. Do not do it when the weather is extremely cold, for bad wounds may result if the wood snaps. Trees that may bleed in spring, such as maples, should be pruned during fall or late summer.

It is important that wounds heal quickly. Painting the places that are over 2 or 3 inches in diameter wards off diseases and keeps out moisture, which causes decay. Wait until the wounds are dry to paint them. Asphaltum paint, free of creosote, is good to use after limbs are removed from shade trees. White lead with linseed oil is often used to paint cuts, and there are preparations that are fungicidal and harmless to the tree.

The time to prune climbing roses is immediately after flowering. Varieties that send up new canes each year, like ramblers, should have the old canes cut back to the ground to allow all the strength to go into new ones. Climbers that send out laterals on older canes, such as Dr. W. Van Fleet, need to have some new shoots pruned, but old canes only when decayed.

Pruning of other roses, not climbers, should not be done until late winter when leaf buds begin to swell but growth has not started. Too early pruning stimulates new growth, which may be killed by late freezes. Old-fashioned roses grown in gardens before 1880 do not, as a rule, require much trimming. The dead canes and crossing branches should be taken out and the plants cut back enough to keep the bushes vigorous and healthy. On hybrid tea roses leave about four strong canes and cut them back slantingly to about the fourth bud or more, about 10 to 18 inches. The top bud should be an outside one, to encourage open growth so that the sun and air ca. penetrate. Some hybrid teas will do better when not trimmed this much; among them are Edith Nellie Perkins and Souvenir de Claudius Pernet. The hybrid perpetuals, which are stronger growing, can be left taller, about 2 feet high, and the polyanthas may be cut lower.

When rose bushes are cut far back they take a longer time to bloom, and there are fewer flowers than on those not pruned to such an extent; but one is repaid with fine long-stemmed roses. When pruning, cut carefully with sharp tools so that no ragged edges are left for insect eggs or disease spores. Then spray with lime-sulphur (one part to eight parts of water) to prevent canker; after a week or ten days follow this with an application of Bordeaux mixture.

Judicious trimming of plants in flower beds helps their form and results in more blooms, or fewer but finer blooms. For example, exhibition chrysanthemums are thinned to a few main stems and disbudded until only a terminal bud is left on each stem. For other chrysanthemums, pinching off the tops of the young growth until July makes side buds develop and produces a great number of flowers. Annuals, such as zinnias and petunias, are pruned, in a way, when their tops are pinched out to make bushy clumps.

TRANSPLANTING, STAKING, LABELING

Transplanting upsets a plant, for it disturbs the root system. A plant stands a better chance of living if transplanted when dormant or after it stops growing. Most dormant trees and shrubs with good roots can be moved successfully in the South from late fall until spring. When transplanting, do not leave roots exposed to air and sun but get them into the ground as soon as possible. Take off all diseased or broken roots.

Nursery stock is usually well packed but for safety the parcel should be opened at once, for sometimes plants overheat if they are packed close. If the plants look dry or shriveled, the roots should be soaked for several hours in water. If they cannot be planted right away, heel them in. Choose a sheltered place, lay the plants slantingly and cover the roots with soil. They will be all right for some time. While getting ready to plant, it is well to cover the roots with burlap to keep them from drying until set in the ground.

Never transplant when the soil is wet. A cloudy day or late afternoon is the best time. Plants need air at the roots and air above them, and some require sunshine. However, many transplanted specimens are killed by the hot sunshine the first few days, when a little shading would have saved them. Plants need special care until the roots are anchored.

Holes should be deep and wide enough for the roots without crowding. Before transplanting, well-decayed manure or other fertilizer should be thoroughly mixed in and covered with several

Plantings in the author's garden—*Euonymus radicans*
climbing the wall, and tall and dwarf boxwood.

The garden of Mrs. Mary Simms Oliphant in Greenville, S. C. The fountain was brought from the plantation of Mrs. Oliphant's grandfather, the novelist and historian, William Gilmore Simms.

inches of soil, because direct contact with it damages the roots. After the plant is placed, pack the soil among the roots until the hole is half filled. Pour in water, and when it has disappeared make the earth firm about the roots and fill in with dry soil. An earth mulch prevents evaporation and keeps the roots damp.

This first watering will keep the roots moist for several days; but if the soil begins to dry, make a hole beside the plant, fill it with water, and replace the dry earth. After rains the surface of the soil should be worked as soon as it is dry enough, so that moisture will be retained. If a plant is balled and burlapped, set it in the hole as it is, picking it up by the ball and not by the stem, which might loosen the soil. Cut the strings and let the sacking lie in the hole; it will soon rot. When transplanting, leave enough room between plants for growth.

Rooted cuttings do better when not put out until spring. Their roots are tender and the soil is firm about them where they are growing. When transplanting annuals or perennials, water them before taking them up; get as much soil as possible with the roots, and replant quickly. Shade them for a few days if the weather is warm.

Some plants need staking to improve their appearance and to make them grow straight. The stakes should be put in the ground deep enough to hold the plant against winds but not near enough to cut into the roots. Stake the plants before they get large enough to fall about on the ground. With some, like dahlias, it is best to put in the stakes at the time of planting so as to avoid disturbing the roots later. Stakes should be tall and strong enough but inconspicuous. As plants grow, the new shoots and foliage will soon conceal the staking. Raffia, which can be obtained in different colors, is a good material to tie plants to stakes. It lasts longer than string and is not noticeable. There are plant ties now on the market with a basis of invisible wire covered with tape, which may be wrapped about stakes and plants. Allow for growth of plants when fastening. If tied too tight, the plant may choke. Tie about the stake first, then to the plant, and back to the stake. Most staked plants have to be fastened at least twice as they grow.

Use well-marked labels for your plants, for everyone likes to be sure of the correct names. Various labels are on the market, or you can make your own. Inexpensive ones can be cut from tin and the names written with acid or paint. Our home-made ones cut from heavy tin have lasted for years. They were cut T-shape and pointed at the bottom, to stick into the ground. Three coats of green paint were applied and the names of the plants printed on them with an ice-pick after the paint dried. Through carelessness some labels get dislocated and need to be replaced. It is well to keep records of the names.

SPRAYING AND DUSTING

There are two general classes of insects, sucking and chewing. The sucking kinds suck juices or sap from foliage, fruit or bark by means of small beaks. Aphids, plant lice, thrips, red spiders and scale insects are the most troublesome. Contact poisons like nicotine sulphate, dry lime-sulphur, pyrethrum, rotenone or oil emulsions with soap are usually applied, either as a dust or as a spray to control sucking insects.

Chewing insects bite off and chew leafy parts or fruits. Tomato worms, potato bugs, cutworms and beetles are well-known pests of this class. They can be destroyed with a solution of poison or a poisonous powder applied to the foliage, stem or fruit. Arsenic compounds are commonly used for poisoning biting insects; rotenone dust is also effective. Rotenone contains derris powder, harmless to man, but a stomach poison to insects; contact with the powder kills soft-bodied worms and insects.

Red spiders cause evergreens to turn rusty. Watch for them in dry, hot summer weather. They are mites that feed on the underside of leaves and deposit many eggs, over which a web is usually spun. Red spiders can be carried by the winds, and they often attack deciduous plants, too. A steady spray of water will knock off some of them. Be careful not to spray an evergreen in the middle of the day, for it may scald. Dusting with sulphur will usually control red spiders, or a spray of Bordeaux and nicotine may be used weekly. A glue spray made by dissolving a pound of glue in 10 gallons of water is also good. The glue should be dissolved first in a little hot water.

Scales are small insects that attach themselves to branches and cover their bodies with self-secreted scales under which they keep sucking plant juices. They multiply fast. Spray if there is a suspicion of scale. Watch especially for hard-shell kinds like San Jose scale and soft black or brown scale. Euonymus scales emerge and begin to spread in spring. For these the early dormant spray should be used. Do not wait until the scales get established. After a plant is infested, it is best to cut it to the ground; new shoots may come up uninfested. Spray in summer, too, in order to kill the young scales, using a solution of 40 percent nicotine sulphate and soap. The winter and early spring spray is most important for the health of plants. It kills eggs and other insects, besides controlling scales.

Cutworms are destroyed with poisoned bait. To keep slugs away, surround the plants with coal ashes or air-slaked lime. Leafhoppers form a thick white mass on the stems of perennials such as phlox. To control them, use a weekly application of some contact insecticide like nicotine sulphate and soap. Spray white flies with oil emulsion or Nursery Volck.

When flower stalks are dying or breaking, look for borers, as in the stems of dahlias. In the early stage they can be taken out with a wire, or they can be killed by getting rotenone into the stem. To prevent the multiplication of borers, clean up and burn dead stalks in the spring and fall. This will get rid of the winter eggs. If borers attack iris rhizomes, lift the plant so that the borer can be cut out and spray the new growth in spring with nicotine and arsenic of lead. (See Chapter IX, Iris.)

Burn webworms with a lighted kerosened wad on a pole. Kill all caterpillars that fall on the ground. Webworms can be cut off and destroyed, or they may be sprayed with arsenic of lead. Destroy bagworms in spring, fall and winter, for the eggs are always there. (For thrips on gladiolus, see Chapter IX, Gladioli.)

To control insects about roots of plants, nicotine preparations and bisulfid of carbon are used. This is poured into holes about a foot apart and 8 inches from the plant. The holes should be kept closed and moist to induce the fumes to go into the soil. Sometimes plant wilt is caused by root aphids. Wood ashes in the soil are a preventive for root aphids, or one may apply ant-killing preparations, for ants seek the honeydew extracted by aphids and thus make the presence of the aphids known. Ants may be killed by pouring a mixture of a teaspoonful of pyrethrum-rotenone spray to a cupful of water in a depression around plants. Sometimes gas is used to kill ants—a tablespoonful of carbon disulphide or a little calcium cyanide.

Dormant sprays are effective if the directions are followed carefully. Improper use may injure plants. These sprays are applied when plants are dormant and less likely to be hurt. The best time is in late winter, before new growth begins. The temperature must not be below 45 degrees Fahrenheit so that the solution (one part oil to fourteen parts water for deciduous shrubs and one to twenty-five for evergreens) will not freeze in the tissues of the plant. Choose a sunny, calm day, and before starting to spray cut out infected parts of the plant and burn them.

A miscible oil spray is commonly used for dormant spraying. There are several kinds on the market that mix readily with water. When using, stir constantly so the oil and water will stay mixed; otherwise the spray may burn the plant. Liquid lime-sulphur is also used for a dormant spray. It will discolor temporarily and has a disagreeable odor, but it destroys scales and spores. For good results spray every branch and twig thoroughly underneath as well as above.

There are parasitic diseases caused by fungi, bacteria and very small worms or nematodes. These attack flowers, vegetables and fruits affecting leaves, bark or fruit. Diseases caused by fungi start as a spore or seed. Spores can be carried by rain or wind. As the spore grows it sends roots into tissues, causing mildew and blackspot on roses and rust, rot and curl-leaf on peaches. There is no remedy after infection. Take off the infected part and burn it.

To prevent fungus diseases, apply fungicide before spores germinate. Spray or dust with compounds of sulphur or copper. The spores, or parasitic fungi, seem to be worse during a damp spell, and fungicide should be applied before rain rather than afterward. Spraying or dusting prevents the spread of blackspot, mildew and other diseases.

Pick up the fallen blackspotted leaves of roses, and pinch the infected ones from the bushes and burn them. Dust or spray regularly, for infection is difficult to detect at the beginning. It is better not to water late in the day. Massey dust, with tobacco dust added for aphids, is an excellent preparation to use. When the weather gets above 90 degrees Fahrenheit, change to copper sulphate spray to prevent burning. Two cupfuls of dry Bordeaux can be mixed with 3 gallons of water and used as a spray. Tri-ogen is a good fungicide and insecticide.

For mildew, dust with sulphur when leaves are dry. Plants subject to mildew should not be grown in low, damp places, and there should be space for air to circulate among them. To prevent rust, dust with sulphur as soon as the leaves appear. Bordeaux is a specific for rust and mildew.

Take leaf-spotted and dead leaves from irises and burn them, for fungus lives through the winter on them. For irregular black spots, like those on delphiniums, rake and burn the fallen leaves and cut off the stems. If your roses have stem canker, a disease caused by a fungus, cut and burn all infected parts. Dormant lime-sulphur spray used in early spring may control it.

30

The leaf mold and deep shade under sizable trees provide ideal conditions for many plants. (See page 97.)

The new southern colonial type home of Mr. and Mrs. Brandon Smith in Anderson, S. C., a perfect modern setting for the traditional boxwood, camellias and azaleas of the old South.

Bacterial diseases attack leaves and buds. Sprays or dusts of sulphur and copper are sometimes effective. Pick off the diseased parts and burn them, or destroy the plants. Treat the soil with formaldehyde or some other sterilizing material. When the crowns of plants rot and the stalks break from roots, take the plants up and burn them, putting fresh soil where they were. As soon as botrytis blight is noticed, the affected flower heads should be cut off and burned; the spores of this blight may be carried to healthy plants. Zinnias are often affected with botrytis, but spraying with Bordeaux mixture checks the disease. Soft rot of tall bearded iris is a bacterial disease. Place the rhizomes close to the surface so that the sun may bake them. (See Chapter IX, Iris.)

All plants with virus infections like lily mosaic and aster yellows had best be destroyed by burning. Small worms or nematodes feed on roots of plants and cause knots to develop on them. A mercury solution made of mercury tablets, 7.3 grains, dissolved in a gallon of water and used on the ground around the plants will help. Frequently it is best to burn the plants and sterilize the soil with a mercurial solution.

To keep down non-parasitic diseases, the gardener must practice crop rotation every few years with such plants as annuals, and must give plants the right food and moisture. Sprays have to be applied at intervals, for they get washed off. No one spray is a cure-all. The applications should cover the whole surface of the plant. The best time for spraying is when insects are in the larval stage, or in time to prevent the start of disease. Begin with a dormant spray in winter and repeat when necessary until autumn. No one treatment will keep down all pests or diseases. A good plan is to start with a lime sulphur spray before the new leaves appear and follow with an insecticide for sucking and chewing insects. A fungicide to prevent fungus diseases can be used in alternate weeks, or "three in one"— pyrethrum, rotenone and sulphur—can be applied weekly.

The wonder insecticide, DDT, does not destroy all insects. Much still has to be learned about what it will kill or control. Other chemicals combined with DDT are also being marketed.

Vigorous plants resist disease best. Notice, for instance, that insects choose dead limbs rather than healthy new growth on which to lay eggs. It pays to maintain clean and healthy plants. The gardener is well repaid for precautions taken to prevent trouble, either by dusting or by spraying. Dusting is the faster method but is more expensive and needs to be done when the air is calm.

Spraying or dusting often kills beneficial insects along with the harmful. The praying mantis, an insect with triangular head that seems to pray with its forelegs extended and wings outspread, is helpful. It destroys grasshoppers, beetles, rosebugs and other insects. Dragonflies pursue and kill mosquitoes and other pests, from hatching time until death. Ladybugs destroy plant lice and scale insects, and bees are indispensable as pollinating agents. Another helper is the toad, which gets rid of numerous garden pests. Lizards feed on small beetles, and tree crickets eat plant lice. Try to cultivate these friends of the garden.

When mole runs appear in gardens, look out! Moles loosen roots of plants and ruin bulbs. They can be eliminated with carbon disulphide gas or poisoned bait, such as a teaspoonful of Paris green mixed with ½ cupful of salt placed in holes in the runways, but the best way is to use mole traps. The runways of moles are used by mice and rats, which probably do most of the damage to bulbs that is ascribed to moles.

PROPAGATING

There are various methods of multiplying plants. One way is by grafting, which is the bringing together of two woods to form a permanent union. One can graft on rootstock or stem, or can make a top-graft. Sometimes a single bud is used and sometimes a young shoot. Grafting is usually understood to mean propagation by the insertion of a scion or shoot in a stock to unite one plant or variety with another. Budding is the insertion of single buds. Such plants as roses, camellias, fruit and nut trees are customarily grafted.

Often plants do not come true from seed or do not do well from cuttings or layers. Then grafting is resorted to, in order to multiply plants rapidly. Generally it is best to have stock and scion of the same species, but frequently other species do as well. The joint must be close and properly protected.

Many perennials, such as those with fleshy roots like bleeding-heart and Oriental poppy, can be propagated by root cuttings. Take a piece of root 1 to 3 inches long, plant about an inch deep in loam or sand, cover it with mulch in winter and by spring rootlets will develop.

Some plants can be rooted from leaf cuttings. Make cuts in the veins under the leaf and place with the right side up on moist sand or loam and fasten it down. Keep the cuttings out of direct light. New roots will come at the cut places. The ornamental Rex begonia

Magnolia grandiflora is a magnificent evergreen tree native in the South and has been named the state flower of both Mississippi and Louisiana. The 7 to 8-inch blooms are followed by large seed pods.

This pool with classic lines acts as a mirror for the plants around it. Evergreen azaleas bordered with boxwood are growing in front of a very fine brick wall, while trees nearby throw cool shadows on the grass.

will root from leaf or shoots, gloxinia from a whole or part of a leaf. The succulent plant, echeveria or cotyledon, roots easily from a leaf. Leaves of certain plants root when the stems will not. Use the leaf stem with the leaf, and place in sand and peat moss. Keep moist; do not let the top of the leaf get dry. Provide shade on sunny days. If chemically treated, they will root faster.

Cuttings of many plants, such as pussy willow, oleander and cape-jasmine, root easily in shallow water. Change the water often to be sure of supplying the oxygen needed for the roots to develop.

Hardwood cuttings from shrubs that have woody stems, evergreen or deciduous, can be put out in early winter or late fall. Use cuttings of year-old wood, 4 or more inches long. They may be placed in bundles in sand, and kept moist. A good rooting medium is half sand and half peat moss. When spring comes, the cuttings will have callous ends and can then be separated and put in a place where they will be protected until the new growth hardens. New-growth evergreen cuttings are taken in late summer; these are put out as individual cuttings.

Cuttings of ligustrum are taken any time during the season of growth. These can be put out where they are to grow and should be kept damp. It is best to shade them a few days from the hot sun. Trimmings of any shrubs can be stuck in sand; if they are placed in the garden in early spring, many of them will set roots.

Softwood cuttings from firm wood are put out in spring and summer. Delphinium cuttings should be taken in spring while the plants are growing. Select a 4-inch cutting of healthy growth with a piece of crown attached; plant in sand, shading at first from sun. As the roots form, more sun should be allowed.

For various cuttings one may use a box with clinkers in the bottom, filled with clean sand and kept moist. Make sure of good air circulation and not too strong sunlight. Hormodin, a root-forming chemical, stimulates rooting in certain cuttings that are slow to form roots. Bulb scales, such as those of lilies, are sometimes used like cuttings.

Many roses do well on their own roots but others have to be budded on stock. The best cutting is from a stem where a rose has bloomed, three or four eyes long. Take leaves off the two bottom eyes, and let these two go under ground; trim leaves on the other eyes to two petals each, where new growth will come. December and January, or late fall, is a good time to put out rose cuttings; then root growth is encouraged rather than top growth. Give them a sunny location in good garden soil that is well drained. Keep the ground about them moist. Glass fruit jars may be placed over them, and on cloudy warm days, but not windy, the glass can be removed for a few hours. When the weather gets warm, the jars can be left off. Radiance roses and other hybrid teas, such as Betty Uprichard which does so well in the South, and polyanthas root easily.

To layer roses and other shrubs, bend a branch and fasten it down; cover this with soil, leaving the end free. Making a cut on the stem to go under ground helps. When the underground stem makes roots and grows new shoots, it can be cut and planted. Some shoots root from the tips of plants, such as winter jasmine, coral-berry and forsythia.

A number of plants can be made by dividing the roots of a plant. A whole shrub can be taken up and divided, or pieces can be dug out by cutting down with a sharp spade, without harming the main bush. When perennials become crowded and do not bloom well, they take on new life when the roots are dug up and divided. However, there are some that resent being divided, and plants with long taproots had best be increased by other means.

Spring and summer bloomers can be divided after flowering or in the fall. Late summer or autumn-flowering plants, like chrysanthemums and hardy asters, are divided and replanted in spring. Each small root will make a new plant. Tall bearded irises need to be divided every three or four years by pulling the rhizomes apart. Japanese or Siberian iris roots can be pulled or cut apart. Day-lilies may be separated every few years to increase the supply.

MAINTAINING A LAWN

Lawns are valuable assets when they are started right and kept in condition. All plantings show to better advantage when there is a green foreground. When the center of the lawn is kept open, a favorable setting is made for the house. An unbroken expanse of green appears larger than one broken with walks. Trees can be used as needed for shade; the trunks do not mar the lawn, and the shadows are effective.

To induce grass to grow under trees, saw off the lower limbs so that sunlight can reach it in the early morning and late afternoon. Trees will put out growth at the top, and the foliage will protect the grass from mid-day burning. Do this every year or two; the latter part of September is a good time, when new grass is planted. It is not always shade that keeps grass from growing; the roots of trees use up fertility, and the leaves keep off rain. Deep-rooting trees, like the oak, do not take much moisture from the topsoil.

A lawn needs both subdrainage and surface drainage. The ground should be graded and thoroughly prepared about a foot deep before the grass is sown. Cowpeas or other legumes turned under will help to improve the soil texture. Fertilizer high in phosphorus, such as 4-12-4, about 20 pounds to 1000 square feet, can be used in preparing the soil. When making new lawns it is well to spade in manure, which gives food and humus. Use 500 pounds of manure to each 1000 square feet. Even if the texture is right, organic matter is needed to improve the soil so that air and water can enter. Some soil in the South is rather acid, and in such cases lime has to be added. (See Chapter II, Soil.)

A good time to plant a lawn is in the fall, though it can also be done in spring and at other times. The rainfall, warm soil and cool nights of autumn are ideal for germination, and since weeds are then dormant the grass gets a good start before spring. October is the best month for planting lawns in most of the South. When the right kind of grass is used, it does not need protection. Leaves should be raked off to prevent smothering. Grassy sod can be transplanted at any season if there is moisture enough in the soil. Cover it so as to leave a smooth surface.

For good appearance, lawns need to be cut once a week or oftener, particularly in damp weather. In dry, hot seasons the job need not be done so often. It is better, however, to mow frequently and not so close. Short grass clippings can be left to decay, for they help to form essential humus. If grass is allowed to grow too long, it will mat and be hard to cut, and the long clippings will have to be raked off. If the grass gets tall, mow it twice, setting the mower high at first; rake off the clippings, then with normal adjustment of the blades, mow again. Grass should not be cut close in hot, dry weather, for fair length is needed to shade the roots. Leave it about 1½ or 2 inches high.

Mowing the lawn will keep weed tops cut and will cause the grass to grow and crowd out most of the weeds. The few that are left can easily be dealt with. There is a weed-killing tool to cut them below the surface of the ground. Annual weeds are usually kept down by the mowing, which prevents them from going to seed. The best way to get rid of the perennials or biennials that persist, like plantain and dandelion, is to get them up by the roots, or they can be destroyed by applying a chemical in the crowns of the weeds.

A velvety lawn is composed of numerous plants growing close together. It needs frequent clipping and applications of plant food.

Water grass lightly but abundantly, to encourage deep feeding roots. It is better to soak once or twice weekly than to sprinkle daily. A light application of peat moss helps the ground to hold moisture and supplies some humus. To repair bare places in a lawn, give them some plant food, preferably old manure forked in, and then sow more seed.

The annual Italian rye-grass is much used in the South for green winter lawns over Bermuda sod, but it should be kept cut so as not to shade and kill the Bermuda roots. A green lawn in winter can be had by raking in an evergreen mixture of seed or Italian rye in the fall. English rye-grass (*Lolium perenne*) is a perennial also good for this locality. The seed may be sown over the grass. Before sowing, cut the grass, rake off the clippings and apply a complete balanced food, 2 to 4 pounds to 100 square feet. Then water, and after two or three days broadcast the seed, a pound to 100 square feet. In sowing the seed, choose a calm day and take small sections of the lawn at a time, in order to distribute the seed evenly; rake in lightly, and water. Keep moist until the grass starts growing and cut when about 3 or 4 inches high. Or let rain make the seed germinate. If you start watering, keep it up until the grass is well started.

After the grass is established in spring, a fertilizer high in nitrogen, such as 10-6-4, 10 pounds per 1000 square feet, can be used. Nitrogen, phosphorus and potash are all necessary, but nitrogen is most needed to hasten growth. About June, lawns will need plant food of a high nitrogen content; then again in the fall, food of low nitrogen content.

If dry fertilizers are spread on when the grass is wet, the lawn should be watered immediately to prevent its being burned. Rain or watering takes the fertilizer into the soil. Sometimes a lawn needs to be rolled to make it even, but rolling can cause harm by packing the soil. The roller should always be a light one and should not be used until frost is out of the ground. Rolling may be done when the ground is moist but not wet.

Bermuda grass is fine for any sunny area in the South, from Florida to the upper Piedmont, except very wet soil. It stays green from April till frost, but frost turns it brown. Bermuda grass may be propagated from seeds or root cuttings. Coastal Bermuda is a hybrid, produced in 1936 by the Georgia Coastal Plain Experiment Station at Tifton, Ga., which has larger leaves and runners than common

To repair an old lawn, first loosen the soil well with a rake.

Sow the seed on a calm day and scatter it evenly.

Never use a roller if the ground is very wet.

A smooth, fine-textured lawn sets off a house to perfection.

St. Augustine grass makes a thick, springy sod in the lower South. It does best when it is started by cuttings in spring and summer and does not object to being grown near salt water.

Bermuda grass. St. Augustine grass is a coarse variety for the middle and lower South. It will grow where other grasses do not thrive. This does well in the sandy soil of the coast. In light sandy soil in the lower and middle South centipede grass is proving satisfactory. Both St. Augustine and centipede grasses are propagated by cuttings.

For the upper South and Piedmont sections, Kentucky blue-grass, which likes cooler weather, or a mixture of hardier grasses, gives good results. White Dutch clover is often used in mixtures, but too much of it will take over the lawn completely. Manila-grass (*Zoysia Matrella*) will grow in sun or shade in dry or wet soil, clay or sandy; it is fine for Florida and the Gulf Coast and does especially well in Alabama. It browns later in the fall and turns green earlier in spring than Bermuda grass. For best results the soil should be limed, so as not to be too acid. *Poa trivialis*, the rough blue-grass, is good for shady places.

Chapter IV

Season By Season In The Flower Garden

SPRING

The spring clean-up helps to keep plants vigorous and healthy. With air in the soil and plant food available to the roots, plants are in condition for another growing season. Systematic upkeep gives a garden a tidier appearance and makes it easier to maintain.

Winter mulch should be taken off gradually because of the possibility of strong sun and late cold, or dug in early in the spring. Otherwise the plants may have tender growth subject to injury by late frost. Certain plants, like azaleas, need mulch all the time. Evergreens and some deciduous shrubs do well with both winter and summer mulch.

The success of summer and autumn gardens depends on the work done in the spring. Plants that bloom in autumn are transplanted at this time. Generally those flowering after the middle of August are planted in spring. Seeds of tender plants may be sown outdoors in the warmer sections in March and in other areas during April and May.

There is special work for March. Loosen the soil lightly about roses. Feed and spray or dust the bushes every ten days, especially for blackspot and mildew. Fertilize the lawn, using a plant food with high nitrogen content. Bare spots need to be reseeded. To make a nice lawn and crowd out weeds, the grass should be cut often but not too close. All paths should be edged and sod borders cut back from plants. New lawns can be started this month.

Perennials need careful cultivation, but do not risk damaging them by digging in the beds too early. Fertilize them in spring when the first shoots come up unless manure was put on the previous fall. Divide and replant perennials such as chrysanthemums, phlox, shasta daisies, gaillardias and pampas grass.

Foliage of early bulbs that have bloomed may be tied down to allow nearby plants more air and sunshine and to make a neater appearance. Bulb foliage must not be cut until it has ripened.

April and May are very busy months for the gardener. In April begins the pruning of shrubs that have finished blooming, such as

38

winter jasmine, breath-of-spring and *Spiræa Thunbergii*. New growth on conifers can be trimmed. Spray peonies, phlox and delphinium with Bordeaux mixture as soon as growth starts.

Roses can be planted and shrubs and trees set out until the middle of April in the upper sections of the South. Early spring is the best time to plant magnolias and dogwoods. Plant food dug in now will make established roses and other shrubs lose their winter-sick look. Manure is the best fertilizer, but bonemeal and wood ashes are good.

May is just cool enough to make one want to work in the garden. Weeds and unwanted grass should be uprooted before they make headway. Continue the pruning of shrubs that have flowered, so that they will not grow out of bounds; those that bloom later in the summer should not be trimmed now. Cut off some of the lower branches of shrubs to make them thicken, and shorten other branches to improve the shape. Many annuals, too, grow bushier and produce more flowers if their tops are pinched back.

After azaleas have bloomed, sprinkle cottonseed meal or special food about them and keep them mulched. Tropical water-lilies may be put outdoors at this time. If the withered blossoms are removed from tulips, the bulbs will be strengthened. (See Chapter IX, Tulips.) Cut wilted peony blooms so as to prevent seed formation. The foliage must not be cut down; it is needed all through the growing season for the future well-being of the plant. A continuous succession of gladioli can be had if early, medium and late varieties are planted until July. If the corms are set about 5 inches deep, the plants will not require much staking.

To keep a garden continually supplied with flowers for cutting in summer and fall, grow annuals. Petunias, for fragrance and color, and zinnias will give a wealth of flowers. The seeds of these and others can be sown where they are to stay and the plants thinned the proper distance apart, or they can be sown in seed flats and transplanted. Vines, such as Heavenly Blue and Scarlett O'Hara morning-glories, cypress-vines, moonvine and others, planted in spring, will make a fine display over an arbor, trellis or fence.

SUMMER

Many amateur gardeners give up in June when the bountiful display of spring bloom is past. But a garden deserves and responds to constant care. In our climate one can have flowers blooming every month in the year. In fact, each month suggests certain flowers.

For example, June brings to mind the fragrance of cape-jasmine, magnolia blossoms, mimosa and roses. But even if flowers are not blooming in the heat of the summer, a garden can be quite attractive and restful.

Keeping faded blooms and yellowed leaves picked off so that plants will continue to bear flowers is a constant task in summer. If one wants to save seed, it is better to select a few plants for that special purpose.

Do not cut perennials back to the ground until the foliage has yellowed; the leaves give vitality to the roots. The plants may be trimmed back a little at a time as the tops die. Sometimes delphiniums are cut down after flowering to encourage a second blooming, but this weakens the plants and makes them less able to go through winter. In the South it is best to treat the delphinium as an annual or biennial.

Now is the time to dry strawflowers and grasses for winter bouquets. They should be picked before they are mature and hung upside down to hold their form. There are numerous strawflowers or everlastings, such as celosia, echinops, helichrysum and statice, that make unusual borders in summer and keep their color when dried in the shade. Many garden flowers retain their color and shape if dried in borax. Lay the flowers in a box with borax beneath and covering them. In room temperature they will be completely dried in about three weeks.

If watering is necessary in summer, soak the ground. Cultivating after every rain, as the soil dries, builds up a dust mulch. A summer mulch of peat moss or leaf mold applied after a rain wards off the heat of the sun and conserves moisture.

In June many perennials begin to die down, such as doronicum and Oriental poppies. Place labels beside them so that you will not dig into the roots. If faded day-lilies are picked off, the current day's blooms will be more effective. Cut off side shoots of dahlias at the ground to strengthen the main stems. Pinching back the tops makes bushier growth.

Blackspotted leaves on rose bushes should be picked and burned. Dust or spray the foliage every week or ten days to prevent the spread of infection. A mulch of dust or peat moss will protect the roots and keep moisture in the soil. A good time to fertilize roses is after the first rush of bloom is over. Give a heaping tablespoonful of balanced food to each plant. With a little care one can have roses all summer.

As soon as the flowering season is over, the transplanting of bearded irises may begin. They do best if the rhizomes are mature. A medium, rather sweet soil and a sunny location are needed for them. Good drainage and air are essential.

If your daffodils did not flower well the past season, they may be overcrowded. When the foliage is dead, dig them up and separate the bulbs. They can be replanted at once or kept in a dry cool place and planted in the fall. Set them in a different location if they have had too much shade or if shrubbery has grown over them.

When transplanting seedlings, water them well before taking them up, and get as much soil as possible with the roots so that rootlets will not be broken. Seedlings must have moisture until they are well anchored. In hot weather it is well to shade them a few days.

During July, verbenas, petunias and other annuals, as well as perennials, are becoming exhausted from flowering. If they are cut back somewhat and given plant food, they will put out new growth and enjoy a long season of bloom. Any seed that has been left to ripen should be gathered when it is ready. Seeds of delphinium and some other plants germinate better if they are sown just as soon as they mature.

Cleanliness in the garden, sunlight, plant food and cultivation are preventives of disease. Cultivation at the right time makes weed pulling unnecessary. The hot sun will kill weeds in a day if the ground is stirred up in the morning. Flowering stems of all irises should be cut back to the ground so that plants will not be exhausted and air and sunshine can penetrate to the roots. To give the garden a neater look, pull up dead larkspurs and cut back hollyhocks. Self-sown seed may not be the kind wanted, and plants coming up in the wrong places are a nuisance.

August is an ideal time to plant Oriental poppies, for they are dormant in midsummer. The long taproot should go straight down into the soil. If any roots are left in the ground when transplanting, new plants will come. Seeds of pansy, calendula, stocks, English daisy, sweet william, wallflower, snapdragon and flax may be sown this month for next year's bloom. Do not let the seed beds dry out nor stay too wet. It is well to place laths over them or to place them in semi-shade. The seedlings will be ready to transplant in the fall.

Do not allow azaleas to wilt. They like moisture, but too much at this time causes leaves to form at the expense of buds.

When the garden has had good care in spring and early summer, one can enjoy a vacation and not be afraid that valuable plants will be sacrificed. They will thrive without artificial watering if they have been cultivated or mulched. If spraying has been done regularly, "bugs" and diseases have been checked.

It will not be burdensome to do a few necessary things in the cool of the morning or evening during this vacation month. Now we can enjoy the full glory of summer. The dew-drenched morning-glories are a joy to see, and at night the garden is full of fragrance. Tree frogs and birds make their presence known, while colorful butterflies match the flowers they court.

AUTUMN

Autumn is a delightful season for outdoor work. The days are short and sunny, the nights cool and long, and there is likely to be some rain. Work done now greatly relieves the gardener during the rush period in spring when the ground is apt to be too wet. Most plants that bloom before June can be set out in autumn. If manure is added to the soil in the fall, plants will do well without other fertilizer the following year.

Lawns made in the fall have many advantages over spring-seeded ones. Weed growth is slower and the temperature and moisture are more favorable, encouraging the grass to become established before winter. A clean-up in the fall not only gives the garden a neater appearance over winter but is a preventive of plant diseases.

The garden is a satisfaction in September if constant care has brought weeds and pests under control. The gardener, however, should not get careless, for this is seedling time and weeds must not be permitted to go to seed. If not destroyed, the roots of perennial weeds will sprout again. Cone-bearing evergreens can be transplanted the last of the month, for they have a fall growing season. Evergreens do best if they have a ball of soil around their roots when they are moved. Shear and clip tender growth on evergreens.

Get the borders ready for perennials, many of which can be put out the last of this month.

Take off small side buds from exhibition chrysanthemums for finer blooms. Feed them about once a week with liquid manure, discontinuing as the buds begin to open. To prevent burning during dry weather, soak the ground with water before manure treatment.

Peonies resent being moved and should be planted where they can remain for years. If yours have become crowded or are in the ground too deep to flower well, they can be divided now. Peonies need cold weather for a resting spell, and for that reason do not flourish in the lower South. In dividing them, leave three to five good eyes and do not plant deep; set them about 2 inches below the surface in a spot where peonies have not grown before. Give them a sunny location in rich, well-drained, heavy rather than light soil and keep them watered until autumn rains come, but do not let water stand over the crowns.

This is a good time to plant Japanese iris, and not too late to move bearded irises. If the ground is dry, soak it well before doing any planting.

October is a busy month in the garden. Labor is well spent getting all beds in readiness before planting time. It is a good practice to prepare the borders for pansies and let them stand for several weeks. In most of the South, it is best not to set out these cool-weather plants until November.

Seedling perennials from seed sown in spring or August can be transplanted now to permanent places. Many perennials thrive when moved in autumn, but there is no ideal time for setting out of them. Some do best if moved in the heat of summer when their resting stage begins, but those that bloom in the fall should go into the ground in spring. The stock of perennials can be increased by sowing seed or by separating the roots.

All spring-flowering bulbs except tulips can be set out in October. In this climate tulips should not be planted until November.

At this time azaleas and camellias need an abundance of water, because their flower buds are being formed. Dogwood and boxwood set out the past winter and early spring must not be allowed to get too dry.

In our temperate climate, where we have a wonderful Indian summer, we should plan our gardens for vivid color in autumn. Evergreens will harmonize the colors. Trees, shrubs and perennial vines that mature wood early can be transplanted as soon as the leaves begin to shed, but do not yet plant varieties that hold leaves late. Nearly all plants do best if moved when dormant. Let the new growth become hardened before setting out evergreens. They do not have a dormant season.

November is the great planting month. Any losses from fall planting are usually the result of allowing the ground to get too dry for the roots to take hold. Continue the moving of deciduous trees and shrubs. New roots will form before winter, and the plants will be ready to grow in the spring. The ground is now warm and the

43

air is cool, which encourages root growth and retards top growth. Success is practically certain with roses planted in November, December or January. Hard growth cuttings of boxwood can be put out and clove pinks layered at this time.

Gather gourds when they are firm. Frost is not likely to hurt them, but it is best not to let the highly colored ones get frost-bitten. Sow seed of sweet peas, larkspur, cornflower, nemophila, phlox and other hardy annuals.

This is an ideal time to gather ferns and mosses for a terrarium. Plants for Christmas are potted early this month. Those in water and gravel should be put in a dark, cool place for about three weeks. Lily-of-the-valley pips will send out blooms in a few weeks. For iris to go into winter in a healthy condition, cultivate about them before the ground freezes.

WINTER

In the South there are many days in winter when one can work in the garden.

Strawy manure can be scattered under shrubbery; it serves as a mulch to prevent thawing and freezing, and the nutrients in it will give the plants a good start in spring. There is pruning and dormant spraying to be done. Most shade trees should be pruned in winter or early spring but not in very cold weather lest the wood crack and cause bad wounds. Trees that bleed, like maples and mulberries, had best be trimmed in autumn.

Roses can be planted successfully when there is steady cold. In the lower South wait until it is cold enough to prevent buds from forming before the roots have developed. Long branches of hybrid tea and hybrid perpetual roses may be cut back to about 18 inches so that they will not be whipped about by winds and loosened in the ground. Winter is a good time to layer branches and put out cuttings of roses. (See Chapter III, Propagating.)

Holly also can be transplanted during the winter months. (See Chapter IX, Holly.) Holly trees and other berry-producing plants are not injured if their branches are cut for Christmas decorations. This really prunes them, if the branches are taken out carefully so as not to mar the shape of the plants. Nor will it harm the broadleaf evergreens and conifers to be pruned in December. Mistletoe should be removed from trees. Smilax, a native evergreen vine, so decorative for Christmas and other occasions, can be cut to the ground. It will come up the following spring and do all the better.

The delicate and lacy white flowers of the fringe-tree are never so lovely as when seen against a blue, blue spring sky. It likes a location in full sun. (See page 52.)

Elaeagnus pungens is a useful evergreen shrub for foundation plantings and hedges, with silvery green foliage and attractive, yellowish red fruit. This is a rapid-growing plant of spreading habit.

Conditions in December are still ideal for planting evergreens. Deciduous trees and shrubs may also be moved. Transplanting can go on through winter, but it is best to get as much done as possible before rains. When transplanting trees, many feeding roots are necessarily cut. The branches in the top of the tree should be trimmed so that the roots left can take care of the tree until new ones develop. It is well to mark the southern side of the tree with a piece of tape before removing it; then when replanting, expose the same side to the sun. Sometimes newly planted shade trees are wrapped loosely with burlap or paper from the ground to the branches to prevent sun scald or the entrance of borers.

Summer-flowering shrubs can be cut back in January. The latter part of the month or early in February, all roses except climbers can be pruned. Continue the planting of roses when the ground is open. Use a dormant spray to kill scale insects. This is a good time to place coal ashes around delphiniums and foxgloves to repel slugs. Bonemeal spread around bearded irises now will take effect later.

Lawns may be given a top-dressing during January, but do not apply dry fertilizer to wet grass. Watering must, however, follow the top-dressing, in order to carry the plant food into the ground. An 8-4-4 fertilizer is a good one to use at this time.

Notice whether bulbs or other plants are heaving; if so, press them back into the earth or put more soil over them. Expanding of the upper layer of soil causes roots to be forced upward; plenty of organic matter in the soil helps to prevent it. Seeds can be sown in hotbeds this month.

Tip-shear conifers in February. See that the slight mulch stays over peony shoots, keeping the cold in and the sunshine out. In the warmer sections of the South, February is a good time to clean lily pools and reset hardy water-lilies. In February flowers are blooming in various parts of the South, and sometimes they are injured by cold. Some, like flowering quince, will bloom again.

If the job of cleaning up the garden was not completed in the fall, it should be finished now. Burn the dead tops taken from hardy asters, regal lilies, peonies and zinnias, if there is any suspicion of disease. It prevents confusion to use two baskets, one for dead foliage of healthy plants to be put on the compost heap, and the other for waste to be burned.

Take dead leaves off rock gardens so that the plants will not smother or rot, and add a dressing of good loam, sand and old manure. What mulching is done should be around rather than over plants that have a winter top. The portions above ground may suffer from sun scorch and wind, but no permanent damage will result.

Many birds will stay with us all year in the South if we provide feeding places for them and enough water for bathing as well as drinking. They take baths even when the water is icy. Their thanks comes to us in cheerful song and in the destruction of numberless insects, larvæ and eggs.

During inclement winter weather horticultural books and flower catalogs are the gardener's constant companions. They are full of fascinating and helpful information.

Chapter V

For Bloom The Year Round

TRUE BULBS

The thick part of true bulbs is made of plates or scales. When the bulbs are in their resting stage, they are tunicated or coated with layers or rings like narcissi, or scales like lilies. The feeding roots usually come from underneath the bulbs, but sometimes from above (stem roots), as in tigrinum and speciosum lilies. Within the dormant bulb is the flower bud and a good part of the food needed for growth, manufactured partly by the ripening and dying of the foliage the year before. The roots ripen and die also, before the bulb goes into a dormant state.

True bulbs require little attention, but it pays to give them light cultivation, some food and water. They multiply fast and soon make a gorgeous display if spaded up and divided every few years. They do not have to be separated until they become too crowded to bloom well. To be sure of having flowers the next year, let the foliage die down completely before moving the bulbs. They can be grown from seed but it takes a long time to get flowering plants.

In the South one can have bulbs flowering in the garden nearly all the year, from late winter through summer, until *Sternbergia lutea* (sometimes called the fall daffodil) makes its appearance. Some winters are colder and then flowers are retarded, but usually Paper-White and Soleil d'Or narcissi are in bloom in the lower South in December. Here the season is a little earlier than in the Piedmont, and the mountain section is still later. The old-time trumpet daffodils, such as Princeps, and double Von Sion, begin to bloom in January in the middle section. They are usually at their height in February.

These are followed by the sweet jonquils. The dainty Queen Anne's jonquil, the double campernelle (*Narcissus odorus*), is found in many old gardens in the South. Then come the snowflakes (Leucojum), snowdrops (Galanthus), various narcissi and hybrids, followed by grape-hyacinths (Muscari), feathered hyacinths (*Muscari comosum monstrosum*), scillas, star-of-Bethlehem (*Ornithogalum umbellatum*), poet's narcissi, tulips, camassias and Peruvian daffodils (Ismene).

47

All kinds of narcissi grow well in the northern parts of the South. Fewer can stand the long summers and warm winters along the South Atlantic and Gulf Coast. Tulips will bloom in Florida if the bulbs are kept in cold storage from late September until they are planted in the garden in mid-November.

Dutch, Spanish and English irises flower about two weeks apart, beginning in spring. The leaves of the Dutch and Spanish stand the winter; but the foliage of English iris, which prefers a cool climate, dies down and reappears each spring. After growth starts, the flower buds form—a different procedure from many true bulbs, such as daffodils.

Lilies start their flowering parade in late spring. True lilies (Lilium) are really herbaceous perennials that grow from scaly bulbs. Day-lilies are lily-like but do not belong to the genus Lilium; they have tuberous roots. A succession of showy blooms can be had from lilies, and by careful selection varieties can be obtained for almost any location. They are particularly effective with a background of greenery. The majority do well in sunny places, in average garden soil with good drainage. They generally dislike lime and prefer part shade.

Wet weather promotes the spread of botrytis and mosaic diseases, which sometimes affect lilies. Bordeaux mixture controls botrytis, but bulbs infected with mosaic disease must be dug up and destroyed.

Some true lilies particularly desirable for southern gardens are:

The early-flowering little coral lily (*Lilium tenuifolium*, now known as *L. pumilum*), which makes a fine display in rock gardens;

Madonna lilies (*L. candidum*), which begin to bloom in the middle South in May;

Regal lilies, which bloom next and are followed by *L. auratum*, *L. tigrinum*, *L. formosanum*, the yellow *L. Henryi* and *L. philippinense;*

Sunset lilies (*L. pardalinum giganteum*), of American origin, which are brilliant and disease-free.

Other good bulbs for the South would include:

Belladonna-lily (*Amaryllis Belladonna*). This needs to be in a warm spot and will bloom in late summer or autumn. It requires protection in the cooler parts of the South.

Fairy or rain-lilies (Zephyranthes). These like moist acid soil. The large, rose-pink *Z. carinata* is summer flowering. *Z. rosea* has smaller flowers in autumn; *Z. Ajax* is a golden yellow hybrid. *Z. Atamasco* and *Z. candida* are white; the first is a spring and the latter an autumn bloomer.

48

This airy and appealing vaseful of hybrid lilies shows examples of the marvelous work being done by lily hybridizers. It keeps a gardener busy to try to keep up with the newest varieties.

Lycoris squamigera needs to be placed where the foliage of neighboring plants will hide its long bare stems. It will grow and bloom in part shade.

Hall's amaryllis (*Lycoris squamigera*). The rosy lilac, perfumed flowers appear in August or September.

Lycoris radiata, often also called spider-lily, and Nerine or Guernsey-lily (hurricane-lily in Florida). These surprise us with their flowers in late summer. The foliage comes later. They should not be planted deep nor be disturbed for years.

Spider-lilies (Hymenocallis). These are fragrant natives of the South. *H. occidentalis* is one of the hardiest; it does well in the middle and upper sections, where it flowers in late spring. The more tender varieties do better in the lower South, in shade and woodsy loam.

Summer-hyacinth (*Galtonia candicans*). Racemes of fragrant flowers are borne in summer.

The swamp lily of Florida (*Crinum americanum*). The bright flowers come in summer; the foliage is tropical looking. It needs protection in winter in the Piedmont and upper sections.

BULBOUS PLANTS

Bulbous plants include those that grow from true bulbs; from corms, which are bulb-like but solid, like gladiolus; from fleshy rhizomes, which have roots on the underside, like bearded iris; from tubers, which have a rootstock under ground, like dahlias; from thickened roots, like ranunculus; from tuberous roots, like hemerocallis; and from pips, like lily-of-the-valley.

There is no end of interesting bulbous plants, and fortunately, the climatic conditions and soil of the South are ideal for them. All are easily propagated and will give a diversity of bloom through most of the year. Potash is their particular fertilizer requirement.

In the middle South crocuses, which come from corms, begin to bloom in January. After these come dwarf and intermediate irises from rhizomes, many taller bearded irises and Siberian iris. An iris good for the rockery is the winter-blooming *Iris unguicularis* (*stylosa*); this has the appearance of the native *Iris cristata*. In protected places it will open with the winter sun, and blooms off and on from November to April. The Kæmpferi or Japanese, sometimes called Oriental iris, flower in late spring, and some of the bearded ones in the fall. Certain kinds can be grown in all parts of the South. (See Chapter IX, Iris.)

Gladioli are important for cutting, beginning in early summer. By planting corms every six weeks, until the end of July, one may have blooms until Thanksgiving. Good companions for them are the shellflowers or Mexican flameflowers (Tigridia), which require the same treatment.

Peonies are familiar tuberous plants or herbaceous perennials, blooming in May and June. Early-flowering ones are best for the South, where they can be grown successfully except in Florida and in sandy soils of the coast.

Some bulbous plants are rather particular about requiring some shade. The ranunculus, produced from tuberous roots and blooming in early summer, is one. Tuberous begonias, with roots near the surface, require mulch and plenty of water; if they are in a sheltered place with partial shade, they will bloom for several months. Anemones do well in the central and upper regions of the South, flowering in early summer. These also want moisture but good drainage. The tall-growing, fibrous-rooted eremurus blooms in early summer and needs partial shade.

Brodiæas flower from corms in spring and valley lilies from pips in May. Oxalis will bloom practically all summer and into autumn. Day-lilies (Hemerocallis) bloom in spring, summer and fall, according to the variety.

The butterfly-lily or ginger-lily (Hedychium) has rhizomatous roots and likes a warm climate, moisture, good drainage and rich soil. The sweet-smelling flowers have the appearance of butterflies on the ends of the stalky foliage in late summer. The foliage, as well as the flowers, is ornamental. The rhizomatous bulbs of the showy native American turks-cap lily (*Lilium superbum*) grow in queer-looking clusters. They flower in late summer in the middle and mountainous regions and like ample moisture and partial shade.

Among the later-blooming bulbous plants are the lordly cannas, which come all summer and into autumn. Dahlias begin to flower in summer, and frost catches some of the late varieties. Hostas, montbretias and tuberoses bloom in late summer, and torch-lilies (Kniphofia) continue into autumn. The calla, a fleshy-rooted plant, thrives in gardens of the South in moist, rich soil. Autumn crocus (Colchicum) makes an effective mass in the fall; it does best if undisturbed until it becomes too crowded.

These are the most popular bulbous plants for the South. Many of them boast a very large family of varieties, which combine to make an ever-pleasing picture and offer the adventurous gardener an endless choice of plant material.

SHRUBS AND FLOWERING TREES

The South is rich in flowering shrubs, to supply bloom the year round. The exact time of flowering depends, of course, on one's location and soil as well as the weather. Many shrubs bloom continuously for several months; others, after flowering in the spring, repeat the performance in the autumn.

Shrubs or low-growing trees can be used as screens, backgrounds or accents about driveways and walks. If kept pruned, they are useful for foundation plantings. Some shrubs that do not look well in massed borders are suitable for specimens. Certain low-growing trees can be allowed to grow shrub-like. Shrubs and small trees are easy to grow but if given some care and pruned as needed, will give more pleasing effects. They look best if room is left for the branches to spread naturally.

Following is a partial list of shrubs and flowering trees that flourish in various parts of the South, with their blooming time in the Piedmont section.

JANUARY

Breath-of-spring (*Lonicera fragrantissima*). Creamy white flowers.

Japanese apricot (*Prunus Mume*). A mass of pink blossoms.

Mahonias. Spikes of bell-shaped, yellow blooms.

Winter jasmine (*Jasminum nudiflorum*). The bright yellow flowers give the illusion of sunshine even on gloomy days, spreading on slopes and around trees.

Wintersweet (*Chimonanthus præcox*). Creamy yellow flowers.

FEBRUARY

Bridal wreath (*Spiræa prunifolia*). Miniature blooms along the branches.

Flowering quince (*Chænomeles japonica*). Showy blossoms.

Laurestinus (*Viburnum Tinus*). Red buds becoming white flower clusters.

Primrose jasmine (*Jasminum Mesnyi*). Flowers much like *J. nudiflorum* but larger; this is almost evergreen.

Spiræa Thunbergii. Dainty small white flowers.

Tea olive (Osmanthus). Blooms at the same time as Laurestinus.

MARCH

Forsythia. Makes a telling display next to the silky gray catkins of pussy willow.

Magnolia Soulangeana, flowering peach and flowering almond. Shades of pink.

Photinia. White flowers in panicles.

Redbud (Cercis). Rosy lavender flowers. There is also a white variety.

APRIL

Abelia. Pinkish white bloom from spring to frost.

Beauty-bush (Kolkwitzia) and azaleas. Unfold charming flowers.

Dogwood (Cornus), crab-apples (Malus), tamarix and rose acacia (*Robinia hispida*).

Ligustrums and highbush cranberries (*Viburnum Opulus*).

Mountain-laurel (*Kalmia latifolia*). Pink-edged white flowers like a calico pattern, giving it also the name calico-bush.

Oleanders. Bear some flowers throughout the summer in the Piedmont and Coastal zones.

Pearl-bush (Exochorda). Pearl-like buds and waxy white flowers.

Scotch broom (Cytisus). Gives a golden touch.

Spiræa cantoniensis (Reevesiana). Clusters of double white blooms.

Spiræa Vanhouttei. Drooping branches of single white flowers.

Sweet-shrub (Calycanthus) and banana-shrub (Michelia). Bloom from April to June.

Viburnum Carlesii. Pink buds opening into white clusters.

MAY

Cape-jasmine (Gardenia). Hardy to Tennessee and Virginia. Waxy blossoms practically all summer.

Deutzias, weigelas and Hugonis roses. Make borders bright.

Fringe-tree (Chionanthus). Known locally as granddaddy's gray beard.

Lilacs (Syringa). French hybrids bear flowers of a more distinct color and larger size than the common old sorts. Persian and Chinese lilacs (a hybrid between Persian and *S. vulgaris*) also bloom now.

Nandinas, barberry and holly. Inconspicuous blooms.

Pittosporum.

Pomegranates (Punica). A display of conspicuous flowers; will continue to bear some blooms all summer.

Rhodotypos tetrapetala (kerrioides). White blossoms.

Silver-bells (Halesia) and zenobias. In full bloom now.

Snowball (Viburnum) and mock-orange (Philadelphus). Old favorites.

Tatarian honeysuckle (*Lonicera tatarica*). Rose-colored flowers.

Abelia is a popular shrub because it blooms for such a
long time and stands shearing so well. It is an evergreen
in the South, used in foundation plantings and hedges.

At Mount Vernon, Va., familiar perennials and herbs link us with colonial times. (See page 2.)

JUNE

Anthony Waterer spirea. Flat heads of rose-colored blooms.

Goldenrain-tree (*Kœlreuteria paniculata*). Not particular about soil but prefers a sunny place. Covered with clusters of yellow flowers.

Hypericum. Single yellow, rose-like blooms on this dwarf shrub until late in summer.

Mimosa, *Magnolia grandiflora* and roses. These perfume the air for many weeks.

Smoke-trees (Cotinus). Loose panicles of flowers that look like smoke when the seeds ripen.

Stewartia. Large white flowers.

Styrax japonica. Graceful flowers.

JULY

Altheas and buddleias.

Chaste-tree (*Vitex Agnus-castus*). Blooms from July to frost.

Crape-myrtles (Lagerstrœmia).

Hydrangeas, blue and pink.

Spanish bayonet (*Yucca aloifolia*). Spikes of creamy white, bell-shaped flowers.

AUGUST

Autumn sage (*Salvia Greggii*). Spikes of carmine flowers from early spring to frost. There is also a white variety.

Beauty-berry (Callicarpa). Small, lavender-pink flowers.

Hibiscus.

Hydrangea, Hills of Snow.

White-alder or summersweet (*Clethra alnifolia*).

SEPTEMBER

Bush clover (*Lespedeza Thunbergii (Sieboldii)*). Forms a shrub in the South; pea-shaped, pink flowers.

Genista tinctoria. A mass of golden yellow flowers.

Tea olive (Osmanthus). Blooms again in September.

OCTOBER

Altheas, buddleias and crape-myrtles. These continue to flower.

Eleagnus. Blooms from October into December.

Flowering quince. Shows some ornamental blossoms.

Mint-shrub (Elsholtzia). Spicy spikes of flowers.

53

NOVEMBER

Groundsel-tree (Baccharis). Downy panicles of bloom.

Holly-leaf tea olive (*Osmanthus Fortunei*).

Loquats (Eriobotrya). These blooms in the lower South in November and December, also in the middle South in sheltered places.

Tea-plant (*Thea sinensis*).

DECEMBER

Camellia Sasanqua. Flowering in parts of the South.

Winter jasmine. Beginning to open its buds now.

Other shrubs and small trees recommended for a succession of bloom in the South are:

Acacia Farnesiana. Called sweet acacia. Globular, golden flowers in April in the Coastal zone.

Bird-of-paradise-flower (*Poinciana (Cæsalpinia) pulcherrima*). Sometimes confused with the poinciana. Makes an attractive planting.

Blue spirea (*Caryopteris incana*). Flowers in late summer in the Piedmont and lower sections.

Bottle-brush (Callistemon). Showy red clusters of flowers shaped like bottle-brushes, in summer and some even into November.

Buckeyes (Aesculus). Handsome foliage. In a moist loamy soil will bear flowers in May and June in the lower South.

Button-bush (Cephalanthus). Will thrive in a moist sandy place and produce creamy flower balls in late summer.

Desert-willow (Chilopsis). A native of Texas, with willow-like foliage. Lilac and yellow flowers from July to frost.

Franklinia (*Gordonia alatamaha*). Blooms from August to frost. Discovered by William Bartram in his travels through Georgia in the 1700's.

Goldenchain-tree (Laburnum). Showy flowers in early summer.

Japonica (Camellia). Varieties bloom from November to April.

Jasminum humile. Blooms in summer and autumn.

Jasminum officinale. Flowers in summer.

Kerrias. Bear flowers nearly all summer.

Loblolly bay (*Gordonia Lasianthus*). Blooms in the lower South in June and July.

Plumbago capensis. A desirable semi-climbing shrub in the lower South. It likes an abundance of water and rich soil and does best in partial shade. The pale blue, phlox-like flowers (there is also a white variety) are borne on the ends of willowy stems. Will bloom continuously if the flowers are kept cut.

Poinsettias. Bloom in December in the low South, and make a spectacular display for Christmas.

Rhododendrons. Beautiful blooms in the upper area in June and July.

Royal poincianas. Panicles of gorgeous flowers in the low South from June to October.

Witch-hazel (*Hamamelis virginiana*). Flowers in late autumn.

VINES

Both hardy and tender vines are used extensively in garden making, for screens on trellises, for shade about porches, pergolas and arbors, and for covering banks and rocks, brick and stone walls and chimneys. They are valuable for screening any undesirable views. Their creeping, clinging or twining habit of growth and the colors of the foliage are often as interesting as the flowers.

In training vines, let them turn the way they naturally grow. Morning-glories, for example, twine from left to right but Hall's honeysuckle from right to left.

In the South vines may be had flowering nearly all the year. For the intervals between bloom, evergreen and berry-producing vines will brighten the garden. Winter jasmine is sometimes considered a vine, for the green stems and yellow blossoms run over banks and rocks to make trailing sunshiny spots in January.

Some good flowering vines, with their season of bloom in the Piedmont section, are:

FEBRUARY

Periwinkle (*Vinca major* and *minor*).

MARCH

Native Carolina jessamine (Gelsemium). Perfumed flowers. This will flourish if planted while in flower, in acid soil.

Wisteria. Sends forth festoons of flowers on wood of the previous season. When the wood ripens and moisture conditions are favorable, the flowers come again and again during the summer.

APRIL

Akebia. Rosy purple flowers in early spring.

Native woodbine or trumpet honeysuckle (*Lonicera sempervirens*) and an improved kind, *L. Brownii*.

MAY

Confederate-jasmine or star-jasmine (*Trachelospermum jasminoides*). Blooms from April until late summer in the middle and lower sections of the South. The yellow-flowering *T. asiaticum* (*divaricatum*) has smaller flowers and is more hardy.

Euonymus radicans. Insignificant blooms followed in late summer by attractive orange-red and pinkish berries.

JUNE

Bignonias. A hardy vine blooming from June through summer and autumn.

Native trumpet-creeper (*Campsis* (*Bignonia*) *radicans*). The blooms are similar to the preceding and can be seen in southern fields and along highways.

Chinese trumpet-creeper (*Campsis grandiflora*). Does not grow tall but is a gorgeous sight in June and through summer. It can be kept to bush shape by pruning.

Decumaria. A native vine with fragrant, hydrangea-like, white flowers. It will climb high and cling without support to walls.

Large-flowering clematis. Begins to bloom in early summer. Nearly all varieties like lime; they prefer shade at their roots, but the tops want sun. They stand the drought and heat of summer and have charming flowers.

JULY

Cinnamon-vine (*Dioscorea Batatas*). Creamy, cinnamon-scented flowers from July until fall. This fast-growing vine can become a nuisance because sometimes its potato-like seeds fall and sprout where they are not wanted.

Perennial morning-glory or blue dawn-flower (*Ipomœa Leari*). Royal blue flowers from July until frost. When frost cuts it down, cover it with mulch and it will come up again the next year.

Porcelain-vine (Ampelopsis). Finely cut leaves; greenish blooms in summer.

Small-flowering clematis (*Clematis paniculata*). Fragrant blooms in midsummer and fall.

Virginia creeper (*Parthenocissus quinquefolia*).

AUGUST

Kudzu-vine (*Pueraria Thunbergiana*). A fast grower for shade or forage, having clusters of pea-shaped flowers in summer.

Madeira-vine or mignonette-vine (*Boussingaultia baselloides*). Comes from tuberous roots; bears delightful small scented flowers in late summer and fall.

May-pop or wild passion-flower. Grows in fields.

Passion-vine (*Passiflora cærulea*). White and light purple blossoms in summer.

Silver lace-vine (Polygonum). Covered with myriads of white flowers in summer and fall. The roots should be protected in winter.

SEPTEMBER

Climbing honeysuckle (*Lonicera japonica*). In September and all during summer and autumn one can enjoy its flowers. Will grow in shade or sun.

Coral-vine (Antigonon). Laden with rose-pink flowers from June to autumn and is at its height in September. If this vine has too much fertilizer, growth will be vigorous at the expense of flowers.

Other vines recommended for the South would include:

Smilax. A native of the Southern States. Will climb to the tops of trees; the blooms of summer are insignificant but the vines are much used for decorations.

Perennial pea (*Lathyrus latifolius*). An attractive sight scrambling over boulders or on fences. If the flowers are kept cut, this vine will bloom from summer to frost.

Bittersweet (*Celastrus scandens*). Will thrive in the upper sections of the South. Orange-red blooms in summer and showy fruit for winter.

Allamandas. Yellow blossoms. Trained as vines or shrubs in lower Florida. In rich leaf mold in semi-shade, they will bloom much of the year.

Bougainvilleas. Desirable climbers in lower Florida.

Ivy. Conspicuous in winter, not for flowers but for the evergreen leaves.

Native evergreen partridge-berry (Mitchella). A graceful trailer. This forms mats, particularly effective under evergreens. The small white flowers with pinkish throats are followed by bright berries in winter.

Balloon-vine (*Cardiospermum Halicacabum*). A perennial grown as an annual. After the bunches of flowers the seeds come, in balloon-like disks.

Cup-and-saucer (Cobæa). A tender perennial treated as an annual; greenish violet, bell-shaped flowers. An interesting climber.

57

There are many annual vines that flower in spring, summer and autumn. They suffer a setback if they come up too early in the garden, and sometimes do not recover. Among the best are:

Sweet peas. Everyone likes these for cut flowers; they can be planted in autumn in a well-prepared trench.

Cypress-vines (Quamoclit). From early summer into October the delicate tracery of vine and leaves, as well as the star-shaped flowers, can be enjoyed.

Heavenly Blue morning-glories. Blooms are produced profusely from July to November. If seeds are planted in the hotbed and the plants put out in April, they begin to bloom in June. In the cool of autumn the blossoms stay open practically all day. All morning-glories (Ipomœa) are attractive on dewy mornings in summer.

Moonvines. Open their flowers in the evening.

Thunbergias. Easily grown annual vines. The flowers, in shades of yellow, are opening all summer.

Balsam-pear (*Momordica Charantia*). Ornamental climber. The yellow flowers are followed by yellow fruits which split open, and the reddish arils show brownish seeds.

Hyacinth bean (*Dolichos Lablab*). White or purple flowers and bean-like seed pods. Another ornamental vine.

Gourd vines. Certain kinds are very attractive in flower and fruit.

Climbing and creeping roses are charming in spring. Some repeat their bloom during summer and fall. Cherokee and Banksia roses are perfectly at home in the South. The Cherokee is good for holding banks, and the Banksia makes an excellent wall covering. Both can be trained over arbors and will climb to the tops of trees.

The following outline of the particular uses to which some of our favorite vines are best adapted, may prove useful:

For trellises and screens
Carolina jessamine	Porcelain-vine
Confederate-jasmine	Silver lace-vine
Honeysuckle	

For house porches
Smilax	Woodbine
Wisteria	

For brick or stone walls
Banksia rose	Ivy
Decumaria	Virginia creeper
Euonymus radicans	

For ground cover
    Ivy
    Partridge-berry
           Periwinkle (*Vinca major* and *minor*)

For banks, fences and rocks
    Bignonia   Honeysuckle
    Cherokee rose   Passion-vine

Herbaceous climbers
    Blue dawn-flower   Madeira-vine
    Cinnamon-vine   Passion-vine
    Coral-vine   Perennial pea
    Kudzu-vine

PERENNIALS

Perennials are plants with roots that will remain alive for more than two years, whether the leaves are held or not. Some are evergreen and others herbaceous, with tops that die annually. Perennials do not live forever, though many do live a long time. They flower in southern gardens practically the year through, but some of them are difficult to raise along the Gulf Coast. If judicious selections are made, they will give beauty to garden borders and rock gardens for many seasons. Most bulbous plants are perennials; shrubs and trees are woody perennials.

The flowering time of a plant depends on how fast it develops. Some plants take longer than others to get to the flowering stage. The time of bloom given for the following perennials is based on our garden in the Piedmont section:

JANUARY

Violets

FEBRUARY

Hardy candytuft (Iberis)
Phlox subulata

MARCH

Ajuga, aubrieta, basket-of-gold alyssum (*Alyssum saxatile*), erinus, *Phlox divaricata*
    Ranunculus repens
    Brunnera macrophylla (*Anchusa myosotidiflora*)
White rock-cress (*Arabia alpina*). *Arabis alpina grandiflora* has much larger flowers, and *A. alpina rosea* has rose-colored ones. All these low growers are suitable for the rock garden.

59

APRIL

Geum

Linum

Painted daisies (*Chrysanthemum* (*Pyrethrum*) *coccineum*)

Transvaal daisies (Gerbera)

Primula, bleeding-heart (*Dicentra spectabilis*) and columbine (Aquilegia). These want part shade.

MAY

Anchusa, Dropmore

Astilbe

Coral-bells (Heuchera)

Delphinium

Doronicum

Lupines

Oriental poppies (*Papaver orientale*)

Snapdragons (Antirrhinum)

Virginia bluebells (Mertensia)

Gaillardia and golden marguerite (Anthemis). Will bloom in May and continue during the summer if withered flowers are kept cut.

Armeria, coat-flower (*Tunica Saxifraga*), corydalis, saponaria and snow-in-summer (Cerastium). These are blooming in the rock garden.

JUNE

Artemisias. Feathery foliage and small flowers.

Azaleamums

Coreopsis

Feverfew. Begins to make a display. If the flowers are kept cut, it blooms intermittently all summer. Silver Ball is a double white variety and Golden Ball a double yellow.

Hardy carnations (Dianthus). Make bright spots of color.

Harebells (*Campanula carpatica*). Bloom in partial shade.

Shasta daisies

JULY

Achillea Ptarmica, The Pearl. Keeps colors toned down.

Bee-balm (Monarda)

Golden-glow (*Rudbeckia laciniata*). Lives up to its name.

Hibiscus

Lantana

Lychnis Coronaria. Silvery foliage.

Magnolia Soulangeana becomes a broad spreading tree
sure to be of high interest at blooming time. The
large, cupped flowers are stained purplish pink outside.

Dependable is the word for phlox. Its huge heads of bloom in many bright colors are often the standby of a perennial border in midsummer. It seems to do well in practically any soil.

Peach-leaf bellflower (*Campanula persicifolia*). Beautiful blooms.
Phlox. A show in itself.
Sweet rockets (Hesperis). Perfume the air.
Thermopsis. Long spikes of yellow bloom.

AUGUST

Boltonia
False dragonhead (Physostegia)
Knotweed (*Polygonum cuspidatum*). The racemes of this bushy
perennial are fine for drying.
Lavender
Plume-poppy (Bocconia)
Sea-lavender (*Limonium latifolium*). Bears mist-like flowers also
fine for drying.
Veronica

SEPTEMBER

Blue sage (Salvia). Blends its color into the landscape.
Centaurea montana. There are both white and blue varieties.
Lobelia
Michaelmas daisies and other hardy asters. These make a showy
effect.
Native eupatorium
Stokesia

OCTOBER

Autumn glory (Helianthus)
Korean chrysanthemums

NOVEMBER

Chrysanthemums
Mammoth hybrid verbenas
Perennial asters. Native in South Carolina and along the coast
into Florida. Can be grown in gardens. They bloom in November
and December.

DECEMBER

Christmas rose (Helleborus)
This by no means exhausts the list of perennials that grow in the
South, but a selection from the list given makes it possible to have
continuous bloom in the garden. (See also Chapter VI.)

ANNUALS AND BIENNIALS

Annuals are useful for bedding and for brightening borders where perennials have finished flowering. They may be used for cut flowers from spring until winter, and in parts of the South every month of the year. Some grow in cool weather and bloom in early spring; some flower in summer and others in autumn.

Annuals die normally within a year after the seed is sown. There are hardy, half-hardy and tender varieties. Many hardy annuals such as larkspur and ragged robin do well with seeds sown in the open in November, but the general practice, when the ground gets warm, is to sow annual seeds where the plants are to grow and later thin the plants. Seeds raked into skipped spots during spring and summer will prevent bare places from showing later.

Seeds of half-hardy annuals are usually sown in frames or seed flats. The plants are hardy after they are established. Seeds of tender annuals, which require warmth, are usually started in hot-beds and the plants set out when danger of frost is over. Some annuals self-sow every year. Others are really perennials treated like annuals in the South.

Most biennials do not flower until the second year after the seed is sown, although some bloom the same season. In order to have flowers each year, it is best to treat them as half-hardy annuals and plant the seed each year. Many biennials self-sow or have off-shoots from which new plants grow; some can be propagated by layering or cuttings.

In January, in parts of the South, hardy sweet alyssum and petunias continue to bloom, especially in protected places. Pansies, which are perennials grown as a winter or spring annual in the South, and English daisies (Bellis), a biennial in some localities and a perennial in others, are treated as annuals. They flower as early as February in the Piedmont area. In the low South many annuals begin to bloom in January. Calendulas, phlox, nasturtiums and sweet peas are planted in Florida in early fall for winter bloom.

In the Piedmont, baby blue-eyes (Nemophila) makes showy mats in March, johnny-jump-ups (*Viola tricolor*) bloom even in unexpected spots, and biennial wallflowers (Cheiranthus) and honesty (Lunaria) become noticeable.

Stocks perfume the garden in April as the annual Shirley poppies put on their show. Cornflowers (Centaurea) and calendulas add brightness to the garden; and such biennials as foxglove (Digitalis),

Siberian wallflower (Cheiranthus), sweet william (*Dianthus barbatus*), and Chinese forget-me-not (Cynoglossum) begin to bloom.

For May there are larkspurs, *Phlox Drummondii*, and sweet sultan (*Centaurea moschata*). If browallia is growing in good moist soil, it will bloom from May till frost, thriving in sun or shade. The biennial mullein (Verbascum) makes a pretty display about this time, with its tall stems lined with clusters of yellow flowers.

Annual candytuft, dainty blue lace-flower (Trachymene (Didiscus)), nasturtiums and calliopsis flower in June. Along fence corners Queen Anne's lace (*Daucus Carota*), a biennial, is unfurling its airy blooms. Annual scabiosas make fine cut flowers throughout the summer; there are perennial varieties, too. Biennial hollyhocks (*Althæa rosea*) display spikes of bloom at this time. There are also annual hollyhocks, which come into bloom in about five months from seed sown early.

During July, sunflowers (Helianthus) and Klondyke cosmos show golden flowers, and touch-me-nots (Balsam) have pleasing blossoms. Zinnias and portulacas will continue through the summer. Snow-on-the-mountain (*Euphorbia marginata (variegata)*), with its small white blooms and white-edged green foliage, adds coolness to the garden.

Various marigolds, salvias and the Madagascar periwinkle (*Vinca rosea*) flourish in August. These periwinkles flower all summer in good soil and a sunny location; they thrive in hot or wet weather. Spider-flowers (Cleome) and asters bloom in September. Crotalaria has lupine-like flowers and will bloom until frost; the flowers are attractive and the plants are soil builders.

Mexican sunflowers (Tithonia) make a tall flowering background in October; and ageratum, cosmos and celosias can be blended for color effects. Dwarf ageratum makes a desirable edging, growing about a foot high. In November, nasturtiums, calendulas, salvias and zinnias carry on until frost cuts them down. Sweet alyssum flowers on in December; and in the lower sections of the South other annuals and biennials continue blooming in winter.

This does not include all annuals or biennials that can be grown for a succession of bloom. There are many others; some rarely used give beautiful effects.

SOME OTHER ANNUALS RECOMMENDED FOR THE SOUTH

African daisy (Dimorphotheca) blooms for many weeks. The new hybrids have rich colors. 12 inches and over.

Blazing star (*Mentzelia Lindleyi* (*Bartonia aurea*)) has showy flowers. This likes sandy soil and hot sun. 2 feet.

California bluebells (Phacelia) bear a profusion of bell-like blooms. 8 inches to 2 feet.

Calceolaria blooms abundantly in summer. It likes shade. 1 foot.

Clarkia blooms in six or seven weeks after the seed is sown and continues for many weeks. 1½ to 2 feet.

Collinsias are of easy culture and flower through the summer. 1 foot.

Cotula barbata has small, globular flowers. It likes full sun and damp roots. Fine for rock garden or edging.

Gilia has a long season of bloom. 1 foot.

Godetias bear sheets of color over a long period. 1 to 2 feet.

Linarias are easy to grow and have a long season of bloom. There are annual and perennial varieties.

Mignonette is not showy, but the flowers are fragrant. This will bloom till frost from several sowings in partly shaded places. 1 foot.

Nicotianas are sweet-scented flowers that like a sunny place and good soil. 2 feet.

Nigella, with lace-like foliage, blooms in late spring and early summer. 1½ feet.

Polygonum orientale is good for autumn display and for cutting. It has drooping, rosy crimson spikes of flowers. 4 to 5 feet.

Salpiglossis is a continuous bloomer. 2 feet.

Silene is a mass of flowers from spring into summer. There are annual, biennial and perennial varieties. 1 foot.

Swan River daisy (Brachycome), with attractive daisy flowers, blooms in the open in four to five months after sowing. 6 inches to 1 foot.

Tidy tips (Layia) blooms freely. *L. elegans* has golden daisy-like flowers with a white edge; *L. glandulosa* bears glistening white blooms. 1 foot.

The belladonna-lily or amaryllis looks especially well when planted in masses in the border, where its immense, bright-colored trumpets will make a brilliant display. (See page 48.)

A pink-flowered climber like the coral-vine would
be a fine background for pink or rose-colored perennials. It climbs as high as 40 feet. (See page 57.)

Chapter VI
Emphasis On Color

Borders developed with various tints of the same color at different heights are extremely attractive. The following lists should prove helpful in planning.

PINK OR ROSE-COLORED PERENNIALS AND BIENNIALS

Early Blooming; Low Growing (12 inches or less); Sun
> Dianthus. Various pink varieties, mostly fragrant; need a lime soil; to 1 foot.
> Maiden pink (*Dianthus deltoides*). Makes a fine display; will also thrive in shade in alkaline soil.
> *Phlox amœna.* Bright pink flowers; to 6 inches.
> *Phlox subulata.* Covered with bloom for a long time; mat forming.
> Rock-cress (*Arabis alpina rosea*). Will thrive in shade, too; 6 inches.
> Soapwort (*Saponaria ocymoides*). A trailer with small flowers; to 1 foot.
> Speedwell (*Veronica pectinata rosea*). Small spikes of rosy flowers; to 1 foot.
> Thrift (*Armeria maritima Laucheana*). Grassy foliage and clover-like blooms.

Early Blooming; Low Growing; Partial Shade
> *Ajuga reptans*, Pink Spires. Pink-flowered bugle-plant.
> English daisy (Bellis). Various shades of pink, also white; will grow in sunny places also.
> *Primula rosea grandiflora.* Rose-color with gold center; needs a moist place.

Early Blooming; Medium-High (1 to 3 feet); Sun
> Oriental poppy (*Papaver orientale*), Pink Beauty. 24 to 36 inches.
> Persian candytuft (*Aethionema grandiflorum*). Rose-colored flowers in long racemes; 1 foot and over.

Early Blooming; Medium-High; Partial Shade
> Bleeding-heart (*Dicentra spectabilis*). Sprays of heart-shaped, rosy flowers; 2 feet.
> Primrose (*Primula japonica*). Clusters of flowers, pink, rose, red; to 2 feet.

Midseason Blooming; Low Growing; Sun
   Dwarf babys-breath (*Gypsophila repens rosea*). Covered with rose-colored flowers.
   Rose campion (*Lychnis Viscaria*). Pink flowers in graceful spikes.
   Tunica Saxifraga. Small, pale pink blooms, profusely produced.
Midseason Blooming; Low Growing; Partial Shade
   Plumy bleeding-heart (*Dicentra eximia*). Finely cut foliage; racemes of rose-heart flowers; to 1 foot.
Midseason Blooming; Medium-High; Sun
   Coral-bells (*Heuchera brizoides*). Red stems of pink bells; 1 to 2 feet.
   Hardy cornflower (*Centaurea dealbata*). Soft rosy pink flowers.
   Mullein-pink (*Lychnis (Agrostemma) Coronaria*). Rose-colored flowers and silvery foliage.
   Painted daisy (*Chrysanthemum coccineum (Pyrethrum roseum)*). Long-stemmed daisies for display or cutting.
   Rosy milfoil (*Achillea Millefolium rosea*). Showy corymbs of rosy pink; fern-like foliage.
   Sedum spectabile. Heads of rose-colored flowers; will also thrive in partial shade.
   Sweet william (*Dianthus barbatus*), Newport Pink. A biennial having clusters of salmon-pink flowers on erect stems.
   Transvaal daisy (Gerbera) hybrids. Coral-pink, long-stemmed flowers for cutting.
Midseason Blooming; Tall (3 feet and over); Sun
   Delphinium, Pink Sensation. Clear soft pink.
   Greek mallow (*Sidalcea malvæflora*). Rose-colored, hollyhock-like flowers.
   Hollyhock (*Althæa rosea*), Princess Rose. Double, salmon-rose blooms.
   Hollyhock, Newport Pink. Double, pink flowers on 6-foot plants.
   Lupine (Lupinus), Cross Roads. A pleasing shell-pink.
   Mallow (*Hibiscus Moscheutos (palustris)*). Pink blossoms on stiff stalks.
   Snapdragon (*Antirrhinum maximum*), Loveliness. A rustproof variety with soft rose-pink blooms on tall stems.
   Snapdragon, Rosette. Deep rose.
   Snapdragon, Pink Glory. Salmon.
Late Blooming; Medium-High; Sun
   Chrysanthemum, Pink Spoon.
   Dwarf aster, Little Pink Lady. To 18 inches.
   Korean chrysanthemum, Rose Glow and others.

Late Blooming; Medium-High; Partial Shade
Anemone japonica rosea. Free flowering; 2 feet.
Late Blooming; Tall; Sun
Aster, Harrington's Perfected Pink. Deep rose-pink.
Dahlia, Jersey's Beauty. Pink with shading of chamois, carried on long stems.

PURPLE TO LAVENDER PERENNIALS AND BIENNIALS

Early Blooming; Low Growing (12 inches or less); Sun
Candytuft (*Iberis gibraltarica*). A lavender biennial with whitish tinge; will thrive in partial shade also.
Erinus alpinus. Reddish violet flowers in profusion; does best in mid-day shade.
Pasque-flower (*Anemone Pulsatilla*). Violet-colored flowers; likes chalky soil.
Rainbow rock-cress (*Aubrieta purpurea*). Spreading; deep purple flowers.
Early Blooming; Low Growing; Semi-Shade
Kenilworth ivy (*Cymbalaria muralis* (*Linaria Cymbalaria*)). Trailing; light green leaves and small lilac flowers.
Primrose (*Primula denticulata cachemiriana*). Compact umbels of lilac flowers; 1 foot.
Violet (*Viola odorata*). Purple sweet violet.
Midseason Blooming; Low Growing; Sun
Lily-turf (Ophiopogon). Bluish lavender flower spikes; will also thrive in part shade.
Verbena erinoides. Violet-colored flower heads.
Midseason Blooming; Low Growing; Partial Shade
Campanula Elatines garganica. Bluish lavender flowers in profusion.
Cup-flower (*Nierembergia cærulea* (*hippomanica*)). Petunia-like, delicate blue-lavender blooms; flowers freely into autumn; likes moist soil; 6 inches.
Midseason Blooming; Medium-High (1 to 3 feet); Sun
Canterbury bells (*Campanula Medium*), Lavender. Biennial with mauve bells.
Centaurea montana. Showy, bluish violet blooms; 2 feet.
False dragonhead (Physostegia). Spikes of tubular flowers; likes wet ground; will thrive in part shade.
Fringed daisies (*Erigeron speciosus*). Bluish violet; likes shade from mid-day sun.

67

Honesty (*Lunaria annua* (*biennis*)). Purple, stock-like flowers.

Lavender (*Lavandula officinalis* (*vera*)). Purple spikes of bloom for drying; 1 to 2 feet.

Scabiosa japonica. Long-stemmed, lavender flowers, fine for cutting.

Sea-lavender (*Statice latifolia*). Branching panicles of lavender flowers; 2 feet.

Verbena rigida (*venosa*). Bright purplish violet flowers; 12 to 18 inches.

Midseason Blooming; Medium-High; Partial Shade

Funkia (*Hosta lancifolia*). Spikes of bluish lavender bloom.

Midseason Blooming; Tall; Sun

Digitalis purpurea. Spotted purple; biennial; to 4 feet.

Foxglove (*Digitalis purpurea gloxiniæflora*). Purple biennial; to 4 feet.

Thalictrum dipterocarpum. Violet-mauve flowers in large panicles; showy and fine for cutting; 3 to 4 feet.

Late Blooming; Medium-High; Sun

Eupatorium purpureum. Reddish purple, ageratum-like flowers, for display and cutting; 2 to 5 feet.

Korean chrysanthemums, Lavender Lady and others.

Late Blooming; Tall; Sun

Coneflower (*Echinacea purpurea*). Purple with cone-shaped, brown center; 3 to 4 feet.

Liatris pycnostachya. Long racemes of little rose-purple blooms; 3 to 4 feet.

Michaelmas daisy (Aster).

Perennial asters.

BLUE PERENNIALS AND BIENNIALS

Early Blooming; Low Growing (12 inches or less); Sun

Aster alpinus, Goliath. Large, soft blue flowers; likes light, rich, moist soil; 1 foot.

Early Blooming; Low Growing; Partial Shade

Blue phlox (*Phlox divaricata*). A profusion of lavender-blue blooms.

Bugle (*Ajuga reptans*). Erect, deep blue spikes from runners; will also grow in sun.

Forget-me-not (*Myosotis scorpioides semperflorens*). Pale blue flowers; pink buds.

Polemonium reptans. Clusters of flowers.

Early Blooming; Medium-High (1 to 3 feet); Sun

Flax (*Linum perenne*), Heavenly Blue. Attractive, feathery, bluish foliage; light blue flowers.

The tiger lily is a fitting companion for many perennials. Of course, it looks best with blue and white-flowering plants and should be kept away from reds and pinks.

Foliage and flowers of many shapes, tints, heights and textures contribute to the good looks of a perennial border. The venerable boxwood in the distance is a pleasing contrast to the colors.

Early Blooming; Medium-High; Partial Shade

Spiderwort (*Tradescantia virginiana*). Showy flowers each morning over a long season.

Midseason Blooming; Low Growing; Sun

Beard-tongue (*Penstemon heterophyllus*), Blue Gem. Spikes of deep blue; 10 to 12 inches.

Globe-daisy (*Globularia trichosantha*). Small globular blue daisies; 9 inches.

Speedwell (*Veronica incana*). A mat of foliage and spikes of deep blue flowers.

Midseason Blooming; Low Growing; Partial Shade

Catmint (*Nepeta Mussinii superba*). Silvery leaves and small flowers; 1 foot.

Harebell (*Campanula carpatica*). Purple-blue, cup-shaped flowers.

Midseason Blooming; Medium-High; Sun

Balloon-flower (*Platycodon grandiflorum Mariesii*). Free bloomer; 1 to 2 feet.

Beard-tongue (*Penstemon unilateralis*). Graceful bloom spikes.

Chinese forget-me-not (Cynoglossum). A biennial that makes a fine display.

Hardy bellflower (*Adenophora Potaninii*). Drooping, light blue bells.

Salvia azurea grandiflora. Long racemes of deep blue; 2 to 3 feet.

Scabiosa Fischeri. Violet-blue flowers on stiff stems; 1 to 2 feet.

Speedwell (Veronica), Blue Spires. Spikes for display or cutting; likes light soil.

Stokes aster (*Stokesia lævis (cyanea)*). Continuous bloomer with large, purple-blue, daisy-like flowers; prefers light sandy soil; 15 inches.

Midseason Blooming; Medium-High; Partial Shade

Brunnera macrophylla (*Anchusa myosotidiflora*). Heart-shaped leaves and forget-me-not flowers.

Columbine (*Aquilegia cærulea*). Long-spurred, blue flowers that shade to white.

Jacobs-ladder (*Polemonium cæruleum*). Bright blue flowers; 1 to 3 feet.

Virginia bluebells (*Mertensia virginica*). Glaucous foliage; pale blue flowers.

Midseason Blooming; Tall (3 feet and over); Sun

Anchusa azurea, Dropmore. Bright blue racemes; 3 to 4 feet.

Balloon-flower (*Platycodon grandiflorum*). Bell-shaped flowers; likes sandy soil and will stand shade; to 3 feet.

Campanula pyramidalis. 3 to 5 feet.
Delphinium Belladonna. Light blue.
Delphinium Bellamosum. Deep blue; over 3 feet.
False indigo (*Baptisia australis*). Indigo-blue, pea-shaped flowers; 3 to 4 feet.
Late Blooming; Medium-High; Sun
    Hardy aster, Little Boy Blue. 2 feet.
Late Blooming; Tall; Sun
    Monkshood (*Aconitum Napellus*). Bright blue flowers; rich soil; does best in sun but the flowers last longer if shaded; 3 to 4 feet.

WHITE PERENNIALS AND BIENNIALS

Early Blooming; Low Growing (12 inches or less); Sun
    Snow-in-summer (*Cerastium tomentosum*). Silvery foliage.
Early Blooming; Low Growing; Sun or Part Shade
    Candytuft (*Iberis sempervirens*). Covered with heads of flowers; dark evergreen foliage; especially fine in sun.
    Maiden pink (*Dianthus deltoides albus*). Compact plant making a good display; alkaline soil.
    Rock-cress (*Arabis alpina*). Big clusters of bloom.
    Sand pink (*Dianthus arenarius*). Fragrant white flowers on 4 to 6-inch stems.
Midseason Blooming; Low Growing; Full Sun or Part Shade
    Babys-breath (*Gypsophila repens*). A trailer.
    Campion (*Silene alpestris*). Shiny flowers in large panicles; likes shade.
    Cup-flower (*Nierembergia calycina*). Cup-like, white flowers tinted lavender; 1 foot.
Midseason Blooming; Low Growing; Partial Shade
    Campanula carpatica alba. Bell-shaped flowers; 1 foot.
    Lily-of-the-valley (*Convallaria majalis*). Fragrant, drooping bells; needs acid soil.
Midseason Blooming; Medium-High (1 to 3 feet); Sun
    Achillea Ptarmica, The Pearl. Double white flowers; acid soil; 2 feet.
    Babys-breath (*Gypsophila paniculata*), Bristol Fairy. Dainty double blooms.
    Balloon-flower (*Platycodon grandiflorum album*). Thrives in part shade; 2 feet.
    Beard-tongue (*Penstemon Digitalis*). Spikes of flowers similar to foxglove; 3 feet.

Bellflower (*Campanula persicifolia grandiflora*). Bell-shaped, white flowers; 2 to 3 feet.

Feverfew (*Chrysanthemum Parthenium* (*Matricaria parthenoides*)). Small round flower heads; 1 to 3 feet.

Hardy phlox, Miss Lingard. Will grow in part shade.

Mullein-pink (*Lychnis* (*Agrostemma*) *Coronaria alba*). Silvery leaves; phlox-like flowers.

Shasta daisy, various hybrids. Fine for display and cutting.

Sweet rocket (*Hesperis matronalis alba*). Fragrant; will thrive in part shade; 2 to 3 feet.

Midseason Blooming; Tall (3 feet and over); Sun

Artemisia lactiflora. Of graceful habit; 4 feet.

Chimney bellflower (*Campanula pyramidalis alba*). A pyramid of white; 5 feet.

Plume-poppy (*Macleaya* (*Bocconia*) *cordata*). Showy, gray-lobed leaves; 5 feet.

Thalictrum aquilegifolium. Creamy flowers and pretty foliage; over 3 feet.

Late Summer or Fall Blooming; Medium-High; Sun

Chrysanthemums, various.

Eupatorium rugosum (*Fraseri*). For cut flowers; 1 to 2 feet.

Gas-plant (*Dictamnus albus* (*Fraxinella*)). Sun or shade; 2 feet.

Late Summer Blooming; Medium-High; Partial Shade

Funkia (*Hosta plantaginea*). Large, waxy white, perfumed flowers; grows in sunny spots but does best in partial shade.

Late Blooming; Tall; Sun

Hardy aster, Mt. Everest. A tall pyramid of bloom.

Late Blooming; Tall; Sun or Partial Shade

Boltonia asteroides (*glastifolia*). Daisy-like; 4 feet.

YELLOW OR ORANGE PERENNIALS AND BIENNIALS

Early Blooming; Low Growing (12 inches or less); Full Sun

Alyssum saxatile compactum. Golden yellow; small, grayish leaves; spreading growth.

Yellow flax (*Linum flavum*). Golden, bell-shaped flowers; 8 to 12 inches.

Early Blooming; Low Growing; Partial Shade

Adonis vernalis. Golden flowers; full sun or partial shade; 1 foot.

Buttercup (*Ranunculus repens*). Double yellow flowers.

Cowslip (*Primula veris aurea*). Golden yellow.

71

Primula veris lutea. Pale yellow.

Primrose (*Primula vulgaris*). True yellow primrose.

Early Blooming; Medium-High (1 to 3 feet); Sun

Geum Borisii. Single, bright orange flowers; 15 inches.

Leopards-bane (*Doronicum caucasicum*). Daisy-like; for display and cutting; 18 inches.

Siberian wallflower (*Erysimum asperum* (*Cheiranthus Allionii*)). Orange-yellow; will also thrive in part shade; 18 inches.

Midseason Blooming; Low Growing; Full Sun

Alyssum argenteum. Silvery foliage and yellow flowers; 1 foot.

Evening-primrose (*Oenothera glauca Fraseri*). Flowers in late afternoon; 1 foot.

Ground-cypress (Santolina). Inconspicuous balls of bloom; gray, cypress-like foliage.

Midseason Blooming; Medium-High; Sun

Blanket-flower (Gaillardia), Tangerine. Coppery orange; 3 feet.

Butterfly-weed (Asclepias). Native plant giving a brilliant effect.

Centaurea macrocephala. Large golden heads; 3 feet.

Coreopsis. For display or cutting; Sunburst is a double variety; 3 feet.

Dianthus Knappii. Light yellow; 2 feet.

Geum, Lady Stratheden. Golden yellow; 2 feet.

Golden marguerite (*Anthemis tinctoria*). Daisy-like flowers and ferny foliage; for display and cutting; 2 to 3 feet.

Inula glandulosa superba. Daisy-like; 2 to 3 feet.

Snapdragon (Antirrhinum), Buttercup and Yellow Jacket. Rust-proof; will stand some shade.

Yarrow (*Achillea filipendulina*). Flat heads of flowers; likes dry soil; 2 to 3 feet.

Midseason Blooming; Tall; Sun

Golden-glow (*Rudbeckia laciniata*). Bright yellow, double flowers; 4 to 5 feet.

Hollyhock (*Althæa rosea*), Golden Drop and Yellow King. Biennial; double flowering.

Mullein (Verbascum). Hardy biennial; woolly leaves and showy spikes of bloom; 4 to 5 feet.

Thermopsis caroliniana. Spikes of bright yellow, lupine-like flowers; needs slightly acid soil; 4 feet.

Late Summer and Fall Blooming; Medium-High; Sun

Helenium autumnale. Fine for cutting; 2 to 3 feet.

Late Blooming; Medium-High; Sun
  Chrysanthemum, Golden Cushion of azaleamum type, and various others.
Late Blooming; Tall; Partial Shade
  Trollius Ledebouri, Golden Queen. Deep orange; 3 feet and over.

RED PERENNIALS AND BIENNIALS

Early Blooming; Low Growing (12 inches or less); Sun
  Erinus alpinus carmineus. Bright red; effective in clumps.
Midseason Blooming; Low Growing; Sun
  Dianthus neglectus. Diminutive tufts with cherry-red flowers.
  Dianthus graniticus. Makes a carpet of bright carmine.
  Lychnis Haageana. Large scarlet flowers; to 1 foot.
  Poppy-mallow (*Callirhoë involucrata*). A trailer with crimson bloom.
  Verbena hybrids, such as Fireball. Brilliant flower heads.
Midseason Blooming; Low Growing; Partial Shade
  Cranesbill (*Geranium sanguineum*). Trailing habit with large, purple-red flowers.
Midseason Blooming; Medium-High (1 to 3 feet); Sun
  Bee-balm (*Monarda didyma*). Bright blossoms with an aromatic odor.
  Columbine (Aquilegia), Crimson Star. Crimson spurs and sepals; white petals; long-spurred; will thrive in partial shade, but long-spurred columbines need more sun than short-spurred varieties.
  Geum, Mrs. Bradshaw. Brilliant scarlet flowers.
  Hardy carnations, various red shades.
  Hardy phlox, such as Beacon, Saladin and Tanager.
  Heuchera, Pluie de Feu. Spikes of red bells.
  Maltese cross (*Lychnis chalcedonica*). Scarlet flower heads on upright stalks.
  Oriental poppies (*Papaver orientale*), such as Joyce (cerise-red; to 3 feet); Empress of India (deep red); Australia (blood-red).
  Painted daisy or pyrethrum (*Chrysanthemum coccineum*), James Kelway. Single; vermilion-red with golden center.
  Red valerian (*Centranthus ruber*). Clusters of crimson to pale red, sweet-scented flowers; needs staking.
  Sweet william (*Dianthus barbatus*), Scarlet Beauty. Subglobose heads of bright scarlet bloom.

Midseason Blooming; Medium-High; Partial Shade
  Astilbe, Granat. Graceful, crimson-red plumes; to 3 feet.
  Indian paintbrush (*Lobelia cardinalis*). Needs a moist spot; 2 feet.
Midseason Blooming; Tall (over 3 feet); Sun
  Beard-tongue (*Penstemon Torreyi*). Spikes of tubular, scarlet bloom.
  Oriental poppies (*Papaver orientale*), such as Beauty of Livermere, Wurtembergia, Lulu A. Neeley.
  Red-hot-poker (Kniphofia). Tall spikes of orange-scarlet.
Late Blooming; Medium-High; Sun
  Button chrysanthemum, Little Dot. Mahogany-crimson.
  Korean chrysanthemums, such as Juno and Mars.

SOME PERENNIALS, BIENNIALS AND ANNUALS FOR A RESTFUL GARDEN

Blue-flowered plants lend a peaceful air to a garden and harmonize with almost all other colors. Among them may be mentioned: Chinese forget-me-nots (*Cynoglossum amabile*), which bloom for a long season in full sunshine or part shade. This is a biennial that reseeds and produces many plants. The dwarf hardy annual summer forget-me-nots (*Anchusa capensis*) bloom in late summer. Dwarf ageratum is fine for edging; the variety Little Blue Star is pale blue and Imperial Dwarf Blue is deeper. Blue lace-flowers (*Trachymene (Didiscus) cærulea*) look like blue Queen Anne's lace, while love-in-a-mist (Nigella) has bright blue flowers.

Blue flax (Linum), a perennial with feathery foliage, produces a profusion of sky-blue flowers practically every morning during summer. *Phlox divaricata* blooms in the spring but some flowers linger on into the summer, as is the case with myosotis. The half-hardy lobelia (*Lobelia Erinus compacta*) makes a nice edging plant that blooms throughout the season. Plumbago (*Ceratostigma plumbaginoides*) is also used for edging; it flowers profusely in autumn. In planning for blue flowers, do not overlook the perennial veronica, Blue Spires, which has spikes of blue flowers through summer, resisting both drought and heat.

Salvia azurea grandiflora, with long racemes of azure-blue flowers all summer and fall, does especially well in full sun. *Salvia patens* produces deep blue flowers freely. *Salvia pratensis* bears tall spikes of violet-blue; the broad leaves are close to the ground. Nothing in gardens gives more pleasure than borders of verbena. There are many varieties and colors; the pale tones are most restful.

Many colors other than blue help to make a garden a tranquil place. Nature intermingles colors with plenty of green, to create a refreshing atmosphere; wise gardeners will follow her example. Gray foliage also is satisfying among other plants, giving a cool look in summer while blending harmoniously with bright-colored flowers. *Nepeta Mussinii superba*, with silver-gray foliage, has blue-lavender flowers in late spring and at times during summer. This prefers a sunny place. The low-growing snow-in-summer (*Cerastium tomentosum*) is particularly suited for rock gardens. It has gray leaves and white blossoms. Lavender-cotton (Santolina) makes a delightful planting in rock gardens, having lemon-yellow balls of flowers and pungent-smelling, grayish foliage.

Basket-of-gold alyssum is an attractive, free-flowering perennial with gray leaves and stems. Dusty miller (*Centaurea gymnocarpa*) is well known, and agrostemma is showy with silvery leaves and bright flowers. The silvery sprays of artemisia are not only ornamental in gardens but are wonderful fillers for arrangements in the house. The large woolly leaves of mullein, growing close to the ground, are pleasing; and plume-poppy (*Macleaya* (*Bocconia*) *cordata*) is striking at the back of borders, with its feathery plumes of flowers and large, gray-lobed leaves.

Stiffness in plantings can be relieved and a misty effect provided by the use of such plants as gypsophila, artemisia and statice.

PLANTS WITH COLORFUL AUTUMN FOLIAGE

Predominating Color Yellow

    Trees
        American elm (*Ulmus americana*)
        Birches (Betula)
        Black walnut (*Juglans nigra*)
        Catalpa
        China-berry (*Melia Azedarach*)
        Chinese parasol-tree (Sterculia)
        Ginkgo
        Hickory (Carya)
        Mulberry (Morus)
        Poplar (Populus)

Redbud (Cercis)
Sugar maple (*Acer saccharum*)
Sycamore (Platanus)
Wild cherry (Prunus)
Willow oak (*Quercus Phellos*)
Witch-hazel (Hamamelis)
Yellow-wood (*Cladrastis lutea*)

Shrubs
Kerria
Rugosa rose
Spiræa Thunbergii
Sweet-shrub (*Calycanthus floridus*)

Vines
Cinnamon-vine (*Dioscorea Batatas*)
Scuppernong grape

Predominating Color Red

Trees
Black-haw (*Viburnum prunifolium*)
Flowering dogwood (*Cornus florida*)
Hawthorn (Cratægus)
Japanese flowering dogwood (*Cornus Kousa*)
Pin oak (*Quercus palustris*)
Red maple (*Acer rubrum*)
Red-osier dogwood (*Cornus stolonifera*)
Red oak (*Quercus rubra*)
Red-twigged dogwood (*Cornus sanguinea*)
Scarlet oak (*Quercus coccinea*)
Silky dogwood (*Cornus Amomum*)
Sour gum (*Nyssa sylvatica*)
Sour-wood (Oxydendrum)
Sweet gum (*Liquidambar Styraciflua*)

Shrubs
Barberry (Berberis)
Bridal wreath (*Spiræa prunifolia*)
Chokeberry (Aronia)
Cotoneaster
Crape-myrtle (*Lagerstrœmia indica*)
Forsythia
Highbush cranberry (*Viburnum trilobum (americanum)*)

76

The ginkgo is an easy tree to recognize, with dainty fan-shaped leaves and branches that like to go their own way. Scientists tell us that it is the only survivor of a plant family that was widespread in very early times.

Coral dogwood bears
large, whitish fruits.

The light blue berries of
silky dogwood.

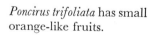

Poncirus trifoliata has small
orange-like fruits.

Itea virginica
Sassafras
Stephanandra
Sumac (Rhus**). Beware** of white-berried varieties growing
in swamps.

Vines
Boston or Japanese ivy (*Parthenocissus (Ampelopsis) tricuspidata Veitchii*)
Virginia creeper (*Parthenocissus quinquefolia*)

PLANTS WITH COLORFUL FRUITS

Red Fruits
American holly (*Ilex opaca*). Glossy, prickly leaves and bright
berries; to 30 feet or more.
Aucuba. Broadleaf evergreen; clusters of large berries; 4 to 8 feet.
Black-alder or winterberry (*Ilex verticillata*). Bright red fruits;
to 10 feet.
Cassine holly (*Ilex Cassine*). A native narrowleaf holly of the lower
South with small berries; to 20 feet.
Chinese holly (*Ilex cornuta*). Glossy, dark green foliage and clusters
of large berries; shrubby growth to 12 feet.
Cleyera. A slow-growing evergreen; reddish new growth turns
glossy green, and the fragrant flowers are followed by showy
berries; to 20 feet.
Eleagnus. An evergreen shrub with silvery green foliage; fragrant
fall flowers and lantern-like fruits; 6 to 15 feet.
English holly (*Ilex Aquifolium*). Spiny leaves and scarlet berries;
to 35 feet.
Euonymus kiautschovica (*patens* or *Sieboldianus*). Spreading shrub
for sun or shade; coral-red fruits; to 10 feet.
Flowering dogwood (*Cornus florida*). Attractive bright berries; to
30 feet.
Highbush cranberry (*Viburnum Opulus*). Fruits change from
yellow and pink to red; to 12 feet.
Japanese barberry (*Berberis Thunbergii*). Spiny branches with
conspicuous berries; 2 to 5 feet.
Jerusalem cherry (Solanum). Makes a lovely low border in the
South; green, yellow and reddish berries at the same time.
Nandina domestica. Bunches of scarlet berries; in winter the foliage
turns bronzy green; 3 to 10 feet.

77

Photinia serrulata. Large, shiny green leaves; showy white flowers in panicles; small red berries in loose bunches; 20 feet.

Pyracantha crenato-serrata (Gibbsii yunnanensis). Spreading habit; a mass of bright fruits during winter; to 6 feet.

Red chokeberry (*Aronia arbutifolia*). Ornamental with red fruits; 6 to 10 feet.

Rockspray cotoneaster (*Cotoneaster horizontalis*). Especially good over rocks in sunny or partly shaded places; dainty pinkish flowers and red berries; 3 feet.

Rosa rugosa. This would be worthwhile for the colorful hips alone; to 6 feet.

Sarsaparilla (*Smilax Walteri*). A vine with red berries in clusters (there are also white-berried sorts); much used for winter holiday decoration.

Strawberry-bush (*Euonymus americanus*). Attractive in late summer with berries that have crimson pods and seed covered with a scarlet aril; to 8 feet.

Sumac (*Rhus aromatica (canadensis)*). Lavender-red fruits; good for a dry, rocky place; 3 feet and over.

Tatarian honeysuckle (*Lonicera tatarica rosea*). Deep pink flowers and red berries; makes a fine screen or hedge.

Umbra-tree (*Phytolacca dioica*). Dark red berries full of red juice; used for shade and ornament in southern California and adapted to tropical and subtropical areas of the South.

Yaupon (*Ilex vomitoria*). Native shrub having small, oblong leaves and numerous small berries; to 20 feet.

White Fruits

Coral dogwood (*Cornus alba sibirica*). Showy from bottom to top with coral-red branches and whitish or bluish white berries; to 10 feet.

Graystem dogwood (*Cornus racemosa*). Effective in the upper sections of the South; gray branches, red stems and white fruits; to 10 feet.

Red-osier dogwood (*Cornus stolonifera*). This bush-like plant likes moisture; dark red branches (*C. stolonifera flaviramea* has yellow branches); to 8 feet.

Rough-leaved dogwood (*Cornus asperifolia*). Brownish red branches and white fruits; 8 to 15 feet.

Snowberry (*Symphoricarpos albus (racemosus)*). Drooping branches and clusters of milk-white berries; 3 to 6 feet.

78

Blue Fruits

Asiatic sweetleaf (*Symplocos paniculata*). Shrub or small tree; sapphire-blue, berry-like fruits.

Dogwood (*Cornus femina*). Purplish branches and pale blue berries; to 15 feet.

Dogwood (*Cornus rugosa*). Branches purplish; berries light blue; 3 to 10 feet.

Fringe-tree (Chionanthus). Pendulous, oval, dark blue fruits; to 10 feet.

Leatherleaf hollygrape (*Mahonia Bealei*). Leaves holly-like but grayish, turning crimson, orange and bronze in the fall; dark blue fruits with silvery sheen; does best in partial shade; 6 feet.

Pagoda dogwood (*Cornus alternifolia*). Branches spreading; dark blue fruits on red stems; to 25 feet.

Red-cedar (*Juniperus virginiana*). Hardy tree; pleasing green foliage and silvery blue fruits; 30 feet or more.

Silky dogwood (*Cornus Amomum*). Purplish red branches and light blue berries; 3 to 10 feet.

Yellow Fruits

China-berry (*Melia Azedarach*). Panicles of purplish flowers followed by globular, smooth, old-ivory fruits that are relished by birds and cattle; for shade or ornament; 40 feet or more.

Cotoneaster Franchetii. Pinkish flowers, then orange-red fruits; an evergreen in the South, growing to 6 feet.

European cranberry-bush (*Viburnum Opulus xanthocarpum*). Cymes of white flowers followed by yellow fruit; to 10 feet.

Firethorn (*Pyracantha coccinea Lalandii*). Laden with bright orange berries in autumn and winter; to 15 feet.

Flowering crab-apple (*Malus floribunda*). Fragrant blossoms followed by yellow fruit with red blush; to 6 feet and over.

Holly (*Ilex decidua*). Orange-scarlet berries; to 30 feet.

Soapberry (Sapindus). Ornamental for the lower South; orange-brown berries resembling china-berries are rich in saponin and can be used in place of soap; to 30 feet and over.

Tatarian honeysuckle (*Lonicera tatarica lutea*). A bushy shrub with flowers in spring and summer, followed by orange berries; 8 to 10 feet.

Purple Fruits

Beauty-berry (*Callicarpa dichotoma* (*purpurea*)). Graceful branches laden with violet-purple berries in clusters; a native growing 3 to 6 feet.

Coral-berry (*Symphoricarpos orbiculatus* (*vulgaris*)). Purplish coral-red berries in thick clusters, giving a red-purple effect; valuable for planting on banks; 4 feet.

Service-berry (*Amelanchier canadensis*). For the middle and upper area of the South; a bushy tree, with leaves white-tomentose beneath and above when young; maroon-purple berries; to 40 feet.

Wayfaring-tree (*Viburnum Lantana*). For the Piedmont and upper zone; the fruits turn from red to blackish purple; to 20 feet.

Black Fruits

Bloodtwig dogwood (*Cornus sanguinea*). Blood-red branches and black fruits; to 12 feet.

Elder (*Sambucus canadensis*). Clusters of purple-black berries; to 12 feet.

Hall's honeysuckle (*Lonicera japonica Halliana*). A vine with white flowers changing to yellow; black fruits.

Japanese hawthorn (Raphiolepis). White flowers followed by black fruits; 10 to 12 feet.

Japanese holly (*Ilex crenata*). Evergreen shrub with black berries; 4 feet and over.

Jetbead (*Rhodotypos tetrapetala* (*kerrioides*)). Attractive, wrinkled green leaves; large flowers and small clusters of bead-like, black berries; to 6 feet.

Leopard-flower or blackberry-lily (*Belamcanda chinensis*). A hardy perennial that bears clusters of shiny black seed resembling blackberries.

Ligustrum, various kinds. Thick bunches of black berries; 15 to 25 feet.

Myrtle (Myrica). Also called sweet gale and bog myrtle; grayish black berries; aromatic shrub thriving in the lower South and Piedmont section if watered well in summer.

Porcelain-vine (Ampelopsis). Bluish black fruits.

Shadbush (*Amelanchier ovalis* (*rotundifolia*)). Bluish black fruits; to 8 feet.

Viburnum nudum. Creamy white cymes of bloom and pink fruits changing to blue-black; to 15 feet.

Virginia creeper (*Parthenocissus quinquefolia*). A vine with blue-black berries.

Withe-rod (*Viburnum cassinoides*). Effective in the upper sections; berries in changing colors; 12 feet.

The Burford Chinese holly has distinctive oblong leaves
with a sharp tip, very dark and shining. (See page 149.)

One of the newer varieties of holly, known as heavy-berry. It has an extremely heavy crop of fruit much loved by the birds. This makes a very good specimen plant and is also recommended for use with other evergreens in borders. (See page 149.)

PLANTS WITH COLORFUL TWIGS AND WINTER BUDS

Forsythia viridissima. Effective erect green branches.

Kerria japonica. Arching green branches in winter.

Laurestinus (*Viburnum Tinus*). Worth having for the clusters of coral-red buds; creamy flowers in early spring.

Leucothoë Catesbæi. Leaves and flower buds attractive purple in winter.

Photinia. The reddish new growth has the appearance of flowers.

Pieris floribunda. Winter buds look like white flowers set off by evergreen foliage, before the early blossoms open.

Poncirus trifoliata. Interesting flower buds and spiny twigs.

Scotch broom (*Cytisus scoparius*). Slender, drooping green branches; for the upper South.

Star magnolia (*Magnolia stellata*). Charming winter buds.

Winter jasmine (*Jasminum nudiflorum*). Spreading and trailing green branches and reddish buds; blooms in January.

Native dogwoods. The colored bark and twigs are effective in the winter landscape; new growth gives the best coloring.

Many deciduous shrubs and trees have interesting branches in shades of green, brown, gray, pink and white, which can best be seen after the leaves have fallen. Climbing roses have branches in various shades of green, and many other plants have flowers or leaf buds or branches to make them worthy of notice. These are effective in the garden and for arrangements in the house.

Chapter VII

Plants For Special Purposes

EVERGREENS FOR THE SOUTH

For Practically All Parts of the South
Abelia. Sun or part shade.
Aucuba. Best in shade.
Azalea. Partial shade and acid soil.
Barberry (Berberis). Likes a moist light loam, sun or part shade.
Boxwood (Buxus). Sun or part shade.
Carolina cherry-laurel (*Prunus Laurocerasus*). Sun or part shade.
Cotoneaster. Sun or part shade.
Eleagnus. Sun, part shade or shade.
Euonymus. Sun or part shade.
Holly (Ilex). Part shade.
Holly-leaf tea olive (*Osmanthus Fortunei*). Does best in rich soil and partial shade.
Leucothoë Catesbæi. Moist soil; prefers shade or part shade but will grow in sun.
Ligustrum. Any soil, even in dry places.
Magnolia grandiflora. Does best in rich soil, sun or part shade.
Mahonia. Part shade.
Mountain-laurel (*Kalmia latifolia*). Prefers part shade but will grow in sun.
Nandina. Prefers sun and slightly sour soil.
Phillyrea. Any soil; prefers sun.
Photinia. Sandy loam; prefers sun.
Pieris floribunda. Best in part shade.
Pyracantha. Sun.
Sand-myrtle (Leiophyllum). Sun or part shade; thrives best in a sandy or peaty loam.
Tea olive (Osmanthus). Any location; prefers part shade.

For Warmer Parts of the Piedmont and Lower Sections
Banana-shrub (Michelia). Sun or part shade.
Camellia japonica. About a half day of sun.
Cape-jasmine (Gardenia). Sun or part shade.

Loquat (Eriobotrya). Prefers sun but will grow in part shade.
Oleander (Nerium). Prefers sun.
Pittosporum. Prefers sun but tolerates part shade.
Tea-plant (*Thea sinensis*). Sun or part shade.

For the Piedmont and Upper Sections
Rhododendron. Acid soil; sun or shade.
Skimmia japonica. Prefers part shade.

For the Lower South
Bayberry or wax-myrtle (Myrica). An evergreen in the coastal plain.
Cabbage palmetto (Sabal). Sun or part shade; will thrive even in poor soil near the coast from Florida north into South Carolina.
Laurel oak (*Quercus laurifolia*). Half-evergreen, glossy foliage.
Live oaks (*Quercus virginiana*). Evergreen trees native along the seacoast; can be used farther north and inland but will not grow so large.
Palmetto trees. Used for avenues.
Royal palms (*Roystonea (Oreodoxa) regia*). Very effective for avenues in southern Florida.
Sabal texana. For south Texas.

Conifers. These narrow-leaved evergreens are not grown to any extent below the Piedmont section. Many are called cedars that are not true cedars.
Arborvitæ (Thuja). For specimen, hedge or windbreak. In the lower South, use *Thuja orientalis.*
Cypress (Cupressus). Desirable for groups, doing best in partial shade. Hardy in the Gulf States. The soft foliage burns in the lower South. Cypress and Retinospora (Chamæcyparis) are similar; both like deep, loamy soil.
Deodar (*Cedrus Deodara*). A true cedar. This has spreading branches and glaucous green foliage; it likes loamy soil but will grow in sandy clay if well drained.
Japanese yew (*Taxus cuspidata*). For low growth, in the upper South especially.
Junipers. For various purposes, with a wide range of color and form. There are tall pyramidal shapes such as red-cedar (*Juniperus virginiana*) and Virginia blue cedar (*J. virginiana glauca*), and spreading or prostrate creepers. Pfitzer juniper (*J. chinensis Pfitzeriana*) is a popular type with horizontal spreading branches that stand severe pruning.

Pine, loblolly, short-leaf, scrub, pitch or black. White pine in upper sections; long-leaf in lower sections; slash and pond pine on the coast.

Spruce (Picea). Rich green; pyramidal shape. Used for hedges in the upper sections.

Conifers for the Upper South

Hemlock (*Tsuga canadensis*) and fir, especially balsam fir (*Abies balsamea*). For specimens and hedges. They like moist, well-drained soil.

DECIDUOUS TREES FOR THE SOUTH

Ash (Fraxinus), white and red.

Australian-pine (*Casuarina equisetifolia*). Sometimes called an oak. Leafless, with light green drooping branches that give the effect of long-leaf pine. Grows in south Florida.

Bald cypress (*Taxodium distichum*). The only southern conifer to shed its needles in autumn. Pond cypress grows in swamps of the low South.

Beeches (Fagus), alder (Alnus), basswood or linden (Tilia), locusts (Robinia), mock-orange or osage-orange (Maclura), buckeye (Aesculus).

Birch (Betula), red. In the upper sections, black and yellow.

Dogwood, flowering (*Cornus florida*). Various other dogwoods have insignificant blooms followed by black, blue, red or whitish berries. Most of them are natives and quite hardy, having colorful bark and branches.

Elms (Ulmus), slippery, American, hackberry, winged (wahoo).

Fringe-tree (Chionanthus).

Gums (Nyssa), black or sour, sweet, tupelo, water.

Kentucky coffee-tree (Gymnocladus). A native of the western section of the South.

Leatherwood (*Cyrilla racemiflora*). Grows in the low South. Though a deciduous shrub or tree, this will hold its leaves. They turn bronzy red in winter. Does best in a shady place in sandy soil.

Lombardy poplar (*Populus nigra italica*). Grows tall and slender.

Maples (Acer), ash-leaved (box-elder), red, silver, sugar.

Mimosa, catalpa and paulownia. Natives of China and Japan, naturalized in the South.

Oaks (Quercus). Black oaks: black, blackjack, pin, red, water, willow. White oaks: burr, chestnut, post, white.

The fragrant, lilac-colored mint-shrub blooms in early
fall and does best planted in the sun. (See page 103.)

The coconut palm is a familiar sight along the seacoast in the low South. More often than not the tree grows at a rather sharp angle, just as the seed sprouted.

Plane-tree or sycamore (Platanus). Wants low, moist soil.

Poplar, aspen or cottonwood (Populus). The southern cottonwood or Carolina poplar. Most commonly found in the coastal plain and the Piedmont region.

Punk-tree (*Melaleuca Leucadendra*). For warm regions. Bears creamy white to pink and purple flowers. This likes an alkaline soil and withstands drought, salt water and slight frosts.

Tulip-tree (*Liriodendron Tulipifera*). Tulip-like flowers. Sometimes called yellow poplar but belongs to the Magnolia family.

Weeping willow (*Salix babylonica*). Drooping branches. Likes a moist location.

Witch-hazel (Hamamelis). Blooms in November and December.

Yellow-wood (*Cladrastis lutea*). Ornamental flowering tree native in Tennessee, Kentucky and North Carolina. Bears racemes of white wisteria-like flowers in late spring. Drought resisting and not particular as to soil.

PLANTS FOR TROPICAL OR SUBTROPICAL EFFECTS

Acanthus mollis latifolius. A perennial that likes light, rich soil and sunshine.

Aspidistra. Hardy in the middle and lower South.

Bamboo. Likes moist, rich soil but will thrive in a wet or dry location.

Buphthalmum speciosum. Showy perennials, easy to grow.

Caladiums. Herbaceous perennials, from tubers or rhizomes.

Cannas. Ornamental foliage and flowers.

Castor-beans (Ricinus). Tall-growing annuals with large foliage; in warm climates they are perennial and grow tree-like.

Chinese angelica-tree (*Aralia elata*). Prickly stems and bold foliage; can be grown in the Piedmont and upper sections.

Cimicifuga racemosa. Tall ornamental perennial in the Piedmont and upper sections.

Cockscombs (Celosia). Annuals with showy flower heads and leaves; for light, rich soil.

Coleus. Gives a pleasing appearance; easy to root from cuttings, or seed may be sown.

Crotons. Ornamental plants with attractive foliage.

Elephants-ear (*Colocasia esculenta*). Large tuberous roots; likes rich, damp soil; rests in winter.

Ferns, funkias and cactus. Luxuriant growth.

85

Heracleum villosum (*giganteum*). A biennial for bold effect.

Mallows (Hibiscus). Very pleasing flowers.

Mullein (*Verbascum olympicum*). A biennial that has a large rosette of green-white leaves.

Palmettos, palms, bougainvillea vines, bignonia and allamanda climbers. All flourish in the lower South.

Pampas grass and various grasses. For foliage and plumes.

Plume-poppy (*Macleaya* (*Bocconia*) *cordata*). A hardy herbaceous perennial with large-lobed, gray-green leaves.

Princes-feather (*Polygonum orientale*). A tall-growing, old-fashioned annual that makes a telling display in autumn.

Sunflowers (Helianthus). Many give a subtropical appearance.

Yuccas. Sandy loam suits them best, but they are easy to grow.

Any plants that have luxuriant foliage or that grow naturally in the tropics, such as bananas, oranges, pineapples, etc., of the low South.

PERENNIALS AND BIENNIALS FOR SUN AND SHADE

Perennials and biennials look best planted in groups, but only colors that harmonize should be near each other. It helps to have white flowers interspersed with the bright colors. Let's plan some borders in various color combinations, for both sun and shade.

SUNNY BORDER; YELLOW FLOWERS

An idea for a border in full sun is to begin with yellow and orange-flowered perennials. On the edge for early bloom basket-of-gold alyssum (*Alyssum saxatile*) with small grayish leaves, could be used, followed by yellow flax (*Linum flavum*) and dwarf geum in colonies. Next to these is a good place for wallflowers (*Cheiranthus Allionii*), which sometimes send out so many bright orange flowers that the plants bloom themselves to death. Set these plants about 6 or 8 inches apart.

Back of them doronicum might be placed in groups of about seven. Their daisy-like, yellow flowers are fine for cutting and make a beautiful display. In summer when they are dormant their leaves disappear, but other plants will fill in the gaps. (It is well to place labels beside them so that they will not be dug up accidentally.) Doronicum will also thrive in partial shade in well-drained soil.

For the front of this border for midseason yellow bloom, I suggest ground cypress (Santolina) with its cypress-like, grayish foliage and *Dianthus Knappii*, which needs a sunny, dry location.

For all-summer bloom back of the lower-growing plants, golden marguerites (*Anthemis tinctoria*) would be useful. They have lacy foliage and daisy-like, lemon-yellow flowers. The plants can be put out at any time and will bloom the first year, doing well even in poor soil if the drainage is good.

The yellow meadow-rue (*Thalictrum flavum*), with attractive foliage, will flower in midsummer. A good companion would be blanket-flowers (Gaillardia), with orange-yellow, daisy-shaped blooms. These stand droughts but in order to live through the winter must not be grown in heavy soil. Back of them is the proper place for the taller-growing coreopsis, from which one can have golden yellow flowers all summer if the dead blooms are kept cut.

Groups of cephalaria, with scabiosa-like, pale yellow flowers, will blend with the other colors. At the back of this sunny border is a good location for golden-glow (Rudbeckia), a plant that grows tall and bears an abundance of golden yellow, double blooms in late summer.

SUNNY BORDER; BLUE FLOWERS

Blue-flowered perennials harmonize well with the yellows to form a pleasing combination. Masses of speedwell (*Veronica incana*) at the front of the border will make a mat of deep blue, and with this *Ceratostigma plumbaginoides* (*Plumbago Larpentiæ*), a dwarf of spreading habit with deep blue flowers and bronzy green foliage.

Back of these could be placed beard-tongue (*Penstemon unilateralis*) with spikes of blue flowers, and then groups of blue flax (*Linum perenne*). This likes well-drained, light soil. The pale blue flowers open in the morning and close in the afternoon, and the feathery foliage is very attractive.

At the rear, *Salvia farinacea* would produce spikes of pale blue all summer. Here, too, belong *Platycodon grandiflorum* with its deep blue flowers, *Veronica maritima* (*longifolia*), delphinium and *Campanula pyramidalis* with its star-shaped blooms. Anchusa, Dropmore, makes a charming display when planted singly to allow the beauty of its branches to stand out.

SUNNY BORDER; WHITE FLOWERS

White-flowered plants for early bloom in the front of the border could include snow-in-summer (*Cerastium tomentosum*) with silvery foliage, then candytuft (*Iberis sempervirens*) with evergreen foliage. For midseason and later bloom the white nierembergia, a spreading plant that does well in either shade or sun, would give a pleasing effect. The flowers are small and petunia-like, white tinted lavender. A border needs gypsophila, with its minute white gauzy flowers. Since these plants like a sweet soil and resent being moved, they should be set about 2 feet apart in a permanent location.

Accompanying them could be achillea, The Pearl, shasta daisies, double feverfew (Matricaria) and sweet rocket (*Hesperis matronalis alba*). Behind these, in a white drift, artemisia, *Campanula pyramidalis alba* and *Platycodon grandiflorum album* could be used; then *Lychnis* (*Agrostemma*) *coronaria alba* and *Boltonia asteroides* (*glastifolia*), of easy culture.

At the back of the border is an ideal spot for plume-poppy (*Macleaya* (*Bocconia*) *cordata*), which bears creamy white flowers in plumy panicles, followed by ornamental plumes of seed. This needs a loamy, rich soil and plenty of room.

SUNNY BORDERS; PINK AND ROSE-COLORED FLOWERS

In a sunny border a good plan is to allow the white-flowered plants to melt into the pink and rose-colored ones. For the outer margin one might use *Phlox amœna* for early bloom, then colonies of English daisies (Bellis), which like a moist but not too rich soil, and *Armeria maritima Laucheana*, which thrives in sandy soil.

Back of these can be clumps of Newport Pink sweet william and Persian daisies (*Pyrethrum roseum*). They like a soil that is very rich but not too heavy. And let's not forget coral-bells (Heuchera), with heart-shaped, notched leaves and graceful coral-pink bloom. This will do well in sun or part shade. Transvaal daisies (Gerbera) can be added. At the back of this part of the border Greek mallows (*Sidalcea malvæflora*), with rosy pink, hollyhock-like bloom, will be effective.

SUNNY BORDER; LAVENDER AND PURPLE FLOWERS

Lavender and purple-flowered plants make a beautiful combination. At the front for early bloom one may like violets (*Viola odorata*) for early spring and late fall, then lilac-colored candytuft (*Iberis gibraltarica*) and bluish purple *Aster alpinus*. Lily-turf (Ophiopogon), which prefers a moist loam, will give midseason bloom. For all-summer color there is *Verbena rigida* (*venosa*), a creeping plant that bears spikes of bluish lavender flowers. The small lavender panicles borne by sea-lavender (*Limonium bellidifolium (Statice caspia)*) will be interesting, and when cut will last for months.

The biennial honesty (Lunaria) with its stock-like flowers is decorative in the garden; after the seed pods are dry, the inside disks make lovely silvery bouquets for winter. Another "must have" for this border is dames-violet or sweet rocket (*Hesperis matronalis purpurea*) with clusters of scented flowers loved by our grandmothers.

Back of these could be planted the early-blooming, hardy biennial foxgloves (Digitalis), and nearby groups of coneflower (*Echinacea purpurea*) for late bloom.

SHADY BORDER; YELLOW TO ORANGE FLOWERS

Perhaps one would like to have a narrow, partially shaded border with the same drifts of color suggested for the sunny border. On the edge for early bloom would be the place for *Ranunculus repens*. The runners take root and send up stems with small, rose-like, double yellow flowers.

Back of these, for midseason bloom, would be primulas—golden yellow *Primula veris aurea* and pale yellow *Primula veris lutea*—and globe-flowers (Trollius). Both thrive in a moist, loamy soil.

PARTIAL SHADE; BLUE FLOWERS

For an early blue effect, a suggestion for the edge of the planting is to have forget-me-nots (Myosotis), then clumps of *Phlox divaricata* that require shallow planting, Virginia bluebells (Mertensia), and *Ajuga reptans*, which spreads by runners and bears purplish blue flower spikes. This will grow in a sunny place also.

For bloom from midseason till late, one can have harebells (*Campanula carpatica*). Near them is a good place for *Brunnera macrophylla* (*Anchusa myosotidiflora*), with heart-shaped leaves and dainty forget-me-not flowers. Here also could be groups of blue columbines (Aquilegia), the plants of each group set about 10 inches apart.

PARTIAL SHADE; WHITE FLOWERS

For a white mixer near the front of this planting, nothing is better than lilies-of-the-valley and white harebells. Plantain-lilies (*Hosta plantaginea*), with fragrant flowers in midsummer, should thrive here.

PARTIAL SHADE; PINK OR ROSE-COLORED FLOWERS

Blending into the white flowers can be plumy bleeding-heart (*Dicentra eximia*), which blooms early in the season. Pink primroses

(*Primula japonica rosea*) would be nice nearby, and back of these, other bleeding-hearts (*Dicentra spectabilis*) with arching branches of heart-shaped flowers.

PARTIAL SHADE; LAVENDER OR PURPLE FLOWERS

Next at the margin *Campanula Elatines garganica*, with heart-shaped green leaves and starry lavender-blue flowers, could be planted, and back of it *Primula denticulata cachemiriana*, which likes a moist leaf mold but will flower in a sunny or shaded location. Plantain-lilies (*Hosta lancifolia*), producing blue-lilac flowers in midsummer, would add to this border.

Why not use irises, hemerocallis and bulbs in drifts about the borders for seasonal accents of beauty? By choosing different varieties in the colors wanted, one can have them flowering from early spring to late autumn, and even in winter.

Countless other combinations for sunny or partially shaded borders may be made to suit individual tastes.

PERENNIALS THAT BLOOM THE FIRST SEASON FROM SEED

(Best sown in autumn or winter in hotbeds)

Anthemis tinctoria. Yellow, daisy-like flowers, fine for cutting.

Buphthalmum salicifolium. A border plant having yellow flowers and willow-like foliage; needs ordinary soil.

Campanula carpatica. Blue or white bell flowers; of dwarf habit; prefers partial shade.

Centaurea montana. Showy plant with dark blue flowers.

Dahlias, certain kinds. The seeds germinate quickly and the plants soon begin to bud; they require a rich, light soil.

Delphinium. Tall spikes of bloom for display and cutting.

Erigeron Coulteri. White, daisy-like flowers and tufted foliage.

Gaillardia. Continuous flowering if in well-drained soil.

Hardy carnations. Attractive perfumed flowers.

Heliopsis. Yellow disks of bloom in summer.

Iceland poppy (*Papaver nudicaule*). Colorful blooms for garden effect and for cutting.

Inula ensifolia. A good rock plant with golden yellow flowers; wants a sunny spot.

90

Linaria dalmatica. Tall habit, with yellow flowers and glaucous foliage; light soil.

Lychnis. Both dwarf and tall.

Nierembergia cærulea (hippomanica). A half-hardy perennial of low growth with light green foliage; the cupped, lavender-blue blooms are borne profusely over a long season.

Penstemon. Spikes of tubular bloom.

Pinks (*Dianthus plumarius* and others). Most are fragrant; give them a lime soil in sun.

Platycodon. Showy flowers over a long season.

Salvia. Various kinds with grayish foliage; a long season of bloom.

Snapdragon. Spikes excellent for cutting.

Sweet rocket (Hesperis). Phlox-like, scented flowers.

Transvaal daisy (Gerbera). Begins to bloom eight months after the seed is sown.

Tunica Saxifraga. Of dwarf habit; likes sandy loam.

Valeriana. A border plant with fragrant flowers; needs a light soil.

Verbena. Profuse and continuous bloom.

Wallflower (Cheiranthus), Early Wonder. Double flowers; often blooms in winter.

PLANTS FOR THE ROCK GARDEN

Rock gardens may be tiny gems or rather extensive displays, depending upon the terrain. Many plants may be grown here that would be out of place anywhere else. The real use of the stones is to supply conditions under which the plants will grow—deep soil and a well-drained location in either sun or shade. Slopes and banks form a natural setting for a rock garden.

In making a rock garden, start at the bottom of the incline and work upward. Large stones are best; bed them down to make them look natural, and leave deep pockets of soil between them. Arrange the rocks so that water will go into the pockets and not run off. Frequent watering will keep the rocks moist and make them look old.

The best soil for rock plants is leaf mold, sand, old manure and loam. Plants that like shade need plenty of leaf mold; for those that like sun it is well to provide some gravel. All will need good drainage. Choose suitable material, such as alpines, plants that grow on high places, or those that grow only a few inches tall. These will trail over rocks or will creep or become low masses. Have some plants that will grow upward too, and not all runners.

91

Such a great variety of plants can be used that a rock garden can be interesting at all seasons. Some evergreens like prostrate junipers will add variety, as well as vines with variegated foliage and low grasses such as fescue. There is danger of overplanting a rock garden. Nasturtiums and petunias are better kept out.

Some Perennials That Will Thrive Even in Poor Soil

Basket-of-gold alyssum (*Alyssum saxatile*). Sun.

Bugle (*Ajuga reptans*). Partial shade or sun.

Columbine (*Aquilegia canadensis*). Sun or part shade.

Five-finger (*Potentilla argentea calabra*). Sun or part shade.

Hardy candytuft (Iberis). Best in sun.

Moss-pink (*Phlox subulata*). Needs good drainage and sun.

Pink (*Dianthus deltoides*). Alkaline soil; sun or shade.

Rock-cress (*Arabis albida* and *A. alpina*). Sun or part shade.

Rockfoil (*Saxifraga decipiens*). Partial shade or sun.

Sedums. Sandy soil; best in sunny spots but some, such as *S. Sieboldii*, like partial shade.

Sempervivums. Sun or shade; sandy soil.

Snow-in-summer (*Cerastium tomentosum*). Sun.

Speedwell (*Veronica latifolia prostrata*). Sunny spots with room to spread.

Sun-rose (*Helianthemum nummularium mutabile*). Sun.

Toadflax (*Linaria vulgaris*). Partial shade.

Tunica Saxifraga. Sun.

Other Effective Plants for the Rock Garden

Adonis. Likes good moist soil in sun or part shade.

Aster alpinus. Needs sun and good drainage.

Babys-breath (*Gypsophila repens*). Sweet soil; sun or part shade.

Baby wintercreeper (*Euonymus Fortunei minimus*). Evergreen trailer.

Bellflower (*Campanula carpatica* and *C. Elatines garganica*). Partial shade.

Brunnera macrophylla (*Anchusa myosotidiflora*). Sun or part shade.

Bulbs, such as snowdrops, scillas, grape-hyacinths and crocuses. Will grow in sun or part shade.

Buttercup (*Ranunculus repens*). Part shade.

Coral-bells (*Heuchera sanguinea*). Prefers sun but will stand part shade.

Corydalis. Sandy loam; likes shade.

Dwarf iris. Sun or part shade.

Erinus alpinus. Sandy soil; shade from mid-day sun.

Quiet water enhances a woodland rock garden.

This formal rose garden edged with boxwood forms a pleasing vista.

Forget-me-not (Myosotis). Moist, shady place.

Globularia trichosantha. Moist soil and partial shade.

Lambs-ears (*Stachys lanata*). Likes a moist place.

Lavender-cotton (Santolina). Likes dry soil and a sunny place.

Low-growing hemerocallis, such as *H. gracilis* (lemon-yellow) and *H. minor* (chrome-yellow; grass-like foliage).

Mugo pines. Will grow in sunny places or part shade.

Petrocoptis (*Lychnis*) *Lagascæ.* Thrives in sun.

Phlox divaricata. Prefers part shade.

Primrose (*Primula denticulata*). Rich moist loam.

Rainbow rock-cress (Aubrieta). Light soil.

Sandwort (Arenaria). Light soil.

Saponaria ocymoides. A carpet of rosy flowers in a sunny place.

Satureja (*Calamintha*) *alpina.* Sunny location in dry soil.

Shrubs like *Cotoneaster horizontalis*, *Daphne Cneorum* and hypericum. Thrive in sun or part shade.

Silene Schafta. Likes shade and sandy loam.

Thrift (*Armeria maritima Laucheana*). Wants a sandy loam; drought resistant.

Thyme. Sun; good drainage.

Violets and other violas. Best in part shade.

Dwarf or Creeping Annuals Adaptable to the Rock Garden

Anagallis. Blue and other colors; similar to annual phlox.

Baby blue-eyes (Nemophila). Shades of blue, lavender, white; sun or part shade.

Candytuft (*Iberis umbellata*). Various shades; common garden soil.

Creeping zinnia (*Sanvitalia procumbens*). Golden yellow flowers, easy to grow; likes sandy loam.

Dew-plant (*Dorotheanthus gramineus* (*Mesembryanthemum tricolor*)). Likes sun and sandy loam.

English daisy (Bellis). An annual in the South; likes a loamy soil and part shade.

Ice-plant (*Cryophytum* (*Mesembryanthemum*) *crystallinum*). Sun and sandy loam.

Kingfisher daisy (*Felicia Bergeriana*). Brilliant blue flowers in midsummer; small grayish leaves.

Sand-verbena (*Abronia umbellata*). Lavender-purple flowers; drought resisting; likes sand and sun.

Swan River daisy (Brachycome). Different colors; ordinary soil.

Sweet alyssum. White and violet; light soil in sun or part shade.

Chapter VIII
Some Features Not To Be Overlooked

HEDGES AND TREES

Hedges have great possibilities, either trimmed to formal shape or allowed to grow naturally into shrubs. They are needed for a background or screen and as a protection for other plants. Windbreaks are a help in preventing soil erosion, especially in light sandy parts of the country. An evergreen hedge provides protection from cold and from hot winds; it gives privacy and is very interesting in winter. Carolina cherry-laurel (*Prunus Laurocerasus*) and the ligustrums are excellent broadleaf evergreens for this purpose in the South. In the middle and upper sections conifers thrive and are desirable.

Some shrubs trained to a single trunk grow tree-like. They are effective when used as single specimens or as accents among other plantings when they have space to develop. A pleasing effect is often made when trees or shrubs are grouped in threes or more. Not only their flowers but also their foliage and texture, fruit, branches and twigs give us pleasure. Evergreens, broadleaf and conifer, are of especial value in the winter landscape.

Some of our native trees, such as the redbud (Cercis) and magnolia, are extremely pleasing, whether in gardens or in woodlands. One of the rare native trees of the South, *Magnolia cordata*, bears canary-yellow flowers in March. This has oval leaves, cordate at the base. It was "lost in the woods" and rediscovered near Augusta, Ga., in 1913. Since then it has been found in several places in Georgia, North Carolina and South Carolina.

There are a number of species of dogwood interesting throughout the year. They have swelling winter buds, then flowers that are followed by clusters of berries. The leaves are colorful and some species have bright twigs. The South is credited with the origin of three outstanding varieties of dogwood. Pink-flowering dogwood (*Cornus florida rubra*) was found wild in Virginia about 1700. The first double dogwood (*C. florida plena*) is credited to North Carolina, and the weeping dogwood (*C. florida pendula*) to Baltimore, Md.

Many species of holly are indigenous in the South. Native trees are a particularly delightful sight in spring, such as hedgerows of

94

hawthorn and wild plums. The delicious odor of plum blossoms is unforgettable. Red maples are among the first trees to send out noticeable flowers. In the mountainous and hilly sections, mountain-laurels and rhododendrons are choice evergreens. The mountain andromeda (*Pieris floribunda*) does well transplanted to gardens; it needs cool, well-drained, moist soil.

At times we like to rest in the shade of trees and enjoy a study of the leaf forms and branches, as well as the perfume of flowering trees. Where shade is needed, trees can make a beautiful frame for the house. If too near, however, they will keep out the air, and the rooms will not be so comfortable as when the trees are farther away. Shade trees not only take in water but also give it off. The drying of the moisture liberated from the leaves makes the temperature lower under a tree. As air circulates, the warm air rises and the cool air falls under the branches.

Desirable shade trees for the South are oaks, hickories, elms, ashes, maples, tulip-poplars and sweet gums. In the lower South the spreading live oaks are a joy to see, and gray Spanish moss, also called Florida or long moss, swaying in every breeze, makes them very picturesque. This moss, *Tillandsia usneoides*, is not a parasite like mistletoe, but an air plant. Few people notice that it has tiny flowers. Frequently the moss smothers the leaves and buds on the tree and eventually kills it.

For best effect, shade trees must be kept healthy and well fed. The trunk of the tree supports the top and branches and is a channel for food and water. The time for feeding is when the trees are dormant in the fall, so that they can send out healthy growth in spring. Make holes 18 inches deep or more, a few feet apart, within the area sheltered by the branches. Into these holes put equal amounts of plant food and soil, and water well. Trees require a pound of food to each inch of circumference of the trunk measured 4 feet above the ground. Bonemeal and cottonseed meal, half and half, will benefit them, or balanced commercial fertilizer may be used, but organic fertilizer and humus are essential, too.

Though evergreens are attractive at all seasons, especially giving life to the winter landscape and restfulness to the autumn picture, plantings of deciduous trees also offer a wide variety from season to season. In spring buds burst open, tender leaves unfold and flowers appear. There is warmth of foliage color in spring as well as in autumn, for as young growth unfurls much of it is bronzy or reddish. At this time one notices the tassel blooms of oaks. One can recognize

95

different oaks by their acorns and leaves. For example, willow oak leaves are long, narrow and willow-like, while water oak leaves are larger toward the end and pear-shaped. The willow oak turns yellow and sheds its leaves before the water oak. It also grows larger and lives longer.

Pines bear their flowers in the spring. There are two kinds: the flower pollen tassel and the fertile flower which receives the pollen, later to develop into cones. Conifers of the pine family have needles; the kind of pine can be determined not only by its cones but also by the number of needles in each cluster. The white pine, for instance, has five needles in a cluster and the pitch pine three.

Sometimes a pine has to be cut down on account of the presence of bark beetles or southern pine beetles. Keep a lookout for borer holes or sawdust on the bark. These insects will go into fresh-cut wood and lay eggs. When the young hatch, they eat the soft material under the bark and spread to other trees. An infested tree should be cut to the ground, the large pieces hauled away and the twigs and bark burned before spring. After the cause of the infection has been removed I have been told, a tree freshly attacked may be saved by squirting carbon tetrachloride into each entrance hole. The opening should be plugged with putty so the gas will be kept in. When pines are needed for timber, they should be cut in winter before the sap begins to rise.

Seeds of plants are spread by winds, birds and animals. Sometimes when a tree grows near water the seeds fall, sprout and find a lodging place far away. Trees like the tulip (Liriodendron) and maple have winged seeds that sail a distance. Often fallen twigs, as from the native willow (*Salix nigra*), take root in moist ground or in water.

Richly tinted foliage and fruits give a cheerful aspect to autumn. Tints and blendings of color are beautiful to see in the foliage of oaks, poplars and other trees, with the green of pines and cedars interspersed. In the woodlands, the sweet gums (*Liquidambar Styraciflua*) and sourwood (*Oxydendrum arboreum*) present a lovely array of brilliant tones.

Fall colors vary in brightness according to the season, but the general color scheme does not change. Autumn coloring is not caused by frost but by the normal ripening of the leaves. As the juices are drawn from the leaves, the minerals that remain produce the coloring. As the days or nights grow cooler, the chlorophyll in the leaf breaks up and the green disappears. This leaves the yellow (xan-

Pink-flowering dogwood makes a charming dooryard specimen. It also looks well planted in clumps and intermixed with the white variety. These are natives over a wide part of the South, where they are rapid growing and long lived. (See page 94.)

A spring garden in the full burst of glorious bloom is a thrilling place. Azaleas, tulips and flowering trees are a riot of color, appropriately toned down by grass and trees in various shades of green.

thophyll) coloring matter. The red pigment (erythrophyll) is not present in such large amounts as the yellow during the activity of the leaves, but when the green color breaks, light penetrates deeper into the cells and, falling upon the sugars, tannins, etc., makes reds. The brighter the light entering the leaves, the brighter the colors, if there is much sugar present. Cold weather is favorable to the formation of the sugars but severe early frosts keep down bright colors, for the conditions are not right for normal ripening. Cool nights, the amount of light, the quantity of sugars and the rapidity at which leaf green breaks down, account for leaves turning yellow, red and brown when life in the leaf is becoming exhausted.

During autumn the leaves are falling from deciduous trees. We enjoyed seeing their tender growth in the spring and the deep color and shade of summer, and now with their beauty gone the leaves still serve a good purpose. They are placed on the compost heap to decay, or they are used as a mulch to be dug back into the soil. When the leaves have fallen, the color and formation of limbs and branches can be enjoyed. During the winter, bright twigs and winter buds are fascinating to study. Each season trees offer a different aspect to please those who take time to observe.

GROUND COVERS AND WILDFLOWERS

The term ground cover refers to low-growing plants that cover the ground like a carpet. A close mat of vines or taller plants not only makes barren spots inviting but prevents excessive evaporation from the soil. A ground cover is pleasing to the eye. It keeps down weeds and saves cultivation, gives a finishing touch to shrubbery borders and is attractive as a footing. It answers the question often asked: "What shall we plant where grass will not grow?"

Often beautiful, well-kept lawns terminate in bare spots under trees. For these places, as well as the shady north side of the house, there are plants that will grow even in dense shade. Ground covers used on embankments prevent the soil from washing away. By conditioning the soil, it is possible to turn many areas where nothing wants to grow into beauty spots filled with ferns and wildflowers.

Various low-growing plants that would die in the sun will thrive in shade. In woodlands many dwarf things grow in deep shade where a heavy layer of leaf mold makes soil conditions right and conserves moisture. To grow plants under trees one must keep them from starving, for tree roots are continual competitors for food and moisture. Tree limbs should be high enough to admit air. It is hard to make plants grow under trees that have surface roots, such as maples, elms and poplars. But even here one can have periwinkle (Vinca) and goutweed (*Aegopodium Podagraria*).

A wild garden of low plants affords as much pleasure as any other planting if care is given to the selection of material and if it is made to imitate nature. Many people think of wildflowers as ordinary weeds; others are learning to appreciate them. The best source for them is nurseries that handle native plants. If you take them from their own haunts, do it in such a way as not to hurt the growth of others. A wildflower enthusiast knows how to move small plants that might die from being choked out, and how to conserve them by transplanting to a suitable place. Wildflower preservation means much to the beauty of our woodlands and countryside. One's supply of wildflowers can be increased by sowing mature seeds in leaf mold in half shade.

Native plants make choice ground covers in a natural setting like a bog, a woodsy spot, a stony slope or a meadow. When these woodland plants become naturalized, they continue to grow year after year. The ground should be made porous with plenty of humus to allow fine roots to penetrate, and the leaf mold should be renewed from time to time and a small amount of well-rotted manure added.

Ferns like best a soil one-third leaf mold, one-third sand and one-third garden loam, with uniform moisture. Some ferns have stems that creep, and others a crown cluster. All of them give a cool, refreshing look to a shaded corner on a hot summer day.

Garden slopes and rocky embankments need not be unsightly with so much plant material at hand that will prevent erosion and help conserve water in the soil. But even with little moisture, the prostrate honeysuckles (Lonicera), trumpet-vines (Campsis) and Virginia creeper (Parthenocissus) will grow and form roots where their stems lie. The memorial rose (*Rosa Wichuraiana*) is fine for places of this kind. Coral-berry (*Symphoricarpos orbiculatus (vulgaris)*) not only roots from the drooping branches, helping to hold the soil in place, but is an attractive sight laden with lavender-red berries all winter. The kudzu-vine (*Pueraria Thunbergiana*) thoroughly controls erosion while improving the looks of the embankment, but it can grow to be a nuisance. The larger evergreen periwinkles (*Vinca major*) are effective planted on banks and have added charm when the blossoms come. *Vinca major variegata* is a beauty with leaves edged white. Wintercreeper (*Euonymus Fortunei radicans*) makes an excellent ground cover. For the upper South the bearberry (*Arctostaphylos Uva-ursi*) is a valuable trailing evergreen shrub for dry poor slopes, in full sun. This is particularly pleasing when the bright fruits adorn the spreading branches.

In crevices between stepping-stones portulacas delight one with their single-primrose or double rose-like blooms. The seeds of this annual do not germinate until the ground gets warm. The plants flower continuously through the summer, enduring drought and hot sun. *Cotula squalida* is a serviceable plant for flagstone paths, being a dwarf ferny carpeter that does not become a pest. Golden moss (*Sedum acre*) is also a pleasing dwarf spreader suitable for use between stepping-stones.

Wild thyme (*Thymus Serpyllum*), with sweet-scented foliage, is an interesting creeper. *Veronica rupestris* forms a carpet bearing bright blue flowers; there is a rose-colored form of spreading habit, too. These perennials do well in sun but can stand light shade part of the day.

Ground covers can give a striking appearance to sunny dry places where grass is not wanted or will not grow, and as the mats spread they shade the soil and keep the moisture in it. Moss-pinks (*Phlox subulata*), which are a mass of bloom in spring, are effective in such locations, and so is snow-in-summer (*Cerastium tomentosum*), with silvery foliage and white blooms. Here the trailing cotoneasters are satisfactory; the creeping species (*Cotoneaster adpressa*) is deciduous but holds its berries until late.

The adaptable lily-turf (*Liriope spicata*) proves an ideal ground cover for either sunny or shady areas. It spreads rapidly; the muscari-like flowers of late summer are followed by blue-black fruits. *Liriope spicata minor* is best for carpeting.

In moist locations the bugle-weed (*Ajuga reptans*) will spread and produce numerous spikes of bloom in sun or part shade. *Ranunculus repens* grows luxuriantly. The runners take root and send up small yellow, rose-like blooms. Fescue-grass thrives in moist places as well as dry. Violets succeed, and little johnny-jump-ups or heartsease (*Viola tricolor*), in their blue and yellow jumpers, are a treat. These are annuals but they self-sow and reappear every year. Forget-me-nots (Myosotis) will blanket damp shady places with clusters of dainty flowers.

Where taller plants are wanted, plantain-lilies (Hosta) are just the thing. These used to be called day-lilies, and then funkias. There are different varieties, some with broad ovate leaves, some with lance-like and some with variegated leaves. Some bear white flowers, others bluish lavender, in late summer. They are all ornamental.

Galax is a lovely ground cover for the sections where it will grow. It is a wild plant living mostly in the mountains of Virginia, North Carolina and Georgia. The leaves are very decorative whether green or bronzy from cold weather. Galax is a suitable ground cover about rhododendrons, for they thrive in the same kind of peaty loam. It likes shade and coolness, with some moisture.

The evergreen Christmas-fern (*Polystichum* (*Aspidium*) *acrostichoides*) is fine for the northern side of a house. It needs moisture and good drainage but not a covering of leaves. Except for field plants, most native plants need protection from direct sun and do well on the north side of buildings in part shade. Trillium, dutchmans-breeches, jack-in-the-pulpit, bluets and wild geranium are interesting types. The creeping fig (*Ficus pumila*) climbs or makes a prostrate mass in parts of the Piedmont and coastal regions and will grow in deep shade.

Perhaps no plant gives us more pleasure than winter jasmine (*Jasminum nudiflorum*), with its green stems and reddish buds that open into sunshiny yellow blossoms in January and February right under trees. All summer the arching green branches and leaves are effective. In the fall give the plants some leaf mold and well-rotted manure. This is all the attention they require except for a little pruning just after they bloom. Wild strawberry vines grow flat on the ground, and the blossoms and bright berries are showy under trees.

Plants will thrive in good soil under such deep-rooting trees as hickories, oaks and pecans. In early spring bulbs will bloom there, for sunshine reaches them before the trees leaf out. Under thick shade trees, the soil gets dry. It may be either acid or limestone, but it can be watered and put in condition. Most vines or low plants that grow in shade like good leaf mold and loam.

Even in a dry spot in dense shade, trailing myrtle or periwinkle (*Vinca minor*) will stay green and provide delightful flowers in spring. The periwinkles will also grow in moist locations. Ivy (Hedera), baby wintercreeper (*Euonymus Fortunei minimus*), and spurge (*Pachysandra terminalis*) are evergreen ground covers that do well in shade under trees. They will also grow in sunny places. In parts of the South, partridge-berry (*Mitchella repens*) is a native evergreen trailer that lends interest under trees. It has red berries in winter and grows in moist or dry soil.

The spring-blooming annual baby blue-eyes (Nemophila) and baby snapdragons (Linaria) will grow in sun or partial shade. A

100

Even rugged oaks look fragile when tender leaves are opening. Daffodils would naturalize well on this grassy slope.

To bring the perfume of the garden into the home is a great pleasure. Lily-of-the-valley and sweet peas are among the most loved and fragrant flowers for cutting.

creeping perennial vine that thrives anywhere is the round-leaved love-in-a-tangle or gill-over-the-ground (*Nepeta hederacea*). It is not evergreen. *Nepeta hederacea variegata* has leaf scallops margined white.

Good Plants for the Wild Garden

Bloodroot (*Sanguinaria canadensis*)
Bluets (*Houstonia cærulea*)
Butterfly violet (*Viola papilionacea*)
Climbing hempweed (*Mikania scandens*)
Columbine (*Aquilegia canadensis*)
Coneflower (*Rudbeckia speciosa*)
Dead nettle (*Lamium album*)
Dutchmans-breeches (*Dicentra Cucullaria*)
False solomons-seal (*Smilacina racemosa*)
Feathered columbine (*Thalictrum aquilegifolium*)
Harebell (*Campanula rapunculoides*)
Lady-slipper (*Cypripedium Calceolus pubescens*)
Large gayfeather (*Liatris scariosa*)
Lily-of-the-valley (*Convallaria majalis*)
Loosestrife (Lysimachia)
Mallow (*Malva Alcea*)
Mullein (*Verbascum Thapsus*)
Native aster (*Aster divaricatus (corymbosus)*)
Roundlobe hepatica or mayflower (*Hepatica triloba*)
Sundial lupine (*Lupinus perennis*)
Sweet rocket (*Hesperis matronalis*)
Wakerobin (*Trillium grandiflorum*)
Wild cranesbill (*Geranium maculatum*)
Wild ginger (Asarum)
Windflower (*Anemone canadensis*)

FRAGRANCE

When plants are selected carefully, even a few kinds can give a long succession of fragrance, as well as bloom and color. In the list that follows are a dozen shrubs or trees, a dozen bulbous plants, and annuals or perennials to provide fragrance in the garden for twelve months. Most of these are well known. Some flower for several months; others, like the tea olive, bloom in spring and again in the fall. The flowering time given is based on their performance in our garden in the Piedmont section.

101

The pleasing flowers of wintersweet (*Chimonanthus (Meratia) præcox*) are delightfully fragrant in January. Soleil d'Or narcissus opens at that time, and sweet alyssum continues to bear dainty clusters of bloom. In fact, sweet alyssum is with us practically all the year, for when the old plants are pulled up in the spring we find they have reseeded.

In February the air seems filled with the odor of breath-of-spring (*Lonicera fragrantissima*), and the fragrance of violets and jonquils or other members of the narcissus family permeates the garden.

The breezes of March will not let one forget flowering crab-apple (Malus), hyacinths and moss-pinks (*Phlox subulata*) as the sweet scents are wafted about.

In April there is mock-orange (*Philadelphus virginalis*); the older *Philadelphus coronarius* bears intensely fragrant blossoms. Poet's narcissus dispenses sweet odors, and showers of rain seem to make stocks smell all the sweeter.

The perfume of lilacs (Syringa) seems to prevail in May, until one gets a whiff of valley lilies (*Convallaria majalis*) and clove pinks (*Dianthus Caryophyllus*). Various fragrances are exquisitely mingled in May; one of the most delicate comes from old-fashioned roses.

In June mimosa puts forth fragrant, ball-like flower puffs and regal lilies perfume the air. If withered flowers of sweet peas are kept cut, fresh blooms keep coming and give pleasure a long time.

Crape-myrtles (Lagerstrœmia) begin to bloom and dispense their much-liked fragrance in July, along with Philippine lilies. One detects the perfume of heliotrope, though not so strong as that of hardy phlox.

In August, summersweet (*Clethra alnifolia*) has perfumed blossoms that appeal to bees, while butterflies hover over the fragrant buddleias. The odor of tuberoses becomes more pronounced toward night, and there is the delicate scent of lavender.

In September, abelia continues to flower and shed its fragrance; large white blooms of the plantain-lily (*Hosta plantaginea*) emit a lemon odor; and one gets hints of the faint perfume of four-o'clocks (Mirabilis).

There is the pungent smell of tea olives (Osmanthus) during October. Some of the gladioli blooming at this time are sweetly perfumed. The butterfly-lily or ginger-lily (*Hedychium coronarium*) has heavily scented flowers, and a delicate perfume is dispensed by cosmos.

Odorous flowers of eleagnus are still open in November when

102

the slightly scented autumn crocus is blooming, and the air is redolent with spicy chrysanthemums.

In December, loquats (*Eriobotrya japonica*) bear fragrant flowers in terminal clusters. These have to be more or less pampered in this section until they are fully climatized, but they thrive in the Coastal zone with little care. Paper-white narcissi are opening and lending their heady perfume to the atmosphere, while the odor of petunias in protected places is perceptible and the scent of wallflowers agreeable.

Numerous other flowers have fragrance, some pleasing and others oppressive. The high-scented Carolina jessamine (Gelsemium) is the state flower of South Carolina. Various true jasmines (Jasminum) are intensely fragrant, but winter jasmine (*Jasminum nudiflorum*) is devoid of odor. Star- or Confederate-jasmine, with sweet-smelling, star-shaped blooms, is a Trachelospermum.

Cape-jasmine is a Gardenia. This flower was named in honor of Alexander Garden, a physician of Charleston, S. C. In gardens of the South the very fragrant gardenia flowers from May until autumn, doing best as a specimen plant since it needs an open space. It thrives in rich soil and leaf mold, with morning sun and protection from afternoon sun.

Early in spring the deciduous magnolias, such as *Magnolia stellata* and *M. Soulangeana*, shed their perfume. The evergreen *M. grandiflora*, typical of the South, shows handsome blossoms with lasting perfume in May and June, and off and on until autumn.

From April until June, banana-shrubs (*Michelia fuscata*) have a delightful ripe-banana odor. In May we get orange-blossom whiffs from pittosporum; the Korean viburnum (*Viburnum Carlesii*) bears flower clusters with arbutus odor; the old-time bush honeysuckle (*Lonicera tatarica*) emits fragrance; and daphne (*Daphne Cneorum*) is a dwarf gem with pleasing perfume. Daphne is sometimes called garland-flower, as is the butterfly-lily. The graceful beauty-bush (Kolkwitzia) distils a scent of pine, and flower spikes of yucca give out a pleasant odor. The old-fashioned flowering currant (*Ribes odoratum*) is worth a place in the garden, for it bears blooms in the spring that have a delicious perfume. Some azaleas, particularly the natives, are sweet-smelling. The interesting mint-shrub (*Elsholtzia Stauntonii*) has leaves with an aromatic odor; the spikes of flowers, borne in the fall, shed a spicy fragrance for weeks.

For the Piedmont and lower sections, *Eurya ochnacea* (*Cleyera japonica*) is an acceptable plant. Here the fragrant flowers come in

103

June. In the fall tea-plants (*Thea sinensis*) bear blooms with a light perfume. Of course, everybody revels in the exotic perfume of the true orange blossoms of the deep South, while in the mountain sections various rhododendrons have an alluring sweetness in early summer.

Many day-lilies (Hemerocallis) and some tulips have a nice perfume, and flowering tobacco (Nicotiana) has trumpet-shaped blooms that are quite fragrant. There are sweet-smelling peonies, irises, various dianthus and nasturtiums. Rose geranium, lemon-verbena, thyme, rosemary and other sweet herbs deserve a place in the garden if for no other reason than their fragrance.

Such vines as honeysuckle, wisteria, clinging mignonette, cinnamon-vine, moonflower and clematis are fragrant, too. On cloudy days or when the sun goes down, the odors become stronger.

Warmth brings out the fragrance of some flowers. In cool weather even roses seem to have little perfume, but when they are cut and placed in a warm room the fragrance is soon perceptible.

The stems or leaves of many plants are fragrant or spicy. Boxwood has a distinct odor; the wood and foliage of cedars have a pungent scent; and the foliage of the sweetbriar rose is highly scented. Vitex, with spikes of bloom from June to frost, has aromatic foliage.

COLOR HARMONY

Harmony of color in a garden can be a source of great delight. Some people are more sensitive to color clashes than others. Planning is necessary for the best results. Planting is done in spring for a "thought-out" summer and autumn effect, and in autumn for a spring picture.

With the right location and well-prepared soil, one can have an all-season garden with no more labor than a one-season garden. Some pruning will have to be done to keep plants from running over others, and there may be disappointments if certain ones do not bloom at the expected time. But gardening for color effects is an artistic experiment well worth a good deal of thought.

By planning before planting, one can be sure of having inspiring pictures through the year, for there will be a balancing of form and color. Very careful planning will be required for a small place. Here greenery and variegated-leaf material may be used for color part of the year in lieu of flowers. It is well to have a dominant note in the different sections of the garden, and to plan for a succession of well-blended hues.

104

All plantings are enhanced by a background to bring out the color. Whether this is composed of trees, formal hedges, shrubs growing naturally, or vines on fences, it can tone in the various plants like bulbs and other perennials and annuals. Shrubs flowering at different seasons offer an opportunity for color all the year.

Annuals can be used for quick color effects. Most of them like sunny locations but some, such as pansies, cornflowers and asters, thrive in partial shade. Picking flowers from annuals increases the number of blooms.

For continuous bloom and best results the perennial border should be 3 to 5 feet wide or more, provided there is access to the back. Several plants of the same variety set in a clump look best. Monotony of height and a too crowded appearance as well as discordant colors should be avoided.

Each season harmonizing tones make a garden an enchanting place. In spring the predominating early color is yellow. The early narcissus does not mind the cold and is with us at a time when we can really appreciate it. For summer, cool green, white, gray or variegated foliage blends nicely with brighter tones. This is when we especially enjoy blue flowers or pastel tints. When autumn comes, one admires the dash of cheer given by berries and fall flowers and vivid foliage. In winter bright fruits, evergreens and deciduous plants with interesting colored twigs and winter buds give warmth to the landscape in the coldest weather.

A few suggestions for securing color harmony each month with well-known plants may be acceptable. Most of the combinations suggested will last for several weeks.

Pansies are very attractive as edgings for borders in spring; they begin flowering here in the Piedmont section in January and continue into June. *Phlox subulata* and *Alyssum saxatile*, also the pale yellow *A. saxatile luteum*, are other good edgers for spring. In March, unless the winter has been severe, one can expect gray-lavender veils of wisteria before the leaves come. It blooms at times all during the summer, but the panicles become shorter as the season advances and show a deeper shade of lavender along with the leaves. During this early springtime the yellow jessamine vine blooms, paulownia trees bear their showy lavender panicles and fruit trees in bloom are as bewitching as any flowers.

There are sudden showers and fleecy clouds in April, and all vegetation seems to be glowing with life. The mornings are cool but the sun comes out and warms the ground, and with a mossy green lawn for foreground, flowers show to great advantage. It seems as if spirea, forsythia, Scotch broom (*Cytisus scoparius*) and azaleas are among the "must haves," particularly when bordered with white candytuft (Iberis) and blue *Phlox divaricata*.

In the early spring a lavender and yellow planting will stand out. Yellow Master and purple Royal pansies may be combined with Yellow Giant and Dream tulips; back of these one may have Persian lilacs and redbud trees (Cercis), with Banksia roses not far away. In a short time purple and yellow tall bearded irises will bloom, followed by giant zinnias.

Ultramarine-blue Lake of Thun pansies and Giant White ones are charming in front of clumps of tall white Zwanenburg and pink Flamingo tulips, backed with pearl-bush (Exochorda) kept pruned so that it will flower from the bottom. Later, Golden Salmon and white Katharina Zeimet polyantha roses will flower just behind the tulips. Late in the summer the lilliput zinnia Salmon Gem will replace the tulips.

Rosy pink Fantasy tulips make an interesting planting when fronted with Blue Boy pansies and backed with the old Lohengrin iris, which is the color of the silvery lilac pansies, intermingling with painted daisies (*Chrysanthemum* (*Pyrethrum*) *coccineum*) the color of the tulips. This is a satisfying combination for the last of April. Lavender and pink verbena will be blooming there by the time the pansies stop.

When planting iris, beautiful pictures can be created if a dominant color is chosen to blend with certain other tones. Irises make a lovely display near shrub roses and with clumps of perennials like long-spurred columbines (Aquilegia) in harmonizing tints.

Dr. W. Van Fleet roses near blue Chinese forget-me-nots, Newport Pink sweet william (*Dianthus barbatus*) and pink verbenas are truly alluring. Japanese irises look pretty with spikes of agreeably contrasting gladioli close by.

In June, borders can be made attractive with regal lilies, delphinium, shasta daisies and blue linum, with light yellow lemon lilies (Hemerocallis) interspersed. An edging of fairy-lilies (Zephyranthes) gives an artistic touch. When the weather gets warm in June a water garden, with water-lilies in delicate colors, is very appealing.

Orange-colored tiger lilies, lantanas and gaillardias can be toned down in July with white and green, using white phlox, feverfew (*Chrysanthemum Parthenium*) and white petunias. An edging of silvery-

106

leaved santolina will make the border enchanting; it may be kept quite bushy if it is clipped. Grasses with their creamy plumes and variegated-foliage plants provide cool colors at this time.

When August comes, one can have pleasing combinations with petunias and zinnias. They will stand a good deal of neglect. Spikes of blue bloom may be had a long time from perennial salvia, such as the azure *Salvia grandiflora*, *S. patens* or *S. pratensis*, and from veronica.

Double altheas or Rose-of-Sharon (*Hibiscus syriacus*) are especially delightful. The double white althea, Jeanne d'Arc, makes a good accent plant near the peach-colored canna, Apricot.

An arbor covered with coral-vine (Antigonon) with its dainty rose-pink flowers and heart-shaped leaves, footed with tall-growing ageratum and edged with Rosy Morn petunias, gives pleasure in September and over a long period.

Various dahlias lend color to a garden in October and are especially interesting when backed with downy flowering groundsel trees (Baccharis). Heavenly Blue morning-glories are a glorious sight over a pergola, particularly when near the daisy-flowered Astrid chrysanthemum, with shell-pink to old-rose blooms.

As November approaches, dwarf blue ageratum makes a good edging for single, gleaming yellow Sunbright chrysanthemums. And with the tints of leaves and chrysanthemums blending together, gorgeous combinations of color can be enjoyed this month.

For December color harmonies there are evergreens and berried plants like the snowberry (*Symphoricarpos albus (racemosus)*) laden with white fruits, nandinas with dainty foliage and clusters of bright red berries, and tall ligustrums with blue-black fruits.

A nice border for January can be had with coral-berries (*Symphoricarpos orbiculatus (vulgaris)*), weighted down with reddish lavender berries, and back of these, laurestinus (*Viburnum Tinus*), with bud clusters toning with the rosy lavender berries. Eleagnus may be added to the border, with its silver leaf linings showing against the green and yellow, lantern-like fruits. These fruits turn red by March. Back of the plants named may be photinia, with reddish new growth. At this time conifers come into the picture as pleasing accents of green.

In February winter jasmine (*Jasminum nudiflorum*) makes sunshiny spots near golden drifts of early trumpet daffodils and jonquils, while close up under oaks the evergreen vine, *Vinca minor*, shows blue or white blooms. Flowering quinces (Chænomeles) are cheerful with bright color, and *Spiræa Thunbergii* and bridal wreath (*Spiræa prunifolia*) are burdened with small white flowers.

107

In addition to the plants already suggested, one may consider the airy white and pink dogwoods (*Cornus florida* and *C. florida rubra*), larkspurs and poppies. *Nemophila Menziesii* (*insignis*) makes a good ground cover about tulips in the spring garden.

Lovely effects may be had with crape-myrtles (Lagerstrœmia) in midsummer and later, from the palest tints of pink or lavender to the deep tones of watermelon-red or purple. For contrast these should be interspersed with the white-flowered kind.

There are golden marigolds and orange or red berries of various pyracanthas for autumn. A holly tree full of glistening red berries and with a mat of small-leaf ivy around the base draws the attention of all at Christmas time.

There are endless combinations of plants to produce different color effects. One gets immense satisfaction from developing the exact picture that he wants.

SOME SOUTHERN BIRDS

Birds are a pleasure in a garden on account of their lovely plumage and cheery melodies. They need protection from enemies and a supply of food and water. In return for hospitality they destroy harmful insects and noxious seeds. Spraying does not kill all insects and will not take the place of birds. Children are being educated to care for birds instead of destroying them. Species that are with us in winter need protection against cold as well as from enemies like cats. The berry-bearing evergreens provide some food and shelter. Birds will come back season after season to places where they can get food and safe homes.

Sometimes birds devour useful fruits. To prevent this, one should plant ornamental berried shrubs. Mulberries will keep birds from strawberries and raspberries. In late summer they will be attracted to dogwoods, hawthorns and beauty-berries, for most birds have a fondness for the fruits of native shrubs. Various plants, such as ligustrums, Carolina cherry, honeysuckle and holly, have berries in fall and winter that entice birds.

All during the year some birds are about for one to study. It is intensely interesting to identify them by color, size, songs or calls and movements, and see what they feed on. Some have hard bills, like the cardinals, and can eat seed; others with soft bills like worms and berries. Some nest in trees, like the woodpecker; others prefer man-built houses. There are permanent residents of the South, such

The Bok Tower located at Lake Wales, Fla., is a famous
bird sanctuary with thousands of visitors every year.

What more could a family want for pleasant outdoor living all season long than a comfortable and home-like spot like this, where bird song mingles with the color and fragrance of the garden?

as cardinals, mockingbirds, some of the wrens, partridges, jays and English sparrows. Others are summer dwellers, like the ruby-throated hummingbird, chimney swift and whip-poor-will. Such birds as juncos and white-throated sparrows stay during the winter while others merely stop when passing through.

During the migratory season we look for unusual birds and listen for medleys. Some birds migrate at night, like warblers, and some in the daytime, like wild geese and ducks. The usual migration route is southwest and northeast, parallel with the Atlantic; in the interior it follows the course of large rivers. Birds have a wonderful sense of direction and appear at the same place about the same time every year. Generally the older ones are the vanguard and return to the localities where they have nested before.

Watch the different birds at a feeding station. Many of them like crumbs and pieces of apple, and many must have grit. Seed-eating birds, such as juncos, relish chicken feed, benne and sunflower seed. Insect eaters have a liking for suet, which is a substitute for insects. This can be fastened to feeding stations or trunks of trees. Birds become more or less tame and will feed near a person if not frightened. They want water to bathe in as well as to drink. Bird baths must be shallow and not slippery and should be so placed that cats cannot hide close by.

When placing bird houses, do not put them in dense shade or facing prevailing winds. Set at an angle so that rain will not beat in. It is well to have drainage holes in the bottom in case of a driving rain. Bluebirds, wrens and martins particularly like to nest in boxes high on poles. English sparrows will frequently leave the eaves of houses where their nests are so annoying, in order to take the homes of more desirable birds. English sparrows were imported into America about 1850. They raise several families a year and do more harm than good, for they eat very few insects.

Sparrows with destructive habits must not be confused with our native kinds, like the song sparrow, which consumes numerous weed seeds. This sparrow has a marked breast, forked tail and stubby bill. It takes a close observer to distinguish the different native sparrows. Some are insect eaters; others devour weed seeds. Most of them are gray and dull brown. The breast and throat of the white-throated sparrow are distinctly white.

If the entrance to a bird house is made very small, wrens can enter when English sparrows cannot. The Carolina wren is the largest species of its kind and stays all the year in the Southern States.

Most birds sing during the mating season, but the Carolina wren sings every month of the year and devours numerous insects.

Many birds like to nest in shrubbery, such as euonymus, red-cedar and other junipers. Some nest in thorny places for protection, as in hawthorn, Osage-orange and climbing roses.

A bird we could do without is the starling, which chatters but does not sing. However, he does eat some insects. These greenish purple-black birds were brought to the United States in 1890 and have become naturalized. They often have two broods a year and are destructive to fruit and to corn in the ear. Starlings and English sparrows will live together, but starlings drive the sparrows from their nesting places just as the English sparrows drive away wrens, bluebirds and martins.

Keep a lookout for cedar waxwings. They are brown, with wax-like spots on the wings, and a black line around the eye to the back of the head; the tail is yellow tipped. They appear in the Piedmont section the latter part of March and feast on eleagnus berries. Both the berries and the birds are attractive.

Bobolinks are not popular in the South but are well liked in the North, where they are useful. While there, the male birds are buff, black and white, but when they come South in late summer the colors change to buff like the female. On their way to warm countries they live in the marshes, where they feed on seeds of grasses and wild rice and are known as rice or reed birds. When rice was grown extensively in South Carolina, they did much damage, for they arrived just as the crop was ripening.

One of our permanent residents, the blue jay, as a rule is beneficial. It is said that jays rob the nests of other birds and feed on the eggs and young. This may be an exaggeration. The blue jays are such handsome, cocky birds and so interesting to observe that we are willing to overlook some of their crimes. As a general rule, male birds have brighter plumage than their mates, but this is not true of the jay. Both sexes have the same plumage and give the same harsh shrieks. If a hawk comes near, the blue jays give the alarm and other birds take to cover.

The mockingbird is the songster of the South. These gray birds, white beneath and on the tail, and on wings when in flight, stay throughout the year in the South. They are quieter in winter, but we are apt to hear their melodious songs in the night in the very early spring. As is often true of birds, the male is the songster. Sometimes he will hold one spellbound with a great outburst of melody and will then introduce a mocking note. Mockingbirds nest in shrubbery or thickets, and their appetite is for dogwood and holly berries, pokeberries and other fruits. They eat insects, too, such as grasshoppers and beetles. Catbirds are sometimes mistaken for mockingbirds. They are drab, with rusty red under the tail, and they like to "show off." The male sings, and if frightened makes cat-like calls.

Cardinals or red birds (sometimes called Virginia nightingales) are welcome helpers in the garden. The male is a vivid color, while the female has a grayish tinge over her red. Both have topknots, though the male's is more prominent. The male and female give varied song notes.

The brown thrasher is reddish brown from head over tail. The wing coverts are tipped white, making two wing bars. Underneath this bird is creamy streaked dark brown, and it has a long rounded tail. It stays in parts of the South all the year. The song is loud and melodious. Brown thrashers like to perch on a high limb and send forth sweet medleys early in the morning. It is interesting to watch them scratch among leaves, seeking worms and insects. This bird is sometimes confused with the wood thrush, which is brown on the back, with head and neck reddish brown. Beneath, it is white with round, brownish black spots. Its tail is short as compared with the thrasher. The wood thrush sings clear, flute-like notes, most often in the evening. It stays near woods but will come around a house where there is shrubbery. For the most part, its food consists of insects and wild fruits.

Many different woodpeckers, from small downy ones to the large red-headed, go up and down trees searching for grubs. They peck under the bark for larvæ and thus take care of trees. The red-bellied woodpecker, however, is a nuisance in Florida on account of its fondness for oranges. Golden-winged woodpeckers, flickers or yellow hammers are beautiful, with black head and red band at the neck. They get rid of a number of ants, beetles and flies.

Brown creepers remove insects from crevices in tree bark with their long curved bills. Their long tails, like the woodpecker's, are held against the tree for support. It is fascinating to watch a creeper climbing up a tree in a spiral. It spends its time going from one tree to the next, for its food is almost entirely insects. The color is somber, toning in with the trees and rendering the birds inconspicuous. The nuthatch, or "upside-down bird," also spirals trees, up and down, head first. It gets its name from hacking with its bill at food held in the claw.

111

We like to have bluebirds in our gardens, for they destroy harmful insects such as cutworms and grasshoppers. The bluebirds have mellow, cheery song notes and such a good disposition that they cannot cope with English sparrows and starlings. They are rather helpless creatures and have a hard time in winter if they are not cared for.

The tufted titmouse, ranging over the eastern United States, generally stays all year where it nests and is active in search of wasps, caterpillars and weed seeds. Its common note is a clear whistle of *peto, peto, peto,* and it has a call somewhat like the chickadee's. The southern or Carolina chickadee is a useful bird that seeks insects and larvæ under crevices of bark, as well as eggs of caterpillar, moth and plant lice.

Everybody knows the robins, with their reddish brown breasts. The cock robin has a black head, the female a gray head and paler breast. They live mostly on worms and wild fruit but will eat cherries and strawberries unless there are other berries convenient for them. An old story is that they get drunk on china-berries.

Towhees, sometimes called ground robins, get much of their food by scratching on the ground, using the feet alternately. Their early spring activity gets rid of numerous insects and weed seeds.

We have snowbirds or juncos with us all winter. These birds are slate-gray, with white underneath; the tail feathers show white in flight. They have a flesh-colored bill. Their song is a trill, and they become friendly when food is provided for them. Juncos live mostly on weed seeds, caterpillars and various insects.

Warblers migrate north in spring and south in fall. These are not loud singers but are many beautiful colors. The yellow-breasted chat is one of the larger species and often sings at night during summer. Watching hummingbirds fly backward as well as forward interests one in the summer. The male has a red throat and the female a whitish one.

Male summer tanagers, also called summer red birds, are rosy red, the females greenish yellow. They spend summers as far south as Florida. Brilliant male scarlet tanagers, red with black wings and tail, delight all who see them; the females are olive-green. These winter in the tropics and return north in spring. The vireo hunts insects on pecan trees. We also have butcherbirds, hooded warblers and screech owls, which do not screech but have a melancholy voice.

There are flycatchers that catch flies on the wing, such as the phoebe and kingbirds and wood peewees; each has a call that can

Sasanqua camellias, such as Hinode-gumo pictured here, bloom earlier than the japonica varieties and do better in areas of higher altitude. (See page 146.)

Although camellias have come to us from the far East, they thrive like natives in parts of the South where they have acid soil, good drainage and a humid atmosphere. Shown here is *Camellia japonica*, Bessie McArthur. (See page 146.)

be recognized as its own. Even chimney swifts, which stay in summer, hold one's attention as they circle over chimneys, snapping insects from the air. Whip-poor-wills, so named for their call, are not seen till twilight when they fly about, catching insects in the air.

Orchard orioles are not so interesting as Baltimore orioles, but they have gay plumage and a cheerful warble. They prefer to live in orchards, where they get such food as worms and beetles. They are said to feed also on boll weevils. The prettiest blackbirds are the greedy red-winged; though they are a menace to crops, they do good by eating weed seeds. Then there are goldfinches that look like canaries, and swallows.

The purple martins are popular swallows that come here early in March. The male is blue and black, and his mate is gray and black. They like to nest in hollowed-out gourds hung on a pole high in the air. They catch insects and will fight crows and hawks. And with what patience they teach their young to fly! We once paid particular attention to a mother bird at this job. All of the young were trying their wings except one timid fellow. The mother pulled and pushed him along until his wings just had to be tested.

Golden-crowned kinglets winter in Florida and along the Gulf Coast to Texas. Sometimes called greenlets for their color, they are the smallest birds next to the hummingbird. The male golden-crowned has a yellow and orange, black-bordered crown, while his mate is adorned with a yellow crown. The male ruby-crowned kinglet has a bright patch on his crown and a whitish ring around the eye. The song is a mellow warble. Kinglets flit from branch to branch seeking hibernating insects.

One of the pleasures of having birds is to watch them with their young and see them feed the gaping mouths. We have noticed how some birds, like the brown thrasher, will do everything to keep one from locating the nest. The mother will roll in the sand, perform various antics and fly in the opposite direction to divert attention. We note that some walk and others hop along the ground. To watch them as they carry twigs and grasses for their nests, and to hear snatches of song is highly entertaining. We whistle to partridges and enjoy hearing their clear *bob-bob-white* in answer. The call of doves, though plaintive, is sweet. All the year, birds add interest to a garden, and it is worthwhile to attract them.

One who makes a study of birds has an entertaining hobby that will continue to be interesting. It is good to know that garden clubs are taking such an interest in birds and sanctuaries.

113

OUTDOOR LIVING

A happy trend is to make the garden a part of home life. People should be healthier and happier, and the children should want to stay at home when the garden is really lived in. Even on wet days one can walk here in comfort if stepping-stones are provided.

In many parts of the garden one can put a seat or unobtrusive bench right among the flowers. This will be appreciated perhaps most of all in spring when the gardener can rest occasionally from his work and enjoy the beauty of the flowering bulbs and shrubs around him. These seats ought to be comfortable and in keeping with the surroundings.

In the South it is possible to be outdoors so much of the time that an outdoor living area sees a great deal of use. It may be furnished like a room in the house, or the hours outdoors can be enjoyed with only a bench and a chair or two. In any case, the furniture should be sturdy enough to be left outdoors when it rains; oilcloth covers for the cushions are an advantage.

Pergolas and arbors to hold vines and to frame desirable vistas are a fitting part of the outdoor living room. As one reclines there in the shade on a warm summer day, it is a joy to see birds splashing in the baths nearby while colorful butterflies flit about. A gazing globe will mirror these pictures if set in the sun. A sundial is another attraction seen in many gardens. It must be level, on a firm base and in full sun. Set the dial when the sun reaches its zenith just at noon; the point that makes the shadow must point to the north star.

A desirable view from the outdoor sitting room would be a rock garden that appears to belong to the landscape and is not just a heap of rocks and soil. A steep incline is not necessary for a rock garden. In our own garden there was a sloping area near oak trees where we couldn't coax anything to grow. We placed rocks here, put rich soil between them and planted these pockets. Now everything started there thrives in the weak sunlight. The place that was an eyesore has been turned into a real beauty spot.

A pleasing feature of an outdoor living room is a pool, which can be made by the family. First draw the design on paper and then lay it off on the ground. It is well to have a 2-inch overflow pipe screwed into a drain pipe to drain the pool. The concrete should be 6 inches thick. A pool may be either formal or naturalistic; if the latter, the cement should be concealed. To prevent injury from freezing, let the pool slope outward on the inner sides.

114

One of the beauties of a pool is to see clouds mirrored there. It is important, therefore, to have a few well-chosen plants for it rather than so many as to cover the surface completely. Water-lilies come first to mind. Hardy varieties start blooming early; tropical ones will bloom from June to frost. The night-blooming kinds are open from afternoon until late the next morning. Water-lilies do best in sun, and the majority of them like to be 1 to 2 feet deep. They can be planted in tubs of good loam (three parts of soil with one part of well-rotted manure and an inch of gravel or sand on top). Have the tubs well weighted down in the water. A good place for water-loving plants, such as Japanese, Spuria and Siberian irises, is around the pool. Even when they are not in bloom, their foliage is charming in combination with ferns and primroses. Fancy-leaved caladiums are fine for summer effects.

Fish, snails and other scavengers help clear the water of aphis, mosquito larvæ and other pests. If there are oxygenating plants, the fish eggs will cling to them and the baby fish can hide there. Goldfish infected with fungus may be dipped in a three percent salt solution. When they show that they are uncomfortable, put them in fresh water.

Another asset for pleasant outdoor living is a fireplace. From time to time the various garden magazines give directions for making many different types; these may be followed easily. A fireplace may be constructed for cooking purposes only, but it will have more usefulness if logs can be burned in it as the days get chilly. Food tastes better when cooked and eaten out-of-doors, even if it is only "wienies" browned on a forked stick, or corn on the cob roasted after being boiled a few minutes. And what is better tasting than barbecue hash cooked in an iron pot outdoors?

In the leisure hours of long lazy summer days, outdoor living is a real pleasure and garden visiting becomes a popular pastime. Of course, there are visitors—and visitors. Some merely notice what is blooming and nothing else; some cannot see "our" garden for talking about "theirs," and others ask if we will "sell" them plants. Some visitors, however, appreciate all the aspects of beauty in the garden and help to heighten our own enjoyment of it.

Any space set aside for relaxation in or near the garden will be popular all the year in the South. Even if the grounds are small, the garden can be livable, and each season brings something new to enjoy there.

115

ENJOYING FLOWERS INDOORS

Everyone likes to send flowers to the sick and to friends and enjoys the sight of them in the home. To make the most of them, it is necessary to know at least the rudiments of arranging cut flowers.

In gathering flowers, they ought to be cut and not broken off the plant. Cut the stems slantingly and place them in water immediately to prevent air from entering. They will soak up quantities of moisture, which will keep them firm.

If you pick garden flowers after sundown, soak them in water all night and arrange them the next morning. If you cut them in the morning, do it early; then plunge the full length of the stems in water and leave them for an hour or two in a cool spot free from drafts and away from direct sunlight. The cooler flowers are kept, the longer they will last. When they are hardened, they stand better and live longer.

It is best to carry a vessel of water in which to place the stems just as soon as they are cut. If this is not done, hold the flowers head down to prevent them from snapping off and to keep moisture in the stem. Flowers wither when they do not get enough water to replace what evaporated through the foliage.

Varieties that have a sticky sap, such as poppies, should be singed at the end of the stems immediately after cutting, or half an inch of the stem may be dipped in boiling water for one to three minutes, with the flowers and foliage protected from steam. When cut flowers look wilted, cut their stems and place them in deep water. If the ends of hardwood branches are bruised or slit before being put into water, they will last longer.

It is best for peonies not to open in the sun; cut them as the buds begin to open. Do not pick daffodils until they expand. Generally, single flowers should be gathered while they are still closed, and double flowers after they have loosened. Tulips wrapped in paper that is fastened with a rubber band, will stiffen when placed in deep water. Morning-glories may be cut in the bud, each one wrapped tightly in wax paper, and the stems immersed in water. Remove the paper a short time before you want the flowers to open. To make water-lilies stay open, pour melted paraffin (just warm enough to run) into the center of the bloom.

After flowers are conditioned, they do not have to be kept in deep water. The depth of the water does not matter so long as the

A mass arrangement by Mrs. Rafe Banks DuPré of Marietta, Ga., of tulips, daffodils and snapdragons with a medley of camellias. The crystal container with silver and gold base imparts the same elegance and graciousness as the flowers.

Above, left. Mrs. Douglas Featherstone of Greenwood, S. C., made this line arrangement of dried material in a bronze incense burner to show how a feeling of rhythm can be expressed by repetition of form. It contains Scotch broom, seed pods and the blossom end of a coconut stem.

Above, right. In this line arrangement by Mrs. Henry K. Thayer of Greenwood, S. C., a gray, orange and brown pottery jug holds kumquats, date palm fruits and cat-tails.

A border of annuals is a good source of flowers for cutting. The oftener you cut, the more you have.

cut surface of the stem is covered and the water is changed when necessary. Anything that kills bacteria prolongs the life of flowers.

Interesting material for winter arrangements may be gathered in summer. Everlastings or strawflowers, Japanese lantern, honesty and pampas grass may be used. If cut when too mature, they will darken. Pampas plumes should be picked when they come out of the husks and are fluffy. All of these, along with cones, seed pods and evergreens, make attractive arrangements for winter.

Flower arrangement is one of the fine arts. Many people take pride in producing original effects and in imitating masterpieces. The container is an important factor but it does not have to be expensive. Its color, shape, size and material should be considered in relation to the flowers, for its purpose is to "bring out" the flower material.

Certain countries have characteristic types of flower arrangement. In Japan the art has been developed to a high degree, but it is comparatively new in America. Some principles are followed here that have been originated by the Japanese; others are borrowed from Victorian and French paintings. Artistic arrangement of flowers is more a matter of appreciation and good taste than knowledge. A few simple rules are observed, but rules do not create beauty.

Flowers for arranging fall into three classes: background, steeple, and dominants or substance. Background flowers are of small form, feathery and light, like babys-breath, artemisia and grasses. They are fillers giving height and grace. Steeple flowers are tall and smart, such as gladiolus, delphinium, foxglove and snapdragon; these break up the form and give style to the composition. The dominants are the body of the design, such as the round flowers—roses, petunias and marigolds. These as centers of interest must not be merely inserted where the lines meet. They are accents of interest leading the eye to the focal point, generally a little over halfway from the table to the top of the arrangement. If there are too many centers of interest, the result is monotonous.

Flower arranging is particularly satisfying when the plants are grown by the arranger. All stages of the flower may be used, from bud to full-blown. Some of the crooked and curving branches give unusual and pleasing effects. The container will determine the height of the material. Whether simple or elaborate, the arrangement should have stability and good balance. To analyze a composition, consider distinction, relation of material and container, color harmony, proportion or measure balance, and perfection of arrangement.

Distinction raises an arrangement above mediocrity. This involves good color, excellent material in an appropriate container, and the correct quantity of flowers. Distinction is to the arrangement what personality is to a person. The unexpected may cause a composition to stand out. It may be a bold color scheme, unusual color harmony, material placed in a way that is different, or the line of the design, that gives the quality of distinction.

The plant material and the container should be good companions in color, form and texture. The attractiveness of the flowers is heightened by the receptacle. A container that seems heavy because of its substance or color should be avoided for an arrangement made wholly of dainty, light-colored flowers. Neither should a vase of delicate appearance be used for large blooms, especially if they are of dark colors.

A clear glass container should not be considered for any flowers with stems that get slimy in water. In clear glass the stems must be arranged to look attractive. A vase can cheapen flowers or it can help create a beautiful picture. Plain white glass and neutral-colored receptacles are always in good taste. Strong-colored flowers are effective in bronze containers. Fine-textured ones, like roses, look well in silver receptacles or fine pottery.

The color of the blooms, the container and the surroundings should harmonize. When there are flowers of several colors, a more pleasing effect is gained by placing those of one color or tone together rather than by mixing them and making a spotty appearance. Combinations of flowers of the same kinds look best. Interesting arrangements may be made with contrasting colors; with complementary colors; with monochromatic shades, or different values of any one color, as gold, yellow, cream; with analogous tints or any group of colors that are closely related, like blue, blue-purple, bluish green.

A law for the proportions of arrangement comes from the Japanese: "Flower material should be one time and a half the height of the container if the vase is tall, or one time and a half the width if low." A stand under the vase is considered to be part of the container. Light foliage and flowers may be higher, but the body of the composition should be about the height stated. One uses this scale unconsciously and gets to "feel with the eye." The width of the arrangement is a matter of instinctive feeling. The heaviness or seeming weight of the container influences the height and width of a composition.

For perfection of arrangement, strong lines should be at the base for balance. Place large flowers and darker colors low, for they seem heavier, and small material and lighter tones at the top. The arrangement ought to appear balanced and not top-heavy or loose enough to fall apart. Do not allow main stems to cross. The blooms should not be placed at exactly the same height nor exactly parallel. Parts of the foliage and flowers may be cut off if that will add to the beauty of the creation, for there should be no crowding. Use only enough material to give a good effect.

In a vase where it is not practical to have a flower block, a wire filler can hold the blooms in position. Chicken wire crumpled up will do. Small twigs of evergreens can be used, but sometimes they will cause stems to decay. Choose only fresh flowers and branches, and do not push them down to the bottom of the holder but place them lightly so that they may soak up water.

A simple rule is to arrange flowers, so far as practicable, in the way they grew. Use plenty of greenery, preferably the foliage of the flowers used in the composition, unless you want to break up the form or relate it to the container. Do not hide the mouth of the vase completely.

A good way of arranging flowers is to insert the tallest sprays first in the container, then the background sprays, and last, the dominant ones. Beautiful results can be produced with a scanty supply of sprays and flowers, or with foliage alone. Blooms and foliage give color, line and mass to an arrangement; sometimes fruit adds just the right note.

The Japanese stress simplicity and economy of material—in other words, restraint and correctness. Strong lines are at the base and are well held together. The lines look simple and natural because they are so arranged that each stem, leaf and flower stands out. The Japanese like plant material rather than color to work with. Buds, flowers, foliage and stems are used in all stages of growth. Symbolism is very important. The highest part of the design typifies heaven; man is half as high as heaven, and earth half as high as man. There is only one heaven stem but as many men and earth stems as desired.

A massed arrangement does not mean the crowding of as many flowers as possible into a container. The composition should be strong and compact, with a center of interest. There may be considerable massing at the mouth of the receptacle, with color combination and the relation of blooms to the container stressed. For example, for a Victorian arrangement use a vase characteristic of that period

119

and appropriate flowers of rich colors to make a mass of interesting form and color. The French or classical type emphasizes the form of the flowers known at the period selected and the dainty coloring of the whole design. The rule that "no flowers should be level or directly above each other" does not apply to Victorian and French arrangements.

In line arrangement there is little massing, and that only at the mouth of the container. The lines are few; each one relates to the others and to the vase. Modernistic arrangements have strong lines in angular style. The material used and the container suit each other or are symmetrical.

An arrangement in the home becomes a still-life picture harmonizing with the rooms and the furniture. It may be meant for one-way or for all-around viewing. All-around compositions should be pleasing from all sides. Flowers with strong lines, like gladiolus, look better in front of a mirror or with a plain background. For formal or dignified rooms, such flowers as callas, irises and gladioli are appropriate. Whether the arrangements in a room are large or small, there should be a feeling of fitness.

Making bouquets, particularly when one gathers the material from his own garden, is a recreation. A "tussy-mussy" (a medieval word) is made of bright-colored flowers and some aromatic foliage. The flowers are in the middle and the leaves, such as sprigs of thyme or tansy, are placed around them. Bouquets suitable for different seasons can give a feeling of coolness, warmth, richness or brightness, as well as exemplify different themes.

Among other pleasures to be derived from growing flowers is the making of potpourri jars. The following recipe uses rose petals and spices: On a sunny day gather the petals of roses, preferably in the early morning while the dew is still on them. Spread them in a cool place where there is little sun; turn the petals lightly. When they are dry, put them in a large covered bowl in layers, sprinkling each layer freely with salt (not iodized). More petals can be gathered for several days. Stir from the bottom every morning, and let the whole mass stand ten days after the last petals have been added. Transfer to a glass fruit jar, in the bottom of which have been placed 2 ounces of crushed allspice and an ounce of broken-up stick cinnamon. Let this stand for six weeks, when it will be ready for the permanent jar. Add to it an ounce of powdered orris root, 2 ounces of lavender flowers, and a small quantity of any other sweet-scented dried leaves that may be desired. Mix all together and put in the permanent rose jar; sprinkle on it a few drops of oil of roses. Pour over all ½ teacupful (¼ pint) of good cologne. The jar may be left open when fragrance is wanted and closed tight at other times. This potpourri will last for years, though from time to time a little perfume, orange-flower or lavender water, can be added. More rose petals may occasionally be placed in the jar. Other flowers than roses may be used for potpourri. An aromatic potpourri can be made from herb flowers and leaves alone.

A terrarium is fascinating, for one can watch this miniature indoor garden grow all winter. Any glass container that has an adjustable glass top is suitable. Most plants, except those that like dry conditions, will thrive in a terrarium; moisture-loving kinds do particularly well. The best soil is a good loam, mixed with sand, leaf mold and powdered charcoal. Place the rocks and soil first; then press the roots firmly into the soil. Water well, spray the plants with water, and attach the top. The best location for a terrarium is a cool place in partial sunlight. It requires little attention. If too much moisture collects on the glass, raise the top for awhile; or if the soil gets dry, spray it with water.

Chapter IX
It's Time To Specialize

ROSES

Beds for roses should be prepared sometime before the plants are set out, in order to allow the soil to settle. Roses need good drainage, humus, air and sunshine. They will thrive with some shade but their tops need to be in the sun and their roots shaded by their own foliage. It is possible to grow them near trees and hedges provided these do not cut off the sunshine more than a few hours of the day or send out their roots to compete with the roses for plant food and moisture.

Roses prefer a deep, rich, porous soil. Spade out the bed to the depth of 2 feet or more and put in about 6 inches of clinkers or gravel for drainage. Into the soil should be thoroughly mixed old manure (cow manure is best), bonemeal and wood ashes, or commercial fertilizer, with clay added if the soil is sandy.

Often failure of roses in the South is caused by poor drainage and not enough humus, and maybe not enough potash or phosphorus, or too alkaline a soil. Roses do best in a neutral or slightly acid soil. Either light sandy loam or heavy clay loam can be put in condition for them. Some species grow wild in various soils.

Generally, late autumn is the best time to plant in the Southern States, since growth stops for a short while in midwinter. In all sections where the temperature does not fall below 10 degrees, it is usually best to plant in the fall. November and December are good planting months except in the mountain section, where late February or early March may be best.

Use number 1 grade, two-year-old plants for best results. The roots must be kept moist until the plants are put out. If they seem dry when you receive them from the nursery, let them soak in a tubful of water for several hours. Dig the holes large enough for the roots to be spread out. Pack the fertile soil between the roots when filling in. Water the plants, then add more soil and firm well. Hill the soil up for a few weeks until the roots get anchored. The grafted part of budded roses should not be more than 2 inches below the level of the ground.

Roses do not need protection in the central and lower parts of the South, but in the mountain section it is safer to keep them hilled with soil through winter. If planting cannot be done until late spring, pot-grown plants had best be used. Be sure to label them and keep records.

Do not apply any more fertilizer to newly set plants the first year. Keep the ground loose on top, and in dry weather soak the beds with water about once a week. As soon as the ground is dry enough, cultivate lightly for a dust mulch. The fine roots of roses come close to the surface, and deep digging will injure them. In summer, if one prefers, pine needles or other material may be used for a mulch. Strawy mulch will keep in the moisture and make frequent watering unnecessary. When established roses begin to grow in spring, they should be given fertilizer. Wood ashes and bonemeal are good to scratch into the ground surface.

Just after pruning bush roses in late winter, it is well to spray them and the ground thoroughly with lime-sulphur. This helps to control stem canker. This disease can enter the garden on nursery plants, regardless of precautions taken. Stem canker is caused by a fungus that gains entrance through wounds. Sometimes it gets in canes after they are pruned, especially if they were not pruned just above an eye. Clean cuts should be made with sharp tools and near a bud, avoiding stubs. If it is not cut away, the canker will work down into the stem and kill the entire plant or parts of it. (See Chapter III, Spraying and Dusting.)

As soon as tender bronze leaves show, spray or dust with a good fungicide like Bordeaux or Massey dust to prevent blackspot. Do this regularly about once a week, especially before rain. When plants are wet, infection takes place. Sprays for fungus troubles are preventive and not remedial. It is necessary for the plants to have good foliage, for the food of the plant is manufactured in the leaf. This spraying or dusting will hold rose insects in check, too.

Just after flowering is the time to prune climbing roses. The others are pruned in late winter. (See Chapter III, Pruning.) Sometimes suckers appear below the graft on budded roses. As soon as they are observed, cut them off below the ground where they start. If left they will outgrow the grafted part of the plant. They are identifiable by their quick growth and smaller leaves, and are usually an outside growth. Seven leaflets do not necessarily indicate sucker growth; many modern hybrid tea roses will show seven leaflets. If the tips of rose canes are black and dead in the spring, cut the parts off; new shoots will appear closer to the ground.

There are bedding roses, shrubs and climbers, and all types thrive in the central and upper sections of the South. Tea roses do best in the lower part of the Gulf states and Florida. In the warmer areas some roses flower in the winter, but then they often tire out and should be treated as annuals.

Soil for roses in the lower South should be prepared as elsewhere and the plants set out about the first of November to early January, when plants are most nearly dormant. They bloom beautifully the first year and sometimes live for several seasons, but many wear out the first summer. In western and northern Florida roses do well. Clay soil is good for them when mixed with sand and humus. Many old-fashioned roses grow in the lower South. Some have been flourishing for years and years, probably on their own roots. Nature seems to take care of them when they are not forced. The Bengal or China rose Louis Philippe is at home in this lower section and grows quite tall; Cherokees and Banksias thrive, too.

Hybrid teas, the mainstay of the rose garden, and often referred to as everblooming, seem suited to formal designs rather than naturalistic. La France, the first hybrid tea rose, was originated in 1867 in France. A number of hybrid teas can be planted even in a narrow border if the plants are set about 18 inches apart. For instance, in a bed 3 feet wide and 8½ feet long, ten alternating bushes can be planted, placing them a foot from the edge. Many of the older tried roses are as effective for display and cutting as newer ones, but the gorgeous new varieties do bring a thrill.

Most yellow roses are short lived and have to be replaced every few years. Eclipse, Mrs. Pierre S. du Pont and Sœur Thérèse are among the best yellows for the South. Etoile de Hollande is one of the best reds for this section; the old dark red Ami Quinard blooms well, and Christopher Stone and Crimson Glory are good. Rubaiyat, with beautiful rosy crimson blooms, likes this climate. White roses that do well are Kaiserin Auguste Viktoria, Mme. Jules Bouché, Caledonia, McGredy's Ivory and Snowbird. Peace is an outstanding rose, ivory flushed with gold and pink.

The two-toned President Herbert Hoover, Brazier, Duquesa de Peñaranda and Condesa de Sástago flourish here. Some of the best salmon-pinks are Edith Nellie Perkins, Mme. Cochet-Cochet, Faience, Countess Vandal, Angels Mateu and Betty Uprichard. Of the deep pinks Editor McFarland is a vigorous grower, and Sterling and light pink Warrawee do well. The older Lady Ashtown deserves a place.

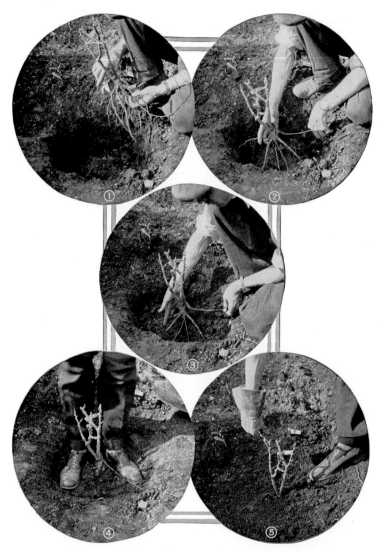

Steps in the planting of a rose bush include digging of an adequate hole, spreading of the roots, filling in with soil, firm packing, and trimming of the top growth.

Floribunda roses make a very fine border that will keep blooming even if the hybrid teas go into a midsummer resting period. A hedge like this needs almost no care.

The Radiance group—red, pink and shell-pink Mrs. Charles Bell—are very satisfactory. Among the "must-have" roses are single hybrid teas like the pink Dainty Bess and buttercup-yellow Cecil. White Wings is a single white with amethyst stamens tipped yellow. The singles, mostly from hybridizers of Ireland and England, have fragile-looking blooms, but the growing plants are not weak.

Hybrid perpetuals are stronger growing than hybrid teas and live for many years. Some of the most noted are Paul Neyron (1869), General Jacqueminot (1852) and White American Beauty or Frau Karl Druschki (1901). If they are combined in beds with hybrid teas, they should be planted back of the hybrid teas and set 2 or 3 feet apart. It is better to give them a place to themselves. They make good pillar roses. Pernetiana roses are a copper, orange or yellow cross of an Austrian Brier and hybrid teas and are not a distinct class.

Polyantha roses or baby ramblers are dwarf and bushy and are suitable for the front of borders. They may be planted about 15 inches or more apart and will bloom continuously through summer and autumn if dead flower heads are removed. Larger-growing polyanthas that have blooms in large clusters, like rose-pink Betty Prior and bright scarlet World's Fair, are classed as floribundas or hybrid polyanthas. These are good in shrubbery borders.

Old-fashioned and tea roses are easy to grow in southern gardens. Tea roses can be used as bedders and are effective among shrubbery planted about 5 feet apart. Their delicate odor is very pleasing. Duchesse de Brabant (1857) shows its cupped pink blooms for about nine months, and buff-apricot Safrano is exquisite in bud and semi-double open flower.

Old-time roses that thrive in the Southland and used to be called "monthly roses" are the Chinas or Bengals (*Rosa chinensis*). They have dainty foliage and few thorns, like Louis Philippe (1834), velvety crimson Agrippina or Cramoisi Supérieur (1832) and pink Old Blush (1780). The curious green rose (*Rosa chinensis viridiflora*, 1856) has a mass of sepals or foliage-texture petals. These flower continuously and are practically free of blackspot and insects.

Another older type is the fragrant Damask rose (*Rosa damascena*), such as York and Lancaster, known in 1551 and named for the War of the Roses. The Yorkists wore white roses and the Lancastrians red; this rose is a merging of the two colors. (There is a difference of opinion about this. Some believe the striped Gallica rose, Rosa Mundi, to be the true York and Lancaster rose.) Of the French or

Gallica roses, Cardinal de Richelieu (1840) is such a blackish crimson that it matures to blue. This will grow in any soil.

Cabbage or Provence roses (*Rosa centifolia*) of the sixteenth century and earlier, are an old group that can be pruned hard. Moss roses were introduced from Holland to England about 1596; many varieties originated in the first half of the nineteenth century. They are thought to be the crested form of the Provence rose (*Rosa centifolia muscosa*).

The Bourbons are closely related to the Chinas. Souvenir de la Malmaison (1845) is a famous Bourbon variety that bears pale flesh-colored flowers. Hermosa, once classed as a Bourbon but now called a China, is a fine rose for the garden. Maiden's Blush (1797), of difficult classification, possibly brought to England by the Romans, will live near trees, in part shade or sun, in wet or dry locations. This can be found in many old gardens of the South. The old musk (*Rosa moschata*) and "burr" or "chinquapin" (*R. microphylla rubra*) roses have almost disappeared. The Noisette is a cross of the Musk and Old Blush China roses, first developed in Charleston, S. C., in 1817 and improved by Noisette in France.

Teas, Bengals, Bourbons and Noisettes (included in the Indica group) are indigenous to warm climates. The old roses do best in medium clay soil in sunny, protected situations, and they respond to attention. However, they will live even when neglected, and with a few exceptions, such as some teas and Bourbons, they should be allowed to grow as they like. The flowers are borne on the old wood.

Some roses are especially suited for growing as shrubs or hedges. Their good foliage is more important than the flowers. Hybrid Rugosa roses are fine for these purposes. They will thrive under adverse conditions and are valuable for gardens near the seashore. A species that is very effective is the Hugonis rose, with arching branches covered with golden bloom in spring. Its foliage is graceful and dainty, the younger parts being reddish. For a hedge the plants should be set about 15 inches apart. As specimens in the shrubbery border they need about 6 feet to develop. They do best in a good but unfertilized soil. There are other species for massing, like the old cinnamon rose (*Rosa cinnamomea*) and *R. xanthina*. Shrub roses like Harison's Yellow (1830) are quite hardy. Sweetbriers have spicy foliage and ornamental fruits after flowering.

For the rock garden there are certain suitable roses, too, such as the fairy rose Rouletti (1848) and the hybrid chinensis minima Pixie (1940). Trailing roses such as the glossy-foliaged Wichuraiana or memorial rose are useful for ground covers. It gives a pleasing appearance at all times.

There are numerous climbing roses such as hybrid teas, hardy climbers, ramblers and pillars. Some flower off and on during the summer, bearing many blooms in the fall, like the everblooming hybrid teas. Climbing Talisman does better in the South than the bush form. Some climbers bloom once a year but make a wonderful display; for example, the early-blooming Spanish Beauty or Mme. Grégoire Staechelin, with long pointed buds opening into delicate pink blooms, and Golden Climber or Mrs. Arthur Curtiss James, which sends forth golden yellow flowers on long stems and does especially well in the South after it gets thoroughly established. A newer one, Sunset Climber, of sunset coloring, is ideal for the South.

Silver Moon with silvery white, semi-double flowers, gives a beautiful effect along with the single creamy yellow Mermaid. The latter is a repeat bloomer. The single Cherokees have become naturalized in the South. The Noisette Maréchal Niel (1864) is short lived, and the weak stems allow the blooms to droop, but it adds much to a southern garden, as does the tea rose Devoniensis.

Banksias are best treated as wall roses, with the shoots fastened to a wall and not pruned for years. These and the ramblers bloom only once during the year but they are worth having. Pillar roses, like orange-scarlet Flash and rose-pink Dr. J. H. Nicolas, are quite popular. They are not so rampant as other climbers.

Roses are grown from seed, from cuttings, by layering, by suckers or divisions, buds and grafts. (See Chapter III, Propagating.) Plants can be obtained on their own stock or budded. Strong varieties do well either way, but less hardy ones had best be budded.

To grow larger roses, it is necessary to remove the side buds from a stem when they are the size of a small pea. Pinch them off close to the stem and leave the topmost bud to develop. In cutting roses, leave the stem on the bush about ¼ inch above a leaf. At least two developed leaves should be allowed to remain; new shoots will form there.

IRIS

Many people know only the tall bearded irises and the Japanese varieties. There are many others. Some grow several feet high, others only a few inches. Some come from thick rhizomes that lie almost on top of the ground; some have thin creeping rhizomes in the ground, and others have bulbous roots. There are irises with beard on the lower petals or falls, as well as beardless and bulbous kinds.

Anyone who makes a hobby of growing iris has an interesting field to explore for variety as well as beauty. There is a choice of different types, with a wide range of color over a long blooming time. Great improvements in irises have been made in the past few years. They are effective for masses of color and look well with other plants, especially when they have a background to bring out their beauty.

The iris withstands summer drought and heat and winter cold. Practically all irises require sunshine, and the quality of the flowers depends on the amount they get; but some thrive in partial shade. The rhizomes of bearded varieties like to be baked by the sun and should not be shaded by the foliage of other plants. They do best in a location sheltered from high winds.

The queen of the rainbow flowers is the tall bearded iris (*Iris germanica*), which gives one a wealth of color and beauty. Some bloom a second time during the year. The shorter bearded irises, 20 to 30 inches tall, such as Amigo and Pink Ruffles, are now called border iris. Bearded irises can be set out after they flower and on into autumn. The best time is when they are semi-dormant, in late summer and early fall, with side shoots and rhizomes well developed. When planted too late in the fall, there is danger of their not getting established in time to bloom the following spring. They increase rapidly and should be divided about every three years so that the rhizomes will not become too matted. When the rhizomes are too close together, they cannot flower well; the bloom stalks will decrease in number and they may stop producing entirely.

Before planting tall bearded irises, prepare the ground by spading deep and breaking up lumps. If the soil is clay, it can be lightened with sand and enriched with wood ashes and bonemeal, or a little complete fertilizer can be thoroughly mixed in it. Be sure there is good drainage. In replanting, it is best to lift the whole clump. The inside crowded rhizomes, however, can be taken out and the remainder of the clump left. Carefully pull the rhizomes apart to a single fan and trim the fan-shaped foliage to about 4 to 6 inches from the base, in order to give new roots a chance to form. Place the top of the rhizome just below the surface of the ground. The roots should be firmly pressed into the soil, to steady the plants.

Iris may be planted singly or in groups of three or five. When groups are set out, space the rhizomes 6 or 8 inches apart. Different varieties should be separated by several feet. The newly planted

Guernsey-lily (*Lycoris radiata*) has been called surprise-lily by those who were astonished to see how quickly the flowers jump out of the ground. They are decorative in early fall. (See page 49.)

Dutch iris are among the most beautiful of their large family. Perhaps we should call orchids the "rich man's iris" instead of iris the "poor man's orchid." Certainly nobody should make excuses for this exquisite flower.

rhizomes must not have much moisture until they start growing, for that may cause rot or bring on growth too early. They dislike standing moisture always, but during dry spells they must not get too baked while becoming established.

Bonemeal is a safe fertilizer for this iris. Bonemeal and wood ashes correct soil acidity, and when they are used lime is not necessary. These irises do not thrive in an acid soil. Healthy foliage on established plants should not be cut unless the rhizomes are taken up and replanted, for its maturing is necessary to the health of the plants. If the foliage gets brown, it may harbor disease or eggs of borers and had best be cut and burned. The chief enemies of these irises are the borer, root rot and leaf spot.

Although tall bearded irises are of easy culture and are not susceptible to diseases, it is safest to take precautions. When shiny trails on the leaves or frayed leaf edges indicate the presence of the borer, look for punctures. The borer lays eggs on the foliage; the tiny caterpillars bore inside the leaves and grow larger. They work down in the leaves and can be crushed or taken out with a wire; or the affected leaves can be cut and burned. If borers are not destroyed, they eat their way down into the rhizome. If that happens, take up the rhizome, cut out soft spots, dry the remainder in the sun, and sprinkle with sulphur before replanting. Dusting or spraying with arsenate of lead in early spring checks the borer.

To escape root rot, rhizomes should be close to the surface, to get sun-baked. Rot is indicated by the falling over of the leaves that have decayed next to the rhizome. It gets into the rhizomes through an injury of some sort and may be caused by borers, too much moisture or crowding. Take up infected plants and after cutting back to the sound part, disinfect with potassium permanganate (a teaspoonful of crystals to a quart of water); or dip in a solution of bichloride of mercury (a tablet to a pint of water), dry and plant in a new location.

Leaf spot is a fungus disease that somewhat disfigures the leaves but is not a serious trouble. If the tops of the plants are burned during the dormant season, the spores of leaf spot are destroyed and the plants will not be harmed. It is helpful to use a spray of Bordeaux in spring after growth starts.

Mustard seed fungus sometimes attacks rhizomes and the base of the leaves. In the beginning this is a fungus-like web; later it gives the appearance of mustard seed. If rhizomes are affected, soak the roots for half an hour in a solution of Semesan.

Among the earliest of the irises to bloom are the bulbous reticulata

129

group, which prefer a position in the rock garden or in a sunny, well-drained place. Miniature bearded types and then pumila hybrids, which are a somewhat taller and larger group of dwarfs, flower early in spring. Hybrids from the oncocyclus and regelia, and other low bearded irises follow. These require good drainage, sun and neutral or rather sweet soil. Later, the intermediate irises come into flower. They are intermediate in season as well as in height between the low and the tall bearded kinds.

In spring we have many beardless irises. The Siberian, with narrow foliage and dainty flowers on tall stems, is suited for waterside planting. It likes moisture but requires good drainage and sun. The spurias, too, like moist spots and give a profusion of bloom just after the tall bearded irises have finished. When planting either of these, place the crowns at least an inch under ground, in slightly acid soil containing humus. Though they like a sunny location, light afternoon shade is desirable. Established plants stand drought but newly planted ones must not be allowed to become dry.

The bulbs of the Dutch, Spanish and English irises should be planted in the fall. The Spanish type thrives in a warm, sandy soil in sun and stands some moisture. Dutch irises descended from the Spanish and are much like them, but the flowers are larger and there is a wider color range. They thrive in good, well-drained soil. English irises look like small Japanese iris and grow in rich, moist loam. They like sun but will grow in part shade. The foliage of these irises must not be cut to the ground after the blooming season, for it is needed to mature the bulbs for the next year's flowers.

The Japanese iris (*Iris Kæmpferi*) appears next in the parade. There are three-petaled and six-petaled kinds. When they have plenty of water especially while the buds are forming, and a rich soil with moisture-holding capacity, the flowers are quite large and showy. Lime or bonemeal must never be used on these. Manure or dried blood are good fertilizers for them. Sunshine is necessary, but they do not have to be in the sun all day. When divisions or roots are planted, the crowns should go 2 inches deep; the roots must not be allowed to dry out in the operation. These irises can be transplanted after flowering and until early fall.

Native species, with rhizomes growing more or less on the surface, thrive in the Southern States along the Atlantic coast, in South Carolina, Georgia and Florida. Among them is *Iris hexagona*, which flowers about the same time as the Japanese iris. *Iris savannarum* is found over large areas in Florida. In the delta regions of Louisiana and in the central as well as the lower Mississippi valley, varieties bloom between the time of the bearded and Japanese irises. The dwarf *Iris cristata* is a native of Virginia, Kentucky and the Carolinas; *Iris virginica* (*caroliniana*) was first discovered in North Carolina. *Iris fulva*, much used in hybridizing, grows wild in Louisiana, Texas and Georgia. The wild irises are interesting; hybrids of the native species like to be in partial shade but need some sunshine.

Some member of the iris family thrives in every state. Tall bearded irises grow well in the South, with the exception of Louisiana and Florida. Possibly because of acid soil from silt, they do not flourish in these states. Here hybrids of native Louisiana and Florida species are beautiful; these will grow in an acid soil.

HARDY CHRYSANTHEMUMS

The genus Chrysanthemum includes Pyrethrum, marguerites and other species, but here we are dealing with hardy types, which have been enormously developed in the last few years. Though the old-time garden chrysanthemums, persevering season after season with little attention, still lend brightness to autumn borders, there are others that start blooming even in summer. Since the late Alex Cumming, Jr., of Bristol, Conn., introduced the Korean hybrid Mercury ("the bearer of tidings") in 1933, new varieties have been appearing frequently, such as the spoon chrysanthemum, with each petal flattened at the tip like a spoon.

Chrysanthemums are the paramount flowers of autumn, for they resist frost. Some kinds freeze stiff before the petals are ruined. On account of the mild weather in the South, even late varieties are satisfactory here. Chrysanthemums are not hard to grow in good average soil containing organic matter. They are heavy feeders and drinkers, and to do their best they need summer feeding, watering and light cultivation or mulching. Their roots are near the surface, and a little stirring of the soil creates a dust mulch that discourages surface rooting and weed growth, and keeps in moisture. However, if they are mulched lightly with other material, it is unnecessary to dig around them.

When preparing the soil for chrysanthemums, spade in well-rotted manure, bonemeal and wood ashes, or a fertilizer rich in phosphorus, such as 4-12-4. Do not set out the plants until danger of a hard freeze is over, though it is best to get them in the ground as early as possible so that they can make a good start before warm weather. From March until the third week in April is the right time for this middle section of the South. Space the plants about 2 feet apart, where they will have full sun and good air circulation. They can be started where they have plenty of room to develop and then may be moved to borders where special effects are desired. This transplanting may be done while the plants are in bud or in bloom if a good ball of soil is taken up with the roots.

Chrysanthemums should not be allowed to suffer for lack of water. When setting out new plants in the spring, never let the roots dry out. If they have been out of the ground for several days, soak them in tepid water for a few hours before replanting.

When the old clumps are divided, each shoot will make a bloom-ing-size plant. If they are not separated for several years, they may stop blooming. It is not necessary to divide azaleamums and other low-growing chrysanthemums every year, but it is advisable to take them up every third year and separate them into small clumps.

When plants are 8 or 9 inches high, they should be pinched back an inch or two to produce stockier growth. In a few weeks the tips of garden chrysanthemums can be pinched again, but once is enough for commercial and exhibition types. The more branches there are, the more blooms there will be. This pinching back of growth can be done until the middle of July and still leave time enough for buds to form. If larger flowers are wanted, all but the best buds on each branch should be removed as soon as they begin to appear.

When the buds come, the plants need water and fertilizer. Soak the ground well, and unless a mulch has been used, cultivate lightly after watering and after each rain, as soon as the ground is dry enough. Liquid manure the color of weak tea can be applied instead of fertilizer every ten days. A little food like bonemeal can be dug into the soil near the plants in August.

A tablespoonful of nitrate of soda to each plant will promote strong foliage and stems and develop the buds. As soon as they begin to show color, discontinue giving the liquid food lest the buds be deformed or the foliage burned. Since the feeding roots of chrys-anthemums are near the surface, it is easy for them to absorb plant food. They are gross feeders, but there is danger of overfeeding with liquid manure. The leaves may become dark green and may grow at the expense of buds. In early fall it is well to place good loam or leaf mold about the plants to protect the roots and keep them moist.

The commonest enemy of the chrysanthemum is aphids. Spray-

It is a hundred years since the grand old peony, Festiva
Maxima, was introduced, but this is still considered to
be about the finest double early white. (See page 50.)

A street typical of areas in the lower South.

ing with water will sometimes get rid of them. Use a hose and spray in the morning; evening dampness may invite mildew. Then spray with nicotine preparations—1½ teaspoonfuls of nicotine sulphate and a cubic inch of laundry soap in a gallon of warm water; a week later make another application. Pyrethrum and rotenone can be used weekly from the time the buds form until they show color. Black Leaf 40, one part to 800 parts of water with soap added, makes a good spray.

When root aphids are bothersome, treat for ants. Make a depression around the plant and pour into it a teaspoonful of pyrethrum-rotenone mixed in ½ pint of water. After this solution disappears, pour a cupful of water around the plant and replace the soil.

Spray with arsenate of lead for caterpillars; pick off grasshoppers or use arsenate of lead. If the foliage suffers from leaf spot or rust, pick off and burn the affected leaves, and spray with Bordeaux mixture.

As a general thing, chrysanthemums begin to bloom when the nights are long and cool and the days short and warm. Since the absence of light hastens flowering, they can be made to bloom earlier if they are shaded. When they have been planted about six weeks, or about eight weeks before blooming time, cover the plants entirely, so that light cannot enter for two hours before sunset and for two hours after sunrise. Cloth that is not transparent, like black sateen, can be used, or a box may enclose each plant. Stop covering them when the flowers show color.

The low-growing azaleamums are hardy perennials belonging to the chrysanthemum family, and the earliest to flower. Sometimes they begin to bloom in May. No pruning is required, but if the first buds come very early it is better to tip back the growth, for hot weather may cause the flowers to be inferior.

Certain Korean hybrids are early blooming and make a garden glow for a long period. Colors range from pale tints to deep shades; the blooms are small to large, single, semi-double and double. For example, the Korean-Pyrethrum hybrid Lavender Lady has large, double, silvery lavender blooms, while Silver Moon has loose, semi-double, creamy flowers and Crimson Splendor is a rich red single.

The types of hardy chrysanthemums are exhibition and commercial, early hardy or garden, early and late hardy Korean, button, intermediate and large pompons, large singles, anemone, feathery, miniature, cascade and species.

The exhibition type comprises varieties with a large flower on a single stalk. For exhibition, large size is important. Some growers pinch back once when the plant is about 8 inches high and allow three shoots to develop one bud each. If the crown bud, which is the first to come, is good, it is retained and the lateral growth is removed. If these laterals are left, terminal buds will form on them. When the crown bud develops well, it will become a fine flower before a terminal bud will. If the crown bud is inferior, the best upright-growing terminal bud should be allowed to remain. Side shoots are kept removed.

Commercial chrysanthemums have a more compact shape and smaller flowers with reflexed or incurved petals. The terminal buds come in a cluster and the best bud on each stalk is saved; three or more stalks are permitted to grow. Side shoots are not allowed. These two types, disbudded for fine flowers, need the same culture as other chrysanthemums. They must be staked and tied up from time to time. There should be room between the staked plants for air to circulate. Canvas is necessary to protect them if a cold spell comes before the flowers stop blooming. Do not allow the canvas to come in contact with the blooms.

The early hardy garden type has larger and less formal flowers than the large pompons. They can be disbudded and grown on a few stalks for finer blooms. Their season is early to midseason. Besides the double kinds, there are semi-doubles with more than two rows of petals and showing the center (called duplex-flowered), and singles with one or two rows of petals around the center.

Early hardy Koreans are usually singles of bright colors; here they begin flowering in September. These and the late Koreans can be disbudded; the spreading, bushy plants will supply many flowers.

Pompon chrysanthemums, of half ball form, are divided into large pompons with flowers over 3 inches in diameter, which are often disbudded; intermediate pompons with flowers from 1 to 3 inches in diameter, sometimes disbudded but oftener not; and buttons with flowers less than an inch in diameter. Pinch them all back for bushy growth and plentiful flowers that will stand cold and keep their color even after a killing frost blackens the foliage.

Large single types include semi-doubles. The largest ones are often disbudded; the smaller ones grow in sprays on plants that have been kept bushy.

The anemone type has one or more rows of petals, which may be tubular with shorter petals of the same or different color forming a cushion in the center. These are grown in sprays; the large-flowered ones are usually disbudded, leaving several stalks to carry one flower each. There are also small-flowered ones with a diameter of less than 3 inches.

The odd-looking feathery, hairy or spidery forms have feathery, thread-like or twisted petals. These originated in Japan. They are usually grown in the same way as exhibition and commercial chrysanthemums.

The miniatures grow about 1½ feet tall. If they are pinched back every two or three weeks after growth starts in spring, the compact little plants will be covered with small flowers. These can be used in the rock garden.

Cascade chrysanthemums have pliable stems that can be trained to grow as one wants. They are suitable for the top of an embankment. Species also are planted on banks; they have sprawling growth and innumerable flowers.

Chrysanthemums make fine cut flowers, which stay fresh for weeks in water. After the tops of the plants are killed by frost, they can be cut down within a few inches of the ground, but not until the sap leaves the stems. In the South a light mulch is beneficial over winter.

NARCISSI

Some narcissus species, natives of the eastern hemisphere, have been known for more than 300 years and have spread with civilization throughout the world, and there are numerous new hybrids. A few bloom in autumn, but they are essentially cold-weather lovers flowering in winter and spring. There are several types of narcissi: giant trumpets to small cupped, clusters of two or more on a stem, doubles and miniatures, ranging through tints of yellow, cream, white, apricot and pinkish. Some have a hint of green, and others a reddish rim about the cup. If the trumpet and perianth petals are the same color, the flower is called a self. A bicolor has a yellow or lemon trumpet and white or whitish perianth.

The botanical name is Narcissus, and the common one is daffodil; the terms are interchangeable. Customarily, here they are divided into three main groups: to the long trumpets, the name daffodil is applied; the medium or small cupped and cluster-flowered ones are called narcissi; and the small cupped types with more or less round, rush-like foliage are jonquils.

The length of trumpet, crown or cup determines the type. When the trumpet is reduced but broadened, it is usually called a crown;

when the trumpet is shortened and cupped, it is referred to as a cup. Following are the divisions now recognized, with typical varieties:

1. Trumpet. Trumpet as long as or longer than the perianth petals.
   King Alfred and Emperor. Yellow trumpets; selfs.
   Mrs. E. H. Krelage and Beersheba. White trumpets; selfs.
   Van Waveren's Giant and Spring Glory. Bicolors; perianth whitish and trumpet yellow.

2. Large Cupped or Medium Trumpet. Cup more than one-third, but less than equal to the length of the perianth petals.
   Bernardino. Bicolor with creamy white perianth and yellow cup edged orange.
   Croesus. Yellow crown edged orange; primrose-yellow petals.
   Helios. Cup a deeper yellow than petals.
   John Evelyn. Bicolor with white petals and lemon-yellow crown flushed with orange, heavily frilled.

3. Small Cupped. Cup not more than one-third the length of the perianth segments.
   Alcida. Creamy perianth and citron-yellow cup with orange frill.
   Expectation. White petals and lemon-yellow cup edged apricot.
   Firetail. Creamy white perianth with orange-scarlet cup.
   Nobility. White petals and orange-yellow cup.

4. Double. The flowers are double.
   Cheerfulness. Double white flowers resembling a gardenia, carried several on a stem.
   Daphne. Double white that likes sandy soil and plenty of moisture.
   Twink. Yellow mixed with clear orange.

5. Triandrus Hybrids. Small trumpets about half the length of the segments; petals narrow and reflexed.
   Queen of Spain. A soft canary-yellow hybrid between Triandrus albus and a small yellow trumpet daffodil.
   Thalia. "The orchid-flowered daffodil," with two to four white trumpets on a stem.

6. Cyclamineus Hybrids. Straight and tube-like trumpets, with perianths reflexed like a cyclamen. They are suitable for rock gardens. Good varieties are Beryl, February Gold and March Sunshine.

136

7. Jonquilla Hybrids. Very fragrant flowers and narrow, up-standing foliage.

Campernelle (*N. odorus*). The old-time jonquil with narrow leaves and fragrant flowers.

Golden Sceptre. A newer variety of deep yellow with star shaped perianth.

Jonquilla simplex. Small, single, fragrant, rich yellow.

8. Tazetta and Poetaz. Hybrids between the polyanthus and poeticus narcissi; cluster-flowered.

Admiration. Yellow cluster.

Laurens Koster. White with orange-yellow cup.

Paper-White and Soleil d'Or. Good for forcing.

Narcissus biflorus, popular in old southern gardens. This is an old one of unknown ancestry, perhaps a hybrid of the tazetta and poeticus.

9. Poeticus. Flat white petals and small cups.

Pheasant's Eye (*N. recurvus*). Cup margined red.

Homer. Newer and later blooming.

10. Species. Dainty small-flowered narcissi and practically all wild forms.

Angel's Tears (Triandrus albus). Two or three fuchsia-like flowers on a stem.

Hoop Petticoat (Bulbocodium conspicuus). Little golden flowers with wide mouth.

New narcissus bulbs are packed with food and will grow even without fertilizer, or in water. Deep preparation of the soil and a good supply of humus are more important than fertilizer, although it is preferable to give them some plant food. The beds should be spaded 18 inches deep or more, so that the roots can penetrate into loose soil. They like a rich sandy loam. If you have stiff clay with poor drainage, place about 3 inches of clinkers or gravel at the bottom; then mix sand and well-rotted manure with the clay. The manure must not come into contact with the bulbs. Wood ashes and bonemeal are helpful, or a complete fertilizer can be used. After getting a bed prepared, it is best to let the soil settle before the bulbs are planted.

In order to bloom at the same time the bulbs in a bed should all be set at the same depth; holes must be large enough for the bulbs to rest solidly on the bottom. The best way is to prepare a wide trench instead of individual holes. Usually bulbs are planted one and one-half times their own depth or with about 4 to 6 inches of soil above the top of the bulb, and two or three times their size apart. They can be set deeper in sandy soil than in clay. It is well to have them deep enough in borders so that they will not easily be dug up. If the soil is loose and well drained, they can be placed at a depth of as much as 8 or 10 inches.

Narcissi look well planted in drifts or clumps in front of shrubbery and in perennial borders. Choose a location where they will not have too much shade and, if possible, will be protected from strong winds. In order to naturalize bulbs, plant them as they would naturally fall from your hand if tossed upon the ground. It is not good to plant them in the lawn, for cutting the grass will also cut the bulb foliage and this must not be done until it has matured. Bulbs are quite effective naturalized in a wooded area where they get enough sunshine to bloom before leaves appear on deciduous trees.

After bulbs go into a dormant state, they can be taken up, divided and replanted. The foliage dies down about June. If the beds are wanted for other things before that, the bulbs can be dug up and heeled in somewhere until the foliage is ripe. It is best to plant them where they can stay until they become so crowded that they no longer bloom well. New bulbs form around the old ones, but the mother bulbs do not die in the process. When dug up, they can be replanted at once or stored in a cool dry place and set out in the fall. In separating the bulbs, a piece of the base from which roots grow must be left on each one.

Shallow-rooted annuals may be planted over narcissi without harming the bulbs unless the bed is watered too much. Stable manure can be spread over them in late fall. As the tips of the narcissi begin to show in late winter, they can be given a food strong in nitrogen to make them produce finer flowers. They will respond the next year if fed after blooming time.

Narcissi bulbs bloom early and last a long time. (See Chapter V, True Bulbs.) They stand cold well and usually recuperate even if their stems get stiff with ice. The bulbs increase rapidly and if divided every few years will soon make a fine display. They are easy to grow if there is good drainage and not too much shade, and they reappear year after year. These plants do not require much attention, but when they are cared for they produce even better flowers. Each type has its own more or less pleasing fragrance—some spicy, some sweet, others distinctly like vanilla.

138

A good way to prepare the flowers for arranging is to dip the ends of the stems in hot water for a minute just after cutting them. Then place them in cool water and put them in a cool place.

TULIPS

Tulips are known to have been growing in Turkey in 1500; from there they reached Vienna in 1554. Cultivation began in Holland the latter part of the sixteenth century, and throughout the Netherlands new varieties were produced. The Turks seem to have been satisfied with red and yellow blooms, but European gardeners developed other colors. Parrot tulips, thought to have been a contribution of the French, made their appearance at the end of the seventeenth century. America can grow good bulbs, and there is great interest now in raising tulips in this country.

Tulips do well in ordinary good soil if the bulbs are good; the size of the bulb is not so important as the quantity of fibrous roots. Unlike daffodils, tulips should be planted in gardens of the South not earlier than the middle of November, and in the warmer sections not till December. Here our temperatures are mild, and if the leaves come too quickly for the roots, the result will be weaker flowers. To do their best tulips must be exposed to cold; bulbs that have been in cold storage are the most satisfactory. They prefer a neutral or lime soil; a sandy loam with bonemeal and well-rotted compost worked into it is good, but manure must not come into contact with the bulbs. Tulips do better in the upper South than in the middle section and are not grown to any extent lower in the South.

To enjoy a display of blooms of a particular variety at the same time, be sure to plant the bulbs at a uniform depth. If some are set an inch or two deeper, they will bloom later. When preparing a place for tulips, it is well to spade out about 15 inches. Put in 2 inches of gravel for drainage; then fill in with well-mixed loam to within 7 or 8 inches from the surface, and next an inch or two of sand to hold the bulbs firmly. This will keep them dry but will allow the roots to reach for moisture.

Tulip bulbs are planted about 6 inches deep (the holes can be dug the right depth with a post-hole digger) and about 6 inches apart, depending on their size. They may be set deeper in a light soil than in a heavy one. They require good drainage; it is important never to permit water to stand over them.

If tulip bulbs are planted year after year in the same soil, they may become infected with "fire" (*Botrytis galanthina*), a fungus disease that makes the foliage look burned. Destroy any diseased plants and spray with Bordeaux. Tulips do not need to be mulched in our climate unless planted too late to make good root growth.

One can have early, midseason and late tulips, for there are many types. Some are dwarf, while others grow 2 or 3 feet tall. The earliest to flower are the single early and the botanical or wild species and rock-garden types. Then come the double early, the triumph (sometimes called the early darwin), the cottage, darwin and breeder.

The bulbs do not have to be taken up every year, though it is advisable to move the cottage and darwin. If they are grown in enriched soil they will bloom for several seasons, but in warmer sections it is best to lift them each year. When they are left in the ground they must not be kept watered; the bulbs need to dry out while dormant. The tops should not be cut off until the leaves mature and turn yellow, but the old blooms should be removed as soon as they fade, for bulb energy is exhausted in ripening seed pods. The petals should not be allowed to decay and remain on the ground. This can cause "fire," which is more apt to appear among bulbs in closely planted borders. It is a good idea to fertilize them after they bloom. The flowers of the next year depend on healthy maturing foliage.

The time to dig the bulbs is after the foliage is ripe but while the stem still holds the bulb. Store them in a cool, dark, dry place. It is well to sprinkle the bulbs with tobacco dust and sulphur.

The life of a tulip bulb is said to be seven years—three of increase, one of top size and three of decline. The largest bulbs are called top size, the next first size, etc. Sometimes moles and mice prevent them from coming up. Moth balls about the bulbs may keep away these pests; or planting may have to be done in galvanized netting baskets, 7 inches deep and large enough to hold a group of bulbs. The top of the basket should be even with the soil surface.

Tulips are effective when arranged the old-time way in beds or in borders, using a well-blended color scheme. They are particularly lovely planted all about the garden in front of shrubbery in groups of a dozen or two of a variety, bringing out touches of color where needed. These spots can be planted later with annuals. When the foliage tips appear in late winter, sprinkle plant food on the ground and dig it in lightly. This will improve the flowers.

Weak stems of cut tulips are strengthened by being placed overnight in water up to the flower head, or by being put in a 2 percent solution of calcium nitrate (2 ounces to 5 gallons of water).

A combination planting of clematis and tulips makes
a charming picture. If clematis is given shade over its
roots and sun over its top, it will survive hot weather.

A green garden can be a very restful place in summer, especially if it features a pool.

GLADIOLI

The exact origin of the gladiolus is not known, but the name, meaning "a little sword," was given to it during the period of the Roman Empire. According to the American Gladiolus Society (not functioning at present), the word gladiolus may be used in either the singular number or the plural. Webster's Dictionary permits either gladioli or gladioluses for the plural but prefers gladioli. In colloquial language the word is often shortened to "glads."

Gladioli are grown from solid, bulb-like corms. (See Chapter V, Bulbous Plants.) Formerly, classification was based on heredity, but now gladioli are grouped according to size, such as exhibition type, decorative and primulinus.

Modern garden gladioli are hybrids far removed from the "sword lilies" of our grandmother's day. Each year new varieties are introduced to surprise and delight the grower. Great progress is being made in producing mammoth size, floriferousness and new colors. Kunderd introduced the first ruffled gladioli. Twisted, recurved, twilled and almost any form, shape and color may now be had.

Gladioli can be grown in any part of the country where there are as many as 80 summer days. Average varieties bloom in 95 days, but as the weather gets warmer they grow faster and bloom more quickly. The earliest ones flower in 70 to 80 days after being planted, the midseason in 90 to 100 days and the late in 110 to 120 days. By careful selection of varieties one can have bloom for more than a month from one planting.

Corms cannot be judged by size alone. Some of the large ones are inferior, and some varieties never have large corms. As a usual thing, high-crowned ones are young and vigorous and bear a single fine bloom stalk. Large flat corms may have two or three spikes of average bloom; if desired, the extra stalks can be cut off to allow all the strength to go into the one remaining. Some of the old flat corms can be cut in two or more pieces if each has an eye. The cuttings should be dusted with sulphur or Semesan. Medium-sized corms will flower satisfactorily, though Number 1 size (over 1½ inches) is the best for exhibition bloom.

Gladioli are generally planted in rows or beds, but they can also be used in front of shrubbery and among perennials. They can be set out as soon as the soil can be worked and there is no danger of their freezing. However, it is not advantageous to plant them very early, for they will not grow until the soil gets warm. In Florida they are planted in late fall or winter, but they ought to be in cold storage at about 40 degrees for two months beforehand.

Gladioli do best in full sun but will stand part shade, particularly in the low South. They grow in good, well-drained, moist soil but do not like lime. A sandy loam is best for them, and they want an abundance of water, in an open situation away from trees and buildings. To have flowers for cutting in midsummer and fall, plant some every few weeks until July. In the Piedmont section of the South planting can be done until the middle or latter part of that month.

It is good practice to get the bed prepared for gladioli in the fall, using manure and bonemeal. Avoid manure at planting time unless it is well rotted and thoroughly mixed with the soil; it must never touch the corms. At the time of planting, cottonseed meal can be mixed with the loam, or a little commercial fertilizer can be put a few inches beneath the corms. Spade the ground about a foot deep. The corms should be planted at a depth of 3 to 6 inches in clay soil, and a little more in sandy soil. If they are deep enough, they do not need much staking.

As a preventive treatment it is safer to disinfect corms before planting, to kill any thrips or eggs that may be present. The tiny thrips get under the husks of corms and stay there during winter; when the temperature rises to 60 or 65 degrees, they multiply. A good disinfectant is 1000 strength bichloride of mercury solution mixed in a vessel that will not corrode. Remove or loosen the husks, place the corms in a cheesecloth bag and leave them in the solution over night. Or soak them for six hours in Lysol solution, 4 teaspoonfuls to a gallon of water; this is an insect killer and a powerful fungicide. Be sure the bags are tagged with the variety names. In planting, place the corms right side up and about 6 inches apart, and do not forget to label them.

The plants need frequent cultivation, deep at first but shallow as they grow higher. The soil can be hilled about them as protection from wind and hard rains. Some of the tallest have to be staked, especially if exposed to wind. Tie raffia around the stake first, and then loosely to the plant.

Gladioli should be kept growing vigorously. When they are 6 inches high they can be top-dressed with bonemeal and wood ashes or any commercial fertilizer richer in phosphoric acid and potash than in nitrogen. The fertilizer must not get on the foliage or stems. They need plenty of moisture to do their best, especially when budding, and should be watered thoroughly once a week. After the

142

fourth leaf comes, weak manure water can be poured about them, or they can be given a light application of 4-12-4.

Begin spraying for thrips when the first leaf develops. These are very small insects about $\frac{1}{16}$ inch long, which attack the growing leaves and feed on young flower spikes; they multiply rapidly. Their life cycle is about ten days, so spray every week or at least after each rain, until the flower spikes push out from the leaves. A good spray can be made with 2 tablespoonfuls of tartar emetic and 4 tablespoonfuls of brown sugar to 3 gallons of water; or rotenone may be used. Even though corms are disinfected and planted clean, thrips can be brought in by new stock or by the wind. Drooping flower spikes and silvery spots or streaks on the foliage point to the presence of thrips. In bad cases the best thing to do is to cut off the flower head and burn it. This will not harm the corms.

The gladiolus is valued first of all as a cut flower. The stalk is ordinarily cut when the second floret begins to open, but some varieties fade if they open in water and are better left on the plant. Leaves are necessary to the maturing of the corm, and three or more should be left in cutting the blooms. Reach down between the leaves for long stems. The best time to cut the stalks is early in the morning. Place them in a cool room in fresh cool water. Change the water daily, slanting off a piece of the stem each time and breaking off the lower florets as they wither. The flowers will open in water up to the last bud.

After gladioli have flowered, the corms need a month or six weeks in the ground to ripen. Continue to cultivate but do not water them. When the foliage begins to turn yellow but before it dies down, dig the corms. Cormels will come up in a lump with them. Cut off the tops (it is best to burn them) and dry and cure the corms in an airy, warm place.

After a few weeks the worn-out corms and roots can be removed and the remainder cleaned. Sometimes there will be one new fine corm or more, depending upon the variety, with small corms or cormels attached around the base. Do not take the husks off the new ones; they need this protection in storage. Discard all damaged corms; if they are only bruised, they can be dusted with powdered sulphur. The little ones can be put in a bag in a cool place, but large ones need more time to dry. They may mold if wet. After they are thoroughly dry, put them in a paper bag and shake naphthalene flakes over them as a precaution against thrips, using a tablespoonful of flakes to a gallon of corms or an ounce or more to each hundred

143

corms. In two or three weeks, remove the flakes and store the corms in a cool spot where the air can circulate. About 40 degrees is a good temperature for them in storage; they must not freeze. If the place where they are stored is a little moist, they will not dry out too much.

AZALEAS

Azaleas are among the most valuable ornamental shrubs. Some are deciduous, some partly evergreen and others truly evergreen. In the mild climate of the South the evergreen types are preferred. There are various species and many varieties in different colors, and the flowering time covers more than two months. Some have a delightful fragrance.

The Kæmpferi or Japanese types and hybrids are the best evergreen azaleas for the middle and upper sections of the South. The hybrids are American grown and come in the same colors as the Indica type. Indica flower buds are frequently killed in severe winters in this area. They do well in Alabama, Mississippi, Louisiana, parts of Texas and Florida, southern Georgia, and as far north on the Atlantic coast as Charleston, S. C. The Kurumes have spreading growth but do not grow so large nor so fast as the Indicas.

A number of native species, often called wild honeysuckle, can be used in gardens. Among them is the desirable pinkshell azalea (*Azalea Vaseyi*), a native of North and South Carolina, with pale rose-colored flowers before the leaves. It is partial to moist locations. Flame azalea (*Azalea calendulacea*) has brilliant orange-yellow to scarlet flowers just after the foliage develops. This grows in the mountain sections and into Georgia, even on dry banks. Pinxterbloom azalea (*Azalea nudiflora*), with delicate pink, very fragrant blooms, is another native of the South.

Azaleas are acid-loving plants, and before choosing a location for them it is well to test the soil for acidity. In the majority of cases it will be too low. Fresh leaves of oak and other trees yield some acid and can be used for mulching. (Maple leaves are to be avoided on account of their alkaline content.) Acidity may also be increased by the use of aluminum sulphate, but the applications will have to be repeated as needed. Yellowing of the leaves, especially in patches, and poor bloom is indication of deficient acidity.

It is important to plant azaleas correctly. The soil must be friable and able to retain moisture, but it should have perfect drainage. The holes ought to be dug 2 feet deep and three or four times as wide

Azaleas are obviously at home in this garden where
the soil and location are to their liking. Here they
increase in size and beauty with the passing seasons
and provide a feast of color for many weeks.

An azalea garden can be as colorful as you please. When massed plantings are made, it is wise to be extra careful in choosing the colors that are to be neighbors. The smooth green lawn is a decided asset.

as the ball of earth holding the roots. Deep digging assures a supply of water in the soil during dry periods. The ball of earth should be broken, for the roots ought to come into contact with the surrounding soil. It is best to dip the ball in water before planting. Set the plant as deep as it had been growing in the nursery, and shake it lightly up and down when filling the hole with earth. The soil should be firmed around the roots and then given a thorough watering. Leave a shallow basin around the plant so that water will run toward it.

Azalea roots lie near the surface of the ground, and cultivating will disturb them. They like the top of the soil to be cool and moist, and the best method of keeping it in that state is to use a mulch the year round, 2 to 3 inches deep. With few exceptions azaleas are sun-loving shrubs. They need the morning sun, or at least diffused sunlight, but do best where they are protected from the afternoon sun and from wind. They will grow near oak and pine trees, and a background shows them off to advantage. They improve with age.

These are plants that can be transplanted in the fall and on into spring, when in bud or in bloom. If they are in bud, break off all the flower buds except one here and there. If all are left to open, the plant may exhaust itself before it gets established. Where the bud is removed, new growth will appear.

After the first year any trimming must be done just after the blooming period. The flowers for one year grow on the new wood of the year before. Cut off the dead blooms before seed pods form, and remove all branches that die back. When plants have finished flowering, fertilize with cottonseed meal, tankage or special azalea food. The best method of propagating is by layering of the branches; cuttings and seeds are too slow.

Azaleas are troubled very little by disease and insects, but the foliage should be sprayed often to prevent red spider. In 1931 azalea blight or flower spot appeared in South Carolina. It has been found that this fungus disease can be controlled by spraying the blooming plants one to three times a week, according to weather conditions, with either of two chemicals—the powder Phygon or the liquid Dithane. Azaleas require a great deal of water; drooping foliage will show the need of it. After a dry fall, the plants should be watered copiously before winter sets in.

These showy flowering shrubs make desirable accent plantings or borders, with their tones of lavender, pink, red, flame, and white. Though they want shade part of the day, they do not thrive in dense shade.

CAMELLIAS

Camellias came originally from eastern Asia. In the warmer parts of the South they make wonderful specimen or border plants with waxy evergreen leaves. Though they suffer from too much sun, they grow well to central Florida and up into the Piedmont district. They are hardy in Georgia, Louisiana, parts of Alabama, Mississippi and the Carolinas. But even after they get established and climatized in the middle areas, a cold snap is likely to ruin the flowers. The types that stand the weather best here in the middle section are the singles and the loosely formed semi-doubles or those with centers more or less open. In the colder parts of the South they make good greenhouse plants and can be grown in tubs.

Camellias need protection from cold and from hot afternoon sun until they are established; they do best with a half day's sunshine. They do not bloom much in complete shade but will grow in full sun if protected the first few summers. Like nearly all hardwood evergreens, they like a slightly acid soil; they thrive in a moist place but require good drainage. It is essential that they be kept well mulched and given plenty of water, especially the first two years. A good loam for camellias is composed of one-fourth leaf mold or peat, one-fourth rotted manure and one-half good garden soil. In planting, be sure to have the holes large enough to hold the balled roots without crowding.

To keep these shrubs growing vigorously, fertilize them each spring with well-decayed manure, bonemeal and a little commercial fertilizer. In disbudding, leave one bud at each point of growth. Single-flowered varieties give a pleasing appearance when not disbudded.

Camellia Sasanqua is a species that blooms in autumn, usually before cold weather. Most Sasanquas are singles and semi-doubles with a faint perfume. They do better than *Camellia japonica* in colder climates. The latter follow the Sasanquas in blooming season, from December through March. Colors range from white to pink to dark red and variegated. Flowers may be single, semi-double, peony form or imbricated. Peony-flowered camellias have a full center and are usually of rather loose formation; imbricated ones have the petals overlapping from the center outward, with no stamens showing. Generally *Camellia japonica* varieties do not have any fragrance, but two or three, like Herme and Preston Rose, do have a slight perfume.

146

This summer garden centers around a water-lily pool, with garden lilies about the edge. Narcissi and iris bloomed here earlier in the season. (See page 115.)

Here Japanese holly is used as a hedge above the wall, with boxwood as an edging below it. The sprawling cotoneaster at the edge of the steps is a nice contrast to the clipped hedges.

Hybridizers are continually introducing new and unusual varieties. Up to 1917 all plants were imported; since then American nurserymen have been propagating their own. A peculiarity of camellias is that varieties with solid-colored flowers are likely to produce a variegated bloom. When budded, these sports often make unusual varieties. Many of the older camellias are holding their place among the new ones and are well worth care and attention.

Camellias are propagated by cuttings, by layering, by seed and by grafting. For cuttings, 4 to 6 inches of firm wood should be taken; it is advisable, though not essential, that they have a heel. Put them in damp sand away from direct sunlight, and leave them until they have made good growth. In a cool place, they do not root so fast as in a warm location, but a larger percentage will form roots. Though the seed method is slow, many new varieties are produced in that way. Grafting is the commonest means of propagating camellias. In transplanting, the graft should be above ground level.

As a rule, camellias are healthy plants not bothered with insects. A heavy spraying with water during the growing season will prevent trouble. Sometimes the leaves are attacked by scale insects; these can be controlled by spraying with Garden Volck, one part to fifty parts of water.

HOLLY

We generally think of holly as a broadleaf evergreen with red berries, but there are also deciduous types, and some with black or yellow fruits. Most are slow growing. The flowers are inconspicuous but the fruits are quite ornamental.

Evergreen hollies do best in partial shade in rich, well-drained soil. Some of the deciduous kinds, like winterberry (*Ilex verticillata*), prefer a swampy location. Holly will stand both sun and shade. Sun produces more berries but duller leaves, while shade makes the foliage glossier and the fewer berries more brilliant in color. Partial shade is just about right. Holly will thrive near the seacoast in any area with low altitude, but at higher elevations it needs protection from wind.

Most hollies do not like lime; the exception is the English holly, which likes a neutral or slightly sweet soil. Humus, leaf mold and abundant moisture are needed. They do well planted among companion trees that will prevent drying winds from striking them. Cultivation should stop in late summer, for too much growth will result in fewer berries.

In preparing a place for planting holly, use plenty of leaf mold and some rotted manure, preferably three-year-old cow manure, mixed thoroughly with the loam. The holes for the plants should be half again as large as the ball of roots, and the plants need to be set a few inches deeper than they were in the nursery, with a depression left around each one. Give them plenty of water, especially the first year. Those from a nursery are easily transplanted, for the roots are in a compact ball, wrapped in burlap.

For transplanting from their native setting it is best to choose plants less than 5 feet tall. Spade them up with good roots and wrap in burlap. Remove most of the leaves to prevent transpiration, and cut back the longest branches. When the leaves are not stripped off, prune heavily to give the roots a better chance. As with all broadleaf evergreens, transpiration goes on all the time, and the leaves are dependent on the roots when they are set out. Holly should be moved at a season when feeding roots will come quickly. The best time is in the fall when the young wood has almost ripened or in early spring before growth starts. Keep it heavily mulched always.

See that established plants have plenty of water in the fall. They can be fed with cottonseed meal each year—a bucketful to a large tree, a handful to a small plant—but do not use commercial fertilizer. In leaf mold they will thrive without fertilizer.

The holly leaf miner sometimes attacks holly. To control it, spray in spring with 2 teaspoonfuls of nicotine sulphate and an ounce of soap to a gallon of water.

Holly is propagated by seed, by cuttings, by grafts or buds and sometimes by layering and divisions. Seeds germinate in one and a half to two years, but there are usually more male (staminate) plants than berry-bearing (pistillate). It takes six to eight years for them to fruit. Some growers freeze the berries before planting them, to help germination. They can be stratified in sifted sand and soil and kept moist, and after a year planted in sandy loam in a shady place. Usually they will come up in six months. Or seed can be put in a coldframe, where a good percentage will germinate in less than two years. Transplant seedlings after the second year. Nurseries graft scions from berry-bearing plants upon seedlings. Male and female flowers are borne on different plants; female trees produce flowers with no pollen, but one male tree can cause large plantings to fruit.

Cuttings sometimes set fruit when three or four years old but not to any extent until ten years old. For cuttings use 4 to 6 inches of newly ripened wood with a piece of old wood attached. After removing the lower leaves, place in half sand and half peat moss, with no soil; label whether from male or female trees. A root-growing substance hastens growth, but cuttings must be kept moist.

Low limbs on hollies can be bent down, and a slit can be made in part of the branch and covered with leaf mold or peat. This will form roots and be ready to be cut loose and transplanted in a few years.

Our native American holly (*Ilex opaca*) grows wild in the Southern States from the upper sections to Florida and west to Texas and Missouri. It has sentimental value, for it is typical of Christmas. The glossy, spiny leaves are pleasing even when the bright berries are not in evidence. Continual cutting of this native plant without replacement will exterminate it.

The English type (*Ilex Aquifolium*) is not so hardy as the American but has larger fruits. This is especially useful for hedges. There are many varieties of English holly, some with variegated yellow leaves and others margined with white.

Many evergreen hollies will grow into trees but can be trimmed to any shape. Chinese or horned holly (*Ilex cornuta*), with spiny evergreen leaves and large red berries, and Japanese holly (*I. crenata*) with small oval but not spiny leaves and black fruits, stay more or less shrubby. The tiny-leaved *Ilex crenata microphylla* is a good substitute for boxwood.

Burford Chinese holly (*I. cornuta Burfordii*) is very handsome, with bright red berries and glossy green leaves. Perny holly (*I. Pernyi*) is a miniature Chinese type of slow, compact growth, while *Ilex Pernyi Veitchii*, a seedling originating in England, has larger leaves and is more rapid growing.

The evergreen yaupon (*I. vomitoria*), native from Virginia to Florida and Texas to Arkansas, has berries on the old growth, while narrow-leaved dahoon (*I. Cassine*) produces its scarlet fruits on new growth. *Ilex myrtifolia Lowei* has yellow berries and will even grow in bogs.

The new varieties of holly being introduced have a tendency toward heavier fruiting and glossier leaves. By grafting, self-fertile plants are produced.

Holly will grow in all sections of the South and is attractive throughout the year either on account of the berries or the thick foliage. It is very valuable in home plantings.

149

BOXWOOD

Buxus or boxwood is native to southern Europe, north Africa and parts of Asia. It is rather slow growing but in the wild state it becomes a small evergreen tree. Formerly it was so common in England that places derived their names from it, such as Boxley in Kent and Boxhill in Surrey. The fine-grained wood is used for engraving, and in past years the foliage was used in making certain medicines.

Common box (*Buxus sempervirens*) was introduced into the United States in early colonial times and is often referred to as English boxwood. Plants over a hundred years old are growing in many southern gardens, where they are closely associated with the traditions of the old South. These evergreens with a pungent odor peculiarly their own make ornamental specimens, clipped hedges or borders. The compact, flat growth is composed of numerous small leaves. Under a microscope the branchlets look more or less square or four-angled. Plants are particularly attractive when they have tender light green growth contrasting with the dark green mature foliage. Not many years ago some Southerners who wanted newer plants or a place for raising cotton ploughed up their boxwood, but fortunately the present generation has awakened to an appreciation of its beauty.

There are many varieties of the common box. Some have oval leaves, some oval-oblong, some roundish and others pointed. The typical tree or tall shrub variety (*Buxus sempervirens arborescens*) usually has oval leaves. Longifolia or angustifolia is shrubby, with oblong pointed foliage; upright-growing Handsworthii grows in all sections of the South. Rotundifolia and glauca have oval leaves. Myrtifolia and rosmarinifolia are lower growing than others mentioned.

Some varieties of common box have variegated foliage. Aurea is yellow variegated, marginata is margined yellow and argentea has leaves edged white. A popular variety of *Buxus sempervirens* is the truedwarf (suffruticosa); often the rounded clumps, a century old, are not over 2 feet high. It will grow to 4 feet. This beautiful plant is useful as an edging for formal borders. It can be pruned and kept as low as desired. Plantings of truedwarf box make approaches, such as walks and drives, very interesting.

Another species, *Buxus japonica*, is hardier but not so tall growing as the *B. sempervirens* varieties. This has spreading branches and shining apple-green foliage. The variety aurea is the golden Japanese

A natural slope provides the good drainage essential in a rock garden, while deep pockets of soil between the rocks give sustenance to the plants. (See page 91.)

This boxwood recalls the days when colonial dames planted box as a reminder of old England.

box for low hedges. The coarser foliage of the Korean box (*B. microphylla*) is oval, narrowing down at the tip. It is hardier than *B. sempervirens* but seldom grows over 15 inches tall. In the growing season the Korean box stays a rich green, but in a severe winter some leaves will turn bronzy. The Chinese boxwood (*B. Harlandii*) is fast growing, though probably not so hardy as the common box. The Spanish type (*B. balearica*) is ornamental, but more tender.

Box has a fibrous root system and is not hard to transplant at any time if handled carefully after being balled and burlapped. The best season to move it is from October to March. If it is done after growth starts in spring, that growth will be lost. In planting, put leaf mold or rich loam in the bottom of the hole, and water well. Boxwood will grow in almost any well-drained soil—sandy and loose or heavy clay, medium alkaline or acid—and does best in partial shade. When it is planted on the north or east side of a building, it will not burn in winter; it can stand cold better than changes of temperature. Boxwood should be protected from winter sun when first set out, for the sun browns the frozen leaf tissue. Slats or thin cloth will give sufficient cover. The first two years are hardest on boxwood.

As a rule, these plants do not need to be fertilized. If established boxwood is not healthy looking, cottonseed meal, bonemeal or rotted cow manure can be used to enrich the soil, but not lime. Humus, moisture and good drainage are most essential; leaf mold is excellent. Box is so hardy in the South that after roots get established it will thrive even if neglected.

Boxwood is grown for its evergreen foliage; few people notice the inconspicuous greenish flowers in axillary or terminal clusters and the tiny seed fruits. Plants are propagated by cuttings and by layering or divisions. The seed can be sown just as it matures, but plants of any size will not be produced for a long time.

From November to February it is possible to root cuttings (about 4 to 6-inch) taken from old hard growth; in spring use the tender shoots with firm stems. Strip the leaves from the part to be put in the ground. Cuttings root well in damp sand in a shady location where there is good drainage; keep them moist but not wet. They can be put out until June, but we have better success in November.

When branches of box touch the ground, they will do their own layering. Branchlets with roots formed on them can be cut and planted. Especially with truedwarf boxwood, propagation is often done by divisions of roots. Plant divisions deep and keep them moist.

Boxwood should be trimmed enough to stay dense and shapely, but not enough to lose its soft appearance. Should your plants suffer from spider mites that cause the foliage to turn orange and drop off, spray every ten days during summer. Use a tablespoonful of soap powder in a gallon of water, with a teaspoonful of nicotine sulphate added to the suds.

To control leaf miner, spray with DDT 25% emulsifiable, a quart to 13 gallons of water, before the adults emerge in early spring. In ten days spray again. Since spring seasons differ, keep close watch on boxwood until the leaf can be seen swollen with the insect. Spray when signs of the flying insects are observed, as well as before the emergence.

Chapter X
Time To Eat!

FRUITS, BERRIES, NUTS, MELONS

Choice fruits can be grown even on a small property. Formerly it was the custom to have a special place set apart for a home orchard, but since the beauty of fruit trees has been appreciated they have been used more and more as a part of the ornamental planting. Apple trees, for example, are splendid for shade; and many fruit trees, such as the peach, are beautiful in bloom and productive of tasty fruits later.

All the Southern States present ideal conditions for growing certain kinds of fruit. In many districts, such as Georgia where peach growing is an important business, fruit is raised on a large scale. In tropical and subtropical areas citrus fruits—oranges, lemons, grapefruit and tangerines—are enticing in flower and fruit. A fruit garden or orchard in almost any part of the South can supply delicious food from varieties of apples, apricots, cherries, pears, plums, peaches, nectarines, quinces, pomegranates, figs, currants, grapes, strawberries, raspberries, loganberries, youngberries, nuts and melons. Bought fruit never tastes so good as that grown in one's own garden.

Where space is limited, dwarf and semi-dwarf trees are very useful. These should not be confused with espaliers trained on walls. Dwarf fruit trees, about as tall as a man, are propagated by budding or grafting on improved dwarfing rootstocks. The smallest are propagated on a very dwarf rootstock; another stock is used for trees less dwarf, and still another for those a little taller. Quince rootstock is used for dwarfing pears. Dwarf trees can be set as close as 6 or 8 feet apart. The union should be just at ground level or a little above. They are a pleasing sight in bloom, and the fruit is satisfactory, too. Several different varieties of a fruit are sometimes grafted on one tree; this saves space and makes an ornamental oddity.

Very dwarf trees should be staked or braced. Semi-dwarf ones do not have to be staked, for they are on larger rootstock. All of the dwarfs require a fertilizer high in nitrogen, like nitrate of soda or ammonium sulphate. When the trees are grown on the lawn, fertilizer can be put around them in holes 6 or 8 inches deep. If it is spread on the surface, the grass will get the benefit. A mulch is advisable for dwarf trees.

All fruit trees need good soil, sunshine and moisture. In planting them, set them about as deep as they grew in the nursery, in holes large enough for the roots to be spread out well. Most can be planted as soon as the ground can be worked in the spring, as well as in the fall and even in winter in most of the South. Some trees, such as pears, apples, cherries and most peaches, are self-fertilizing, but usually more than one variety is needed in order to provide for cross-pollination. The blossoms are pollinated by winds or insects.

Sometimes fruit trees, especially old ones, do not bear fruit; this is not so much from lack of pruning as from starvation. They may bloom but not set a crop, or the fruit may drop before it ripens. This condition usually indicates the need of nitrogen; stable manure is often a good remedy, or nitrate of soda or sulphate of ammonia applied about two weeks before the trees bloom.

Figs thrive in many southern gardens; some bear several crops in a season. They respond to an application of bonemeal; phosphorus helps to prevent the fruit from dropping before it is ripe and improves its quality. The bushes can be pruned after a heavy frost. Take out the weak growth, prune as severely as necessary, and paint the cuts with white lead.

An unusual and ornamental fruit is the Japanese persimmon, which is hardy in the middle and lower South. Pomegranates are attractive enough to be planted in the shrubbery border, for they bear bright flowers intermittently all summer. The fruits are juicy and interesting. Anyone with room enough should plant at least one mulberry, if only for the sake of the birds. Mulberries thrive in any soil and will stand neglect, drought and cold.

Fruit trees are pruned at any time between the dropping of the leaves in the fall and the swelling of the buds, but not when the wood is frozen. Dead wood may be taken out whenever convenient. To promote growth of the tree, prune in late fall; to develop fruiting branches, prune in late winter. Leave the center open for air and sunlight to enter, and cut the limbs that grow very tall, to make maintenance easier and bring the fruit within reach. Get rid of suckers and make all cuts smooth. Never leave the trimmings lying on the ground; they may be diseased or may harbor insects over winter. It is best to burn them, as well as mummified and diseased fruits. Cut out and burn any infestation of black knot on plums and cherries.

A vegetable garden can be very attractive when it is
well planned and kept in top condition. Even a small
space can be made to yield a great deal. (See page 157.)

Pecan orchards have proved to be very profitable in many parts of the South. The pecan tree provides good shade as well as nutritious nuts and has been chosen as the state tree of Texas.

Spray with oil emulsion, Bordeaux or lime-sulphur after pruning, while the trees are still dormant. Choose a mild, calm day for the job. Keep the mixture well stirred, and see that it reaches every branch and twig. The necessity for spraying will depend on the region and the pests present. For a complete treatment, spraying is done before the buds begin to swell, after the petals fall, about two weeks later, and again in about three weeks, before the fruit colors. Sucking insects like scale are controlled by a contact poison (nicotine sulphate). Chewing insects, like the codling moths that make apples wormy, are destroyed by arsenate of lead.

Fungus diseases sometimes affect leaves, bark or fruit; they are caused by a fungus that starts as a spore or seed. As the spore grows, it sends roots into the plant tissues; rot and curl leaf of peaches are examples. To prevent this, apply a fungicide before the spores germinate. A miscible oil spray can be used while the plants are dormant, followed by a combination spray of rotenone for sucking insects, arsenate of lead for chewing insects, and wettable sulphur to control diseases, before the blooms unfold.

All southern gardens with any space to spare should have some raspberries, as well as strawberries and grapes. In the upper sections currants and gooseberries (Ribes) thrive. Blueberries (Vaccinium) grow in the middle and lower Piedmont and coastal areas. Bramble fruits take up little room and supply delicious fruit. Raspberries give splendid crops in mild climates. The roots live for years but the canes are biennial; old canes should be removed, for they do not bear again. When pruning in November or December, remove all canes of the year before and cut the new ones back to 3 feet. Raspberries can be grown successfully on various soils, although rich land is best. A heavy mulch of leaf mold or straw will take care of the moisture.

There are many varieties of raspberries: black, red, purple and even yellow and white. Their worst disease is mosaic. Buy plants only from inspected nurseries, and destroy at once any that show signs of disease when the leaves appear. Wilted canes with crumpled leaves tipped yellow and green should be cut away. Spray or dust with sulphur-arsenate or copper-lime-arsenate when the leaves are nearly out, just before the flowers open, and when berries are small. Girdling marks or swellings on raspberry or blackberry bushes indicate the presence of cane borers. Cut the canes to the ground and burn them. It is a good practice to mulch raspberries, as well as blackberries and currants, with manure about November.

155

Strawberries grow in almost any well-drained, carefully prepared soil. Nitrate of soda can be used as a side dressing, for they are heavy feeders. The everbearing varieties particularly need attention in midsummer. Excess runners should be removed and the plants watered in dry weather.

Strawberry plants are set so that the crowns are even with the surface of the ground and the roots made firm, with no air pockets. A mulch of well-rotted manure in November protects the plants, keeps them from heaving and prevents deterioration of the soil, but it must not mat on the crowns. In early spring, the winter mulch is removed and a top-dressing of plant food worked into the soil around the plants. After the berries have formed, a fresh straw mulch is applied to keep the fruit clean and free of grit. For limited space a strawberry barrel is interesting. Fill it with rich soil. Space holes in the barrel about 8 inches apart, and set a plant at each hole.

There are various other fine berries for the garden. Youngberries are improved dewberries, and boysenberries and nectarberries are glorified youngberries. The loganberry is a red-fruited variety of blackberry.

Grapes are one of the oldest domesticated fruits. They need all-day sun and good drainage. The ground can be enriched with barnyard manure, bonemeal, cottonseed meal, hardwood ashes and leaf mold. They can be planted in early spring or fall. The purely southern muscadine grapes are free of disease. There are black-fruited varieties like James and Thomas and light brown scuppernongs. To insure heavy fruiting, some male plants should be included. Self-fertilizing varieties like Burgaw (dark) and Wallace (light) have been developed. These are usually grown on arbors and are rarely pruned; the correct time to do any pruning is after the leaves fall.

Other grapes may be pruned at any time they are dormant and not frozen. Cut off a large part of the last season's growth in order not to have too many new shoots to get out of bounds. Then only enough grapes will be borne for the vine to take care of; there is an average of two clusters to a shoot. The fruits will be carried near the base of shoots of the present season's growth, on wood from the previous season. We generally prune so that each branch will produce five or six shoots. Each year the fruit will be farther from the main vine unless new shoots are allowed to grow near the main trunk. The wood is renewed and the older ones cut out later.

Grapes are usually trained on two wires by the upright system, or by the four-arm or Kniffin system. By the former method two canes are tied on the bottom wires, and as the shoots grow they are fastened to the top wires. In the Kniffin or drooping system of training, two canes are tied on the top as well as the bottom wires (four arms), and the shoots that bear are allowed to hang. Just before the buds swell is a good time to fertilize grapes; 4-8-6 fertilizer can be used. Spray with nicotine and lead arsenate to keep the vines free from any infestation.

Domesticated native nut trees, such as pecans, hickories and black walnuts, make good shade trees and provide healthful and nutritious nuts. The black walnut is a native as far south as Florida and as far west as Texas. The English or Persian walnut is also cultivated about home grounds. Most chestnuts in the South have been destroyed by blight. The whole tree is attacked by this chestnut bark disease, which is caused by fungus that penetrates the bark and girdles the trunk or branch. Any infected parts should be cut off and destroyed. Chinese chestnuts have been developed that resist the blight. Chinquapins can be planted on waste land. Peanuts, which are really a forage or grain crop, can also be grown advantageously in the South.

Melons of all kinds need plenty of space and warm ground. Watermelons do best in a well-prepared, light sandy soil with plenty of organic matter in it. If melons are grown on the same land year after year, they are apt to suffer from wilt disease. Rotate the crops about every five years. Sometimes cowpeas are planted among them after the melons are cultivated for the last time. They shade the fruit and help to improve the soil. Cantaloupes like warmth, too, but not so much as watermelons. Four to five months is required from sowing the seed to harvest time.

VEGETABLES

A good vegetable garden is a source of both pleasure and profit. A small, well-worked plot gives better returns than a large garden that has been neglected, although in spring it is a great temptation to undertake a larger planting than the summer's heat will allow one to care for properly. The vegetable garden can be made a very attractive and enjoyable place, for many vegetables, such as feathery-leaved carrots and reddish-topped beets, are highly decorative. A neat picket fence or an evergreen hedge around the garden adds much to its appearance. A culinary herb border will make it interesting.

The South has an ardent sun and a generous soil. With a little labor gardens here will supply an abundance of delicious food for all seasons. Two important points to remember in growing vegetables are: plant at intervals and keep the vegetables gathered while they are young and tender.

Vegetables are health insurance, for they supply proteins, carbohydrates, mineral salts and vitamins—all necessary for a balanced diet. Beans, peas and others give proteins; artichokes, beets, carrots, potatoes, parsnips, onions and turnips provide carbohydrates; and leafy vegetables are rich in mineral salts and vitamins. Sources for iron are collards, kale, spinach, chard, turnip greens, mustard and beet greens, broccoli, Brussels sprouts, parsley, green lima beans, snap beans, peas, carrots, celery, radishes, potatoes, squash, turnips and others. For calcium there are broccoli, carrots, cauliflower, collards, kale, mustard greens, beet tops, etc. There are many vegetable sources of vitamins A, B, C, E, G and K.

The needs of a vegetable garden are sunshine, good drainage, plenty of humus and fertilizer, deep soil preparation and frequent cultivation. Any existing slopes should be terraced, and space enough should be left for the use of a wheelbarrow. Use plenty of stable manure for soil enrichment; bonemeal and wood ashes are good, too. It is well to spread manure on the top of the soil each fall. Areas not planted should be plowed in the fall or winter and the manure turned under. This destroys many insects and allows moisture to enter the ground; freezing will pulverize the soil.

Before planting, the ground should be put in good condition by plowing or spading, harrowing and raking. Soil must not be worked when wet. It should be dry enough when squeezed in a ball to fall apart again. Although many gardeners think that a hand plow with different "hoes" that can be attached is indispensable in the vegetable garden, the work can be done with a spading fork or spade, a hoe and a steel rake. The rows should be about 2 feet apart, or 18 inches for the smaller vegetables.

Germination depends upon moisture. If seeds are sown outdoors just after the row has been opened, they get full advantage of the moisture in the soil. It is better to sow seeds after a rain than before. The soil should be made as fine as possible, and no fertilizer should be allowed to come in direct contact with the seeds.

In planting, one is guided by weather conditions. In the lower South frost is apt to occur in March, in the middle section in April, in the upper mountain section in May. In the upper part a killing frost may be expected in October and in the middle South in No-

A vegetable garden near the house is likely to receive good attention and to be handy. Succession planting keeps a family in the South well fed by their own garden.

The makings of a healthful, appetizing fresh vegetable salad are always within easy reach when you "grow your own." Try counting how many vegetables of your own raising are in it.

vember. Hardy vegetables stand frost and can be planted as early as the ground can be worked in spring. Kale, carrots, beets and garden peas can be sown in the fall, two weeks before the last killing frost is expected. Half-hardy vegetables stand light frost and germinate in cold ground, but it is better not to plant until danger of frost is over. Those like beans are sown in Florida in February. Do not plant the seeds of tender vegetables, such as squash and cucumbers, until all frost danger is past and warm nights are assured. Squash, cucumbers and cantaloupes should not be next to each other, for bees mix the pollen and the flavor of one may be transferred to another.

Early in the season cultivate the garden about once a week to keep down weeds. Neither grass nor weeds should be allowed to ripen seeds. Cultivate lightly after the plants start growing so as not to disturb roots close to the surface. Work the soil between the plants as well as between the rows. Stir the surface after each rain to prevent a crust from forming.

When watering, it is advisable to soak the ground, for this encourages the roots to go downward. A good idea is to have a trench 6 or 8 inches from the plants, and let water flow from the hose down the trench. Water makes plants grow fast and makes vegetables tender. With plenty of humus and cultivation, watering is usually unnecessary.

Perennials like asparagus and artichokes are best planted at one side of the garden where they can remain undisturbed for years. The asparagus bed must be well prepared. Asparagus is a heavy feeder and can be covered with manure in February. Do not cut any tips until the second year, and always leave a few stalks each year for the sake of the roots. When the plants are killed by frost, cut them to the ground. If rust appears, the old stalks must be burned and a light dressing of lime applied.

Jerusalem artichokes are grown for their underground tubers. A good place for them is along the fence or back border of the vegetable garden. They like rich, sandy soil. The globe artichoke is a perennial that should be renewed after a few years by suckers or seed. The heads are gathered before the florets come; the fleshy parts are boiled and seasoned, and the blanched leaves are used for salad. These are heavy feeders.

If one expects to grow his own plants, it is well to have a coldframe and a hotbed in a corner of the vegetable garden in order to have such plants as tomato, eggplants, pimento and pepper to put out whenever one wants them. The canning of pimento peppers has become quite an industry in parts of the South, particularly Georgia.

In transplanting tomatoes, celery, collards, cabbage and other vegetable plants, firm the soil well about the roots. Set the plants deep but do not cover the buds. Tomatoes set 2 inches deep will be stockier, with more rootlets on the stem to strengthen the plants. It is best to cut off the suckers and side shoots of tomatoes and tie the plants to stakes. When they are about 4 feet high, the tops can be pinched out. Some people put straw under tomato plants and do not prune and stake them, but the fruits are then not so large. Keep tomato plants growing until frost; the fruits can be gathered as they turn color. Mature green tomatoes stored just before frost will be edible into the winter.

Transplant cabbage during September, October and November in the middle South for fresh heads all winter and about the last of August for fall heads. In the mountain sections varieties like Flat Dutch can be transplanted in June and July. Plants thrive in the open ground all winter in the middle and lower South; in the mountain sections they can be moved to coldframes. Or the heads can be bent over into a deep trench and protected with soil. Seed can be sown in October and the transplanting done in February. Freezing does not harm the leaves but it does injure the stems. Set the plants deep so that the stems will not freeze; the leaves will keep the soil from freezing and hurting the roots.

From the cabbage were developed Brussels sprouts, cauliflower and kale, all of which stand cold but not heat. In the South the best crops from these vegetables are obtained in late fall, late winter and early spring. Broccoli is treated like cauliflower but is more hardy. Kohlrabi, a species of the cabbage family, is grown for its turnip-like stem.

Crops ought to be rotated, for different plants take different elements from the soil. The same crop grown in the same place year after year may exhaust the supply of what the plant requires. Besides, the diseases and insects peculiar to that plant may enter the soil, or the disease peculiar to that soil may attack the plant. Fungus parasites multiply if they are in the same soil year after year. By changing crops one may get rid of these pests. Plants grown for leaves should be followed by those grown for fruit, and vice versa. For example, beans can follow lettuce and spinach; or collards can take the place of beets, carrots and turnips. Some plants have deep roots that penetrate the subsoil; such vegetables are nitrogen col-

A real old-world atmosphere has been preserved in this herb garden in Williamsburg, Va., which is both ornamental and useful. (See page 163.)

Gladioli can easily be grown in rows at the edge of the vegetable garden. Their long spikes last for days when brought into the house, for the buds continue to open as the older flowers fade. (See page 141.)

lectors or legumes, like cowpeas. Legumes get nitrogen from the air for their own growth and leave it in the soil for other crops to utilize. Most vegetables are consumers of nitrogen that they get from the soil; it is well for nitrogen consumers to follow nitrogen collectors.

Do not plant all the garden at one time. It is much better to make several sowings. Succession planting means the sowing of a second crop to follow one that has already matured, or the sowing of the same variety at intervals of a few weeks so that the second crop will mature as the first one finishes. Several plantings can be made of corn and beans, but one planting of lima beans, peppers and egg-plant will bear till frost. Rows planted straight across a garden simplify succession and rotation; straight rows look better and are easier to work. As many as four crops can be grown in alternate rows as companion crops, such as collards, beets, corn and turnips. Thus space is utilized best, for the early-maturing vegetable is generally out of the way when room is needed for another. Alternate row planting can be combined with succession crops. When one crop passes, get the ground in condition to plant another. To save space there can be "partnership" crops, such as pole beans to grow up cornstalks or cowpeas between corn.

Vegetables like corn, peas and beans lose some flavor after a few hours, but when we grow them ourselves they can go from "vine to pot" in less than an hour and are always tasty and appetizing. Garden peas and carrots taste just right when cooked together. One reason we like home-grown garden peas is that the outside pods are so green and fresh that they may be brought to a boil and the juice, which has sugar in it, poured over the cooking shelled peas. Edible-podded sugar peas have pods to be eaten like snap beans. Okra and tomatoes also "go together"; and a dash of minced onion brings out the flavor of squash. Some raw vegetables should be eaten at least once a day.

Growing one's own vegetables is worthwhile even when there are weeds, drought and insect pests to fight, which force one to keep materials on hand for dusting or spraying. It is best to avoid insecticides poisonous to birds and animals. Pyrethrum and rotenone dusts are not harmful to man. The latter is made from derris root and is much stronger than arsenate of lead as a stomach poison; as a contact poison it is more powerful than nicotine. Ground lime is effective against beetles that riddle leaves of plants. To control borers on squash, destroy the eggs or the young before they go into the squash. Rotenone can be used during the egg-laying period to poison the larvæ.

A reference chart of varieties of vegetables that do well in this section follows, with the time to plant.

Crop	Varieties	Time to Plant
Beets	Detroit Dark Red Early Wonder	March, April, September
Carrots	Chantenay Imperator	March, April, September
Cabbage	All Seasons Charleston Wakefield Succession	February, March, August, September
Chard	Fordhook Giant Lucullus	March, April, September
Collards	Cabbage Collard Georgia Louisiana Sweet	March to September
Cowpeas	California Black Eye Early Ramshorn Sugar Crowder	April to July
Cucumbers	Boston Pickling Early Fortune	April, May
Eggplant	Black Beauty	April, May—plants
English Peas	Hundredfold Laxton's Progress	Late fall, February, March
Irish Potatoes	Bliss Triumph Irish Cobbler	Last of February, March
Kale	Green Curled Scotch Siberian	February, March, September, October
Lettuce	Grand Rapids Imperial 44 Imperial 847 Mignonette	February, March, September
Lima Beans	Henderson Bush—bush Carolina Sieva—pole	April, May
Mustard	Fordhook Fancy Southern Curled	February, March, August, September, October
Okra	Clemson Spineless Perkins Long Green	April to middle of May
Onions	Prizetaker Yellow Globe Danvers White Pearl	February, March, September, October

162

Crop	Varieties	Time to Plant
Pepper	California Wonder Cayenne—hot Long Red—sweet Pimento—sweet	April, May, June—plants
Radish	French Breakfast Scarlet Button	March, April
Spinach	Long Standing Bloomsdale—spring planting Virginia Savoy—autumn planting	February, March, October, November
Summer Spinach	New Zealand	Last of March, April
Snap Beans	Stringless Greenpod—bush Tendergreen—bush U. S. No. 5—bush McCaslan—pole Kentucky Wonder—pole	March 15 to May 15, August
Soybeans	Easy Cook Rokusum Seminole	May
Squash	Early Prolific Straightneck Summer Crookneck	April, May, August
Sweet Corn	Aristogold Country Gentleman Golden Cross Bantam Trucker's Favorite	March to July
Sweet Potatoes	Porto Rico	May, June—slips
Tomatoes	Marglobe Pritchard Rutgers	April, May, July—plants

CULINARY HERBS

The word herb applies to plants that do not become woody. Culinary herbs are aromatic kinds used for flavoring or garnishing. They include sweet, pot-herb and medicinal species; many can be used for all these purposes or for potpourri mixtures.

The oils in these plants give them fragrance and taste. The leaves of some herbs and the seed of others add a zest to soups, salads and meats. Dried leaves have a distinctive flavor but green ones have a fresher taste. Pot-herbs are cooked before being eaten, while sweet

163

herbs are generally used raw as flavoring for salads, drinks or soups. The minced leaves should be dropped in the soup just before serving rather than cooked in it. Medicinal herbs possess curative power.

In early days herbs were grown because they were needed for culinary and medicinal use; now they are coming into prominence again for flavoring meats and salads. When early settlers came to this country they brought herb seed with them; the Indians already knew the value of the native species. In history and legend we find mention of various herbs. One could have an herb garden using only the ones mentioned in Shakespeare: hyssop, lavender, parsley, mint, marjoram, marigold, rosemary, rue, sorrel, sage, saffron, savory, thyme and wormwood.

These old-fashioned plants bring remembrance of other years and have a sentimental value whether used for fragrance, flavor or medicine. Often they turn insipid food into a delicacy and give a garden uniqueness and charm. At all seasons an herb corner is interesting. It may be the foliage or the flowers or the odors of the different plants that attract attention. After a rain the fragrance is more noticeable.

The best location for a planting of herbs is near the kitchen. Various herbs give a pleasing effect in rock gardens. Many can be planted in a border 2 to 4 feet wide and 6 to 8 feet long. Different kinds can be grown in the same bed, or they can be placed in borders among flowers. There are annual, biennial and perennial herbs. The majority of them grow readily from seed. A packet of mixed seed will give one the pleasure of learning the names of the plants by smell and by sight. All like sunshine, at least most of the day, and light garden loam. Not all of them will grow in the warmest part of the South, and some have to be in shade there. Weeds should be kept down and the soil loosened; otherwise they require little attention. Plants should be cut back as they reach full size so that air can circulate easily. Perennials are propagated by cuttings, layerings and root divisions; some, like mint, have underground stems that take root. For cuttings, strip off the leaves except at the top. In summer the tips of growth will root in a moist, shady spot. Herbs are not bothered much by destructive insects; in fact, some repel insects.

To dry leaves of herbs properly, gather them in the morning after the dew has evaporated, or in the late afternoon. It is essential that the leaves be dry when picked. Put them in a warm but not hot place; the sun makes them lose color and some essence. When they

164

Hairy panicles of ripening seed prompted the name for
smoke-tree. It grows about 15 feet high. (See page 53.)

The vegetable garden at Mount Vernon, Va. (See page 2.)

have dried a little on one side, turn them about. If dried well and stored in airtight jars, they will keep their qualities a long time.

To make spikes of flowers hold their form, cut them as the top floret begins to open and dry quickly in the shade. Fragrance is best in the bud stage. Seeds should be gathered when they are ripe, dried thoroughly, cleaned and put in tight containers. Leaves, stems and flowers can be tied in bunches and hung in a dry, warm room to cure.

Probably the herb best known to most people is parsley (*Petroselinum crispum* (*hortense*)), a biennial from which a beautiful edging can be made for a border. This is used extensively for a garnish; there are now varieties with leaves plain, curly and moss curled. Chopped up, they are used as seasoning in salad, omelets and sprinkled over new Irish potatoes in cream dressing. Parsley is a valuable source of iron. Keep seed stalks cut off the plants, or allow only a few seeds to mature to have plants always.

Another well-known culinary herb is sage (*Salvia officinalis*), a small perennial shrub with grayish leaves and spikes of small flowers. After the leaves are dried and pulverized, they are fine for seasoning meats, especially sausage, and poultry stuffings, and are sometimes used in soup and cheese. Sage tea in olden times was taken as a cure for colds. Plants are rather hard to grow from seed, so it is better to use divisions.

A showy herb border can be made in the vegetable garden with tall herbs like horehound (*Marrubium vulgare*), a perennial growing 3 feet high and bearing whitish flowers; it is used in cough remedies. Fennel (*Fœniculum vulgare*) is another tall perennial but it is treated as an annual or biennial; it bears yellow flowers. The young leaves are used in flavoring soups and fish or as a garnish, and are sometimes eaten raw. The seeds have an aromatic or bitter taste and can be used in beverages. Fennel has become naturalized and is a nuisance in pastures. There is a low-growing kind (*Fœniculum dulce*) that is an annual; the large leaves at the base are used as a vegetable.

Some rather useful annual herbs are anise, borage, caraway and coriander. Anise (*Pimpinella Anisum*), growing about 2 feet high, has yellowish white flowers in loose heads. This has an agreeable odor and is pleasant to the taste. The leaves are useful as potherbs, for flavoring and for garnish; the seed and oil are used for flavoring and perfumery. Borage (*Borago officinalis*) has hairy, prickly leaves and attractive, rose-pink flowers changing to blue. The young leaves have a cucumber flavor and are used as a pot-herb, in the

165

making of salads and in beverages. Caraway (*Carum Carvi*), annual or biennial, and coriander (*Coriandrum sativum*) have small white flowers. The seeds of caraway are used on cakes and bread and the seeds of coriander in mixed spices and on candies.

Three perennials indispensable in an herb border are mint, lavender and rosemary. Each has an enticing appearance and a refreshing odor. Mint suggests beverages and mint jelly for serving with lamb. An easy way to propagate the mints is to cut running rootstocks and replant them. They will thrive in a dry place, but moisture brings out their odor; they do not like lime. The name mint is generally applied to plants of the genus Mentha, with square stems and opposite leaves.

Leaves of spearmint (*Mentha spicata*) are not so narrow or so pointed as those of peppermint (*Mentha piperita*). Spearmint, native to Europe and Asia, is naturalized about old gardens in the United States. This herb is used for flavoring drinks, gum, mint sauce, etc. It is cultivated in gardens especially for the sprigs, which are put in drinks. Peppermint, although introduced into cultivation from England, is often called American mint. The white mint variety of peppermint, officinalis, has light-colored stems and leaves; the black mint, vulgaris, has purple stems and dark foliage. Oil of peppermint is used in medicine, to perfume soap and for flavoring. The native American wild mint (*M. arvensis canadensis*), found in wet soil about streams, is often mistaken for peppermint. Pennyroyal (*M. Pulegium*), another mint of European descent, is useful for seasoning and for oil. The American pennyroyal (*Hedeoma pulegioides*) has some medicinal oil.

Bergamot (*Mentha citrata*), naturalized in Florida, is called lemon and orange mint. It is a low grower with reddish stems and green leaves tinted red. This is used for flavoring conserves, and the oil for perfumes. Apple mint (*M. rotundifolia*) is sometimes substituted for spearmint and peppermint; the variety variegata has variegated leaves. The oil in mint makes a good furniture polish. Possibly our great-great-grandmothers used the leaves to rub their furniture.

True lavender (*Lavandula officinalis*) has delightful leaves, flowers and fragrance. It grows shrub-like, with narrow gray leaves and azure bloom spikes that are attractive in arrangements. Pick and dry the flowers while in bud to put with linens. The oil is used in perfumery. Cuttings having a heel of older wood root readily in moist soil.

Rosemary (*Rosmarinus officinalis*), worthy of a place in a garden,

166

has aromatic leaves, glossy on top and white underneath, and blue flowers. Plant this for the bees and for "remembrance and friendship." The herbage is used for seasoning; it adds a pungent flavor to pot roast. The oils are good for perfumery and soaps. To carry some of the herbs, such as balm and rosemary, is said to make one "happy, merry and loved."

Low hedges can be made with thyme. There are many varieties, differing in flavor, fragrance, foliage and color. Some are creepers; others are upright growing. The leaves are good for seasoning meat loaf, poultry dressing and soup; the oil is used in perfumery. Golden lemon thyme (*Thymus Serpyllum aureus*) has green-edged yellow leaves. It spreads considerably and is not particular about soil or exposure, although it does not like wet feet.

Tea from some herbs has a delightful aroma and taste. To make good tea, pour boiling water over fresh or dried leaves and let it stand a few minutes. Our ancestors liked "bitters for health," and from tansy (*Tanacetum vulgare*) they concocted a bitter brew. Chamomile, catnip and sage teas are soothing, while a tea or tonic with marjoram in it is said to "bring out" measles. A mild stimulant is made from dittany (*Cunila origanoides (mariana)*). Balm needs boiling to give it a lemon flavor. A tea with a chewing-gum scent is made from the yellow-green leaves of costmary or mint geranium. Refreshing teas can be brewed from lavender, rosemary and thyme.

Other "sweet herbs" can be used in beverages and cookery and for seasoning or flavoring; it is interesting to watch them grow. The tall garden angelica (*Angelica Archangelica*) has tropical-looking leaves and umbels of small, greenish white flowers. Chives (*Allium Schœnoprasum*) reaches about 6 inches in height and bears round heads of purple flowers. Its foliage has a mild onion flavor. Bulbs can be planted separately or the clumps divided to make an edging.

Lovage (*Levisticum officinale*), with dark shiny leaves, has celery-like stems that are cut in small pieces and used in confectionery. The cool gray foliage of the evergreen rue (*Ruta graveolens*), called the herb of grace, always attracts attention. This was formerly used in medicine. Superstitious persons thought that it helped to give one second sight. Germander (*Teucrium canadense*) is fine for a hedge around the herb garden, and ground cypress (Santolina) makes a lovely clipped border edging.

The savories are bushy fillers for the base of taller plants. They are covered with small, strong-scented, pink, white or lavender flowers. Summer savory (*Satureia hortensis*), with small, light green

167

leaves, is an annual; winter savory (*S. montana*) is a perennial. They have the same flavoring qualities but summer savory is less woody.

Southernwood (*Artemisia Abrotanum*) and tarragon (*A. Dracunculus*) are both artemisias. The young shoots of southernwood are used as a flavor for cake and those of tarragon in vinegars and sauces. This vinegar should stand two weeks before straining. Tarragon is closely related to wormwood (*A. Absinthium*), which is used in medicine. The oil of wormwood added to water makes an intoxicating drink. Clary (*Salvia Sclarea*) is a biennial with ornamental leaves; wine can be made from the flowers. Burnet (*Sanguisorba minor*), a perennial, has leaves that will give flavor to salad and soup.

Other annual herbs that are easy to grow are chervil (*Anthriscus Cerefolium*), which has a parsley-like flavor, and cumin (*Cuminum Cyminum (odorum)*), the seeds of which are an ingredient in curry powder. The leaves of sweet basil (*Ocimum Basilicum*) taste like cloves and look like pepper leaves. The purple variety is dwarf and has rosy blossoms; the green variety bears delicate pink blooms. They are a pretty sight together or with artemisias. Garden cress (*Lepidium sativum*), called pepper-grass, is used as a condiment and garnish; sow it at intervals to have it always at the best stage. The pungency of upland cress (*Barbarea verna (præcox)*) is like that of water cress and horse-radish.

One may want dill (*Anethum graveolens*) for the herb garden and for making pickles. The flowers are like those of the carrot, and the feathery gray-green foliage is aromatic. Dill does not transplant easily. Sow the seeds where the plants are to stay and thin them out. Samphire (*Crithmum maritimum*) is a perennial with leaves that are pickled in vinegar. This is known as sea fennel and flourishes near the seacoast. The aromatic leaves are a glaucous gray and the flower heads white and yellow.

Some herbs have coloring powers. Lady's bedstraw (*Galium verum*) has been used to curdle milk, and a red dye is made from the roots. This has dainty, thread-like, yellowish leaves and yellow flowers. False saffron (*Carthamus tinctorius*) bears florets that give a deep yellow color to cakes and liquors, as well as fabrics. The flowers of the annual pot-marigold (*Calendula officinalis*) will color butter and flavor soups. Another herb, though not culinary, formerly grown for a blue dye for cloth, is woad (*Isatis tinctoria*), an ornamental biennial bearing yellow flowerets. The dye was obtained from the blue-green leaves.

There are other herbs for medicine, for pot-herbs, for fragrance, garnish and ground carpets. Hyssop (*Hyssopus officinalis*), used for medicine, grows 2 feet high in sun or shade. The flowers entice bees all summer. This perennial evergreen can be clipped or allowed to grow as it will.

Chicory is considered a weed but it makes a handsome tall plant with blue flowers. The tender leaves and roots are cooked as a pot-herb. The roots, dried and ground, are a substitute or adulterant for coffee. The tender, low-growing lemon-verbena (*Lippia citriodora*) has lemon-scented leaves; when crushed, they add flavor to beverages.

Many geraniums (Pelargonium), like the rose, apple, nutmeg and lemon, have pleasant scented leaves. Try putting a leaf of a geranium on a glass of jelly. Sweet woodruff (*Asperula odorata*), which likes partial shade, makes an interesting ground cover. The dried leaves have the aroma of new-mown hay. This can be used to give a tang to vegetables and drinks.

A moth repellent may be made by combining ½ pound rosemary, thyme, tansy and mint with 2 tablespoonfuls of ground cloves; store the mixture in tight boxes.

Chapter XI

A Garden Diary

FIRST QUARTER OF THE YEAR

A WARM JANUARY
Leafless are the trees; their purple branches
Spread themselves abroad, like reefs of coral,
     Rising silent
In the Red Sea of the Winter sunset.
                              —*Longfellow*

January 1. In the Piedmont section of South Carolina this New Year's Day is just cold enough to be invigorating, with the sun shining and birds singing. Violets, sweet alyssum and a few pansies are in bloom, and paper-white narcissi have buds ready to open; dandelions are blooming, too, and many wild onions are coming up. Calendulas, linum, sweet william, Siberian wallflowers and gerberas are looking fine. In the rock garden basket-of-gold alyssum is showing silvery foliage, and the moisture-loving, cool-season, hardy primulas are out of the ground. They like rich soil but no lime and do best with about half sun.

Mullein plants (Verbascum) have a gray-green rosette that resists frost, for the downy covering protects it in winter and also acts as an umbrella in summer. Most of the verbascums thrive in a warm, sunny, well-drained, sandy soil, but purple mullein (*V. phœniceum*) blooms best in part shade. The common mullein (*V. Thapsus*), a well-known weed, is showy with tall spikes of yellow flowers in spring. Later the goldfinches have a fondness for the seed stalks.

January 4. Today is like a mild March day with light winds. We saw a few old-fashioned tea roses blooming among shrubbery in protected places. The pansies look healthy; I don't believe we lost a single pansy plant put out in November. We were careful not to bury the crowns. With so much moisture, moss between the rocks of a naturalistic pool is a rich green. Lichens and tree ferns are conspicuous on trees. During damp winter and spring days they are things of beauty, but when drought comes they shrivel up and look dead. The natural color of lichens is gray or yellowish; the green shades are algæ. Lichens are flowerless, with no distinction between

170

leaf and stem; they form spots or patches and generate by spores. A true moss has tiny leaves on the stems. It is intensely interesting to look at these through a microscope.

January 5. Though the mornings and late afternoons are cold, the middle of the day is pleasant. I put coal ashes around delphiniums and foxgloves to repel slugs, help drainage and conserve moisture.

If this weather continues, we'll soon have bulbs blooming, for their foliage is showing all around. Yesterday people asked if it isn't too early for bulbs to be up—"They'll surely be killed!" One forgets from year to year, but they always come at about the same time and are not hurt to any extent by cold.

January 7. We speak of weather as a "spell"; this is a warm spell! Cardinals may be seen slipping wet leaves between their beaks, squirrels are jumping from tree to tree and red-headed woodpeckers are pounding away.

We prepared a place in our garden for some plants with variegated foliage. Rich soil was placed about the pansies; it pays to feed them about every six weeks with commercial fertilizer or manure. My, there is so much chickweed! One way to eradicate it is to brush over the patches with a solution of a pound of iron sulphate in a gallon of water.

January 9. We walked in the garden this damp afternoon. Noticing a border of lavender and white, I went over to see it closer and discovered it to be bold clumps of crocus. We divided and replanted these in summer when the tops were brown, believing they were star of Bethlehem. Now we are glad we made the mistake.

The bamboo background is tall and thick. We have given away many roots, but it keeps throwing out new shoots. We have it in a damp place where it can keep spreading. Being near a large oak does not stop it from growing. Here's hoping this will not get to be a nuisance!

January 13. Rain all night and again today. On days like this it's fine to read garden magazines and imagine changes in our plantings as we wonder which new things to try. We can look out and see the mistakes in our landscaping and plan improvements. We will remember that putting pale-colored flowers farthest from the house makes the place look larger. We can even plan a June garden on a day like this!

January 19. The sun is shining, and it is not so cold. Winter jasmine with flowers making sunshiny spots, breath-of-spring wafting its pleasing fragrance over the garden, and winter sweet with sweet-scented, creamy yellow flowers, seem to enjoy having the wind bend their branches. The ground is in good condition and we put out plants grown in the open—shasta daisies, hardy phlox and double ragged robins.

Boxwood, euonymus, ligustrum, *Magnolia grandiflora*—the grand broadleaf evergreen native of the Southern States—and conifers are particularly noticeable now. We are watching for evidences of scale insects on shrubs. It is best to spray while trees and shrubs are dormant.

January 27. We planted the grape vines and rose bushes that came this morning. The roses were banked with earth about 6 inches high to keep the stems from drying out and as a protection from cold.

White Roman hyacinths are blooming. These were given to me flowering in pots several years ago, and I planted them in a border. Now we enjoy the lovely gift every year.

Today I bought seed from a local seed store. The hotbed will be in condition for planting in a few days.

January 29. I always look forward to the annual camellia show of the Sand Hills Garden Club of Augusta, Ga. Yesterday I motored there with friends. We enjoyed an instructive lecture while seeing the natural-color slides of camellias. The lecturer said that there are very few scented varieties of *Camellia japonica*. All of the varieties of *C. Sasanqua* have blooms that are somewhat fragrant. These begin to flower in autumn; the foliage is smaller and the plants grow faster than *C. japonica*.

Among the thousands of blooms on display, Lady Marion (Kumasaka), a solid deep pink, was outstanding. Lotus was charming with creamy white gossamer petals. There was a non-competitive exhibit of over a hundred camellia blooms on a mirrored staircase. On each step stood a row of medium-height, clear glass containers; in front of these were low crystal containers, each holding a specimen camellia and a little of the glossy green foliage. Reflected in the mirror risers, these made an exquisite picture. Several valuable and rare prints of camellias were displayed in cases; some were more than a hundred years old.

January 30. When one sees plants that he wants, it is well to find a place for them. I decided on a special spot for camellias today. It is half-sunny, protected from winter winds and afternoon sun; the soil is a leafy mold. Camellias will grow in full sun if protected for several summers with lattice, but they do best in part shade. I am going to try my luck with cuttings started in sand under glass.

172

Bulbs provide the first important color effects of spring
and are a forerunner of the exciting pageant to come.

Blue and white hyacinths are especially striking when
combined with yellow daffodils. Their sturdy spikes are
a good source of color and fragrance in early spring.

January 31. Our wide borders of early trumpet daffodils are attractive now. The buds rise as they open, and now the stems are quite long (they used to be called angel's trumpet). Daffodils stand severe cold, even when they bend with ice in their stems; the flowers liven up when the sun shines and the wind blows. Some blooms are appearing on flowering quinces. Often cold turns them brown, but they will flower again. The blossoms are even more ornamental with the tender green leaves showing.

A Cold January

The whispering trees were laden down,
With frozen fog and mist;
And baby buds, all safe and brown,
By icy drafts were kissed.
—*Margaret Emma McNinch*

January 1. I was surprised to see the housetops white with snow this morning. So I telephoned relatives sixty miles away that our family could not come for New Year's dinner, since we might be snowbound. For good luck we'll have hopping-John at home—our field-grown peas and smoked meat, cooked with rice in an iron pot.

January 4. Well wrapped, I walked about the garden at noon. The lily pools are sheets of ice, but berries still hang on nandinas, *Pyracantha crenato-serrata*, hollies, coral-berry plants and ligustrums. I took note of the deciduous trees. Some branches are greenish, some gray, others brown or pink-toned. Some do not shed all their leaves until new buds are swelling. The parasite mistletoe clinging to the limbs of older trees is attractive with its clusters of milky berries, though we try to get rid of it in order to keep the trees vigorous and healthy.

Broadleaf evergreens and conifers accent the winter landscape. One can see a good distance now. I shall have to replace a few low-growing conifers and remove some shrubbery to improve the vista. Bulb tips are showing all about our garden, and some Soleil d'Or narcissi are blooming in a protected place.

January 5. There was sleet in the night, which melted quickly. It would be delightful in the sunshine today except for the dampness and wind. I'll look over the many colorful new catalogs and check the seeds and plants I would like to have, visualizing where they will be most effective in the garden. My glance goes frequently to a pitcher arrangement of silver honesty (Lunaria) and tannish dried grass (Uniola), which lightens a corner of the room.

January 7. As I sit by a window this morning I can see sleet bouncing as it strikes the terrace. It's a hard time for birds, and I am glad we have feeding stations for them. English ivy is looking green around a bird bath, which is constantly used by some visitors.

Even on a day like this, our winter landscape is colorful. Green shades are provided by the conifers, glossy green by boxwoods and pittosporums, yellow-green by bamboos. Arborvitæ has a golden tinge and Colorado spruce is silvery blue.

Late in the afternoon a freezing rain hangs icicles on fences and trees. Shrubs are bending with ice, electric wires look like silver cords and birds are scratching for grit.

January 8. Lights went out all over our city last night, and ornamental candles came into use. I heard two heavy crashes. A large limb weighted with ice fell and broke down a fence; another hit an outbuilding. The snapping of small pines in the grove nearby sounded like pistol shots. Everything outside is coated with ice. I am hoping there will not be much harm done. This is the most severe weather that I have experienced.

January 9. In the afternoon we went out to survey the damage. The melting of the ice has permitted many plants to rise again. I had been worried particularly about boxtrees and arborvitæ, which were badly bent over. A good deal of ice still coated many plants. We gently knocked it off with sticks, not scraping but shaking it off. The *Pyracantha coccinea Lalandii* will have to be pruned and some twisted branches of tall ligustrums taken out. These are thick and dense from having been pruned, but they are full of clusters of berries and ice made them too heavy. A limb from an oak had fallen on a large boxwood and broken it badly. I stuck cuttings of the boxwood into the soft moist earth of the rooting garden.

Pansy and English daisy plants look fresh, as well as stocks, candytuft, painted daisies, hardy carnations, clove pinks, sweet william and calendulas.

January 10. Frost looked like snow this morning, and frozen mist on the conifers was a beautiful sight. The sun shone in full glory all day, and work in the garden was stimulating. As I put sifted wood ashes about bulbs and lilacs, I noticed many birds eating seeds of paulownia trees. A few bulbs had heaved out of the ground, but I pressed them back.

Tender plants are dead, but flowering quince, winter jasmine, forsythia and laurestinus (*Viburnum Tinus*) have tight buds. They swell even in cold weather. In the vegetable garden, collards and turnip greens are not hurt to any extent and will taste better from having an icy coat.

January 23. It snowed all night, and this morning I enjoyed seeing the big flakes as much as the children do. I am making old-fashioned lye hominy with our own shelled corn, clean ashes and lye. Hominy makes a good dish served with red ham gravy.

January 24. The sun is shining on a landscape of dazzling white. The snow is over 7 inches deep, but it didn't seem very cold when I went out, fully wrapped and rubbered, to have some snow knocked off evergreens. Many branches are bending to the ground, and we found it best to knock those underneath. There are tracks all about the garden—squirrel and rabbit, as well as cat and dog. Cats make a comical appearance trying to walk in the snow.

January 27. The snow is frozen over the top, and there are shadows on the white carpet. Last night the full moon shining on it made a weird and lovely scene. The papers say this is the longest cold spell here in forty-nine years. (This diary 1940.)

As I write, I can see from a window that nandinas with bronzy foliage and red berries and broadleaf evergreens are beautiful with patches of snow on them. Birds are at a feeding station; and on the terrace where we threw crumbs, peanuts, and sunflower and benne seed are cardinals, wrens, towhees, chickadees, flickers, ruby-crowned kinglets, tufted titmice and, of course, jays and sparrows.

Some of our friends are afraid their bulbs and various perennials are being damaged by this hard winter. For my part, I am glad to get cold weather now; maybe we will not have it so late in spring.

A WARM AND COLD FEBRUARY

I hear the wind among the trees
Playing celestial symphonies,
I see the branches downward bent,
Like keys of some great instrument.
—*Longfellow*

February 2. The clouds moved so fast we hardly knew when it was cloudy and when sunny today. A groundhog darting around could see his shadow at times; does that mean the worst of winter is ahead? There are blank spaces in our shrubbery borders and I had ligustrums and mock-oranges (Philadelphus) set out to fill them.

February 5. Fertilizer was scattered on lawns to make grass develop quickly and crowd out weeds. We are preparing places to put tree (standard) roses as soon as they are received, and digging

175

up chickweed ruthlessly. Lily pools were drained and the lilies re-potted; when this is done early, the first baby fish are saved. I picked a few Transvaal daisies, the first we have had at this time of year. They thrive in full sun and like good loam and drainage.

February 7. On this breezy day there are many things to observe. Snowflakes (Leucojum) and blue and pink Roman hyacinths are making a show, and dwarf irises are beginning to bloom around a pool. The red growth on *Photinia serrulata* looks like flowers. Tender green is appearing on boxwoods, and the lantern-like berries of eleagnus are changing from yellow to red.

I had a layer of coal cinders placed in a long box; then the box was filled with sharp sand for rooting boxwood cuttings. An old method is to use a teaspoonful of vinegar to each gallon of sand to root cuttings.

February 8. I arranged garden flowers to send to sick friends—daffodils, jonquils, Chinese sacred lilies, snowdrops, forsythia, flower-ing quince, tea olive, laurestinus, *Spiræa Thunbergii* and bridal wreath. And this is February!

We planted the camellias that came today. The soil had already been enriched with leaf mold and well-rotted manure, and large holes had been dug. After planting, the shrubs were mulched with half-rotted leaves.

February 9. Drifts of daffodils give the illusion of sunshine this dreary day. There is tender green on *Spiræa cantoniensis (Reevesiana)* and other shrubs. February is such a fickle month that one does not know whether to expect cold or mild weather. Wearing rain-coat and galoshes, I was enjoying a walk in spite of the dampness, observing the green lawns and different birds, when a friend drove by and asked why our daffodils had such abundant bloom. My answer was that they had responded to an application of fertilizer given after they flowered last year.

February 10. There's moisture in the ground and moonlight nights; we planted corn as an experiment! (Later: It came through all right, and we were among the first to have corn on the cob.)

Members of our family went for a walk in the afternoon and got sassafras roots for pink tea. These have an aromatic odor and a pleasant taste. It is said that when Captain John Smith sent his first ship back to England it was loaded with sassafras.

February 13. Though the wind is disagreeable, we walked about the garden in the sunshine. Breath-of-spring (*Lonicera fragrantissima*) is not only shedding fragrance over the garden but is adding creamy

Naturalized daffodils are inspiring enough to move anyone to poetry! In a planting like this they will get full sunshine, for they bloom before the leaves come out on the trees. (See page 135.)

For a tulip display like this, it is necessary to plan ahead. Here the lovely color scheme was well thought out. From November to December is the proper planting time in most of the South. (See page 139.)

bloom to the borders. Mahonia has drooping, bell-shaped flowers in clusters.

Fruits continue to hang on berried plants—coral-berry, aucuba, Chinese firethorn, nandina, ligustrum, Jerusalem cherry and sweet myrtle. Berries and birds make a garden cheerful.

The evergreens are especially ornamental. Compost scattered in the borders in December improved the soil texture and gave food to the plants. When they are well fed they have an attractive green color, except some, of course, that turn brownish naturally.

There's moss on part of our lawn, indicating the need of fertilizer. Moss is not necessarily a sign of acidity. Most lawn grass likes a soil that is slightly acid. More and more we realize the value of plant food, especially where trees compete for it.

February 16. The wind prunes our trees by breaking off dead branches. Flowering almond is full of blossoms, and in the orchard pear trees are unfolding their buds.

I had leaves turned under in shrubbery borders; this will destroy some insect eggs. Cultivation and the addition of some well-rotted manure or commercial fertilizer to the soil benefits shrubs. The fertilizer should reach the roots, not the stems.

Irish potatoes were planted in a patch reserved for them; they like moist soil and an early start. "They say" we should plant in the dark of the moon, so this is the right time.

February 17. It's such a fine day that I raised the frames of the hotbeds. Friends with us in the garden this afternoon admired the flowering quinces. The bushes are a mass of bloom clustered along the branches. There are many varieties of this favorite, such as Rosa grandiflora, Apple Blossom and others running from white, pink and salmon to crimson. One person asked why I allowed a flowering quince to grow close to an oak tree. Well, it "took up" there and blooms beautifully, so I am going to let it stand. When plants find a place that suits them, I leave them alone unless they mar the picture.

February 20. On a day like this, between light showers, one likes to transplant snapdragons, columbines, delphiniums and other perennials. Many persons want to get roots of plants while they are blooming instead of at the proper planting time. A good idea is to jot down the names when they are in bloom and plan a location for them, remembering the color and height; then get the place in condition for planting at the right time.

February 21. When out riding today, we saw a pink *Magnolia*

Soulangeana in full bloom in a protected spot with southern exposure. This plant will probably be damaged; it would stand a better chance on the north side, although it would bloom later. Broadleaf evergreens and English ivy stay in better condition on the north side, too.

February 23. Ice and frozen ground today! Daffodils and hyacinths are bending down, and the foliage of snowflakes lying flat. I am hoping they are not so badly injured as they look. The flowering quince blooms are brown, and the large, pretty, long-stemmed calendulas are bent to the ground, with the leaves scorched on account of freezing and quick thawing.

February 28. Rain, sun and wind have revived many plants that appeared to be ruined by the recent cold. A visitor asked whether bulbs should be held back. A mulch might hold the cold and in that way do good, but more than likely this would only encourage tender growth that would be less able to stand the cold. If the ground were frozen it would be all right to mulch bulbs, but in this section of the country it is better to leave it to nature.

A Cold and Warm February

Dame Nature lost her smile today
'Twas stolen by a cloud
And leaden heavens, cold and gray,
And winds both harsh and loud.
—*Margaret Emma McNinch*

February 2. Places where snow melted yesterday were frozen hard enough for skating this morning. Later in the day when the sun was shining, collards that I had thought would surely be "done for" were found to be fresh and green above the snow. In the flower garden I noticed that pansies were unhurt. Buds of daffodils and other narcissi are standing erect, and the ground looked dry where shrubs were mulched with leaves and the snow had melted.

February 5. I scattered sifted wood ashes about peonies and bulbs showing tips. Two things gardening has certainly made us conserve—leaves for humus and wood ashes for potash.

Cold has not injured vegetation much. Aspidistra is green, and in the herb border curled parsley and other herbs are looking fine. Many people are worried because the tops of their bearded irises were killed back, but they will grow again later. Pyrethrums and shasta daisies are not hurt at all.

Kerrias deserve attention now with their green branches. Later the flowers are attractive, and in autumn the foliage turns clear yellow. They thrive in good soil and prefer light shade. Five-petaled, single yellow *Kerria japonica* is lovely in the spring; the graceful flowers and stems make beautiful arrangements.

February 7. I found this to be a very windy day when I went out to see how the plants are bearing up. Some shrubs are almost uprooted by the weight of recent ice and will have to be packed and staked to get their roots anchored again. I had the tree roses tied fast to their supports, and a number of conifers will need to be staked until they straighten. Plants like calendulas and wallflowers are looking a little sick, but stocks, hardy carnations, candytuft, sweet william and snapdragons look healthy.

February 8. It was cold this morning, but some exercise in the garden, or yard, as we often say, warmed me. By noon the weather was like spring. Carolina cherry-laurels look more winter-killed than I have ever seen them. The leaves are brown, but when new growth comes out and they are trimmed they will have an attractive color again. The dead leaves will drop eventually. Bamboos are a whitish brown. I shall have them cut back somewhat to make them thicker.

February 9. The weather is again spring-like, and I had plants cut back and propped to get rid of the effects of last month's ice. Euonymus plantings were given a thorough spraying with miscible oil because young scales hatch in early spring. I saw to it that the under-leaves and stems were drenched. These have to be watched for the whitish substance and dying twigs that indicate scale. Sometimes a soap spray is effective. If the insects are not killed, a nicotine-sulphate and soap solution can be used during summer to keep the scale from becoming established.

February 10. Yesterday I worked as hard as the two hired men and would have been at it again today to limber up if it had not rained last night. We are enjoying the cardinals. The bright scarlet ones are males; the females have a gray over-dress. I like especially their song note that sounds like *Sugar babe!*

February 13. Today we did some pruning and cleaning up in the orchard that is usually done in January. Ice and snow prevented this year. Suckers were trimmed off, tops cut back and the centers left open for air to enter. The trees were sprayed with lime-sulphur.

February 16. Conditions are just right for pruning polyantha, hybrid tea and hybrid perpetual roses. Sometimes I can do the job the last of January. I took out weak growth and left only strong canes. On the hybrid teas I left three or four canes and cut them to about the fourth bud, the top one being an outside one. The cuts

179

were made about 10 inches from the ground, the polyanthas a little lower and the hybrid perpetuals somewhat higher. The cutting was done carefully so as to leave no ragged edges. The bushes were then sprayed with lime-sulphur; the solution was allowed to go down the canes and onto the soil to prevent canker. In another week I will spray with Bordeaux mixture.

February 17. I cut budding branches of winter jasmine, forsythia and flowering quince to force open in the house. A young niece was walking in the garden with me. When she saw me holding brown twigs of flowering quince, she began to pick up little broken branches that the wind had blown from oak trees, and said, "Aunt Mannie, I have some sticks for you, too." In order to have my "sticks" open quickly in water, I place the stems in hot water a half minute, then in deep cool water. Winter jasmine flowers open full in two days. The carrots and beets that I recently cut off enough to lay flat in bowls of water now have tender growing tops. They make unusual foliage arrangements.

February 21. Today our vitex was cut back a little; some branches were taken out to let others develop. Crape-myrtles were pruned to admit air and light; these can be trimmed to either tree or shrub form. Buddleias were cut severely and altheas lightly. All dead or weak branches were removed. These flower in summer and autumn.

In the afternoon I sowed seed in the hotbeds. Many seeds germinate in a short time in the warm soil under glass. It is interesting to see them grow and also helpful to have plenty of plants at such little cost.

February 28. On this windy day, partly cloudy, partly fair, flowers are opening. Violets are making a fine display; single white ones, like Snow Queen, are especially effective. White flowers are favorites with me, for they bring out bright colors and are such good mixers. I heard a friend say she didn't want white flowers in her garden, because they were too funereal. But bright flowers are used for funerals, too!

MARCH

Ah, passing few are they who speak
Wild stormy month! in praise of thee;
Yet, though thy winds are loud and bleak,
Thou art a welcome month to me.
—*Bryant*

March 1. The month is coming in quiet but cold. In March one always feels that spring has arrived, even when ice still lingers. I

Yellow seems, above all colors, to typify the springtime,
and one of the best rich yellows is furnished by forsythia.
Allowed to grow as it likes, it becomes very graceful.

Through a great part of the South are marvelous azalea gardens in a woodland setting.

received a present by mail—a beautiful garden scrapbook. All garden-minded people ought to have one. Mine has a wooden hinged back, and additional leaves can be inserted.

March 3. We walked around, this windy day, to see what damage three cold nights had done to advanced vegetation. Open flowers on Chinese magnolia, spirea and flowering quince are brown but the buds are not hurt. We saw many birds; their early spring activity is of great value, for an insect destroyed now is worth many later. The back-yard was alive with blackbirds and robins, which found the china-berry trees. This tree becomes troublesome as it spreads from roots, but it furnishes quick shade.

March 7. In the garden I observed trailing periwinkle (*Vinca minor*) with its blue flowers and evergreen foliage under big oaks, and in another place the white-flowering periwinkle; and there are blue, pink and white hyacinths. In a rock garden are the blue flowers and heart-shaped leaves of *Brunnera macrophylla* (*Anchusa myosotidiflora*) and the white of arabis. Blue and pink scillas bloom nearby. Chinese magnolia, flowering peach, flowering almond and *Phlox subulata* unfold various shades of pink. Borders of snowflakes (Leucojum) and Sir Watkin and Phoenix narcissi are at their height of bloom.

While I planned what to plant in spring in order to have a variety of harmonious colors in summer and autumn, I noticed cedar waxwings feasting on the berries of eleagnus. Perched close together on a limb, birds will pass fruit that they have just picked to their next companion; sometimes it is passed back along the line before any bird tastes it.

March 8. A dreary, drizzling day but birds are warbling, particularly the mockingbirds. Some Northerners came into our garden, and one of them said she could understand why there is so much yellow bloom now—it is Mother Earth's way of being bright and cheerful in inclement weather. They wanted to know if it was usual for the mockingbird to sing melodiously at this time. I told them he likes especially to sing on damp mornings. Every year a mockingbird nests in a thorny hardy orange bush (*Citrus trifoliata*) near the back porch. Children say he knows me to be a friend and flies from tree to tree in the neighborhood of where I am at work.

March 9. Just such a day, warm and cloudy, as to coax the garden-minded to test their strength. Even those who garden early and give up when hot weather comes are out now with hoe and rake. I was glad to read in the daily that one can get labor by calling the Garden Center.

Bonemeal for water-lilies was placed in the pool; this will not harm the fish. A friend told me she places a good-sized tin pipe in the lily tubs and puts fertilizer through the pipe. The lilies get food from the earth in the tubs.

As the leaf buds of roses have opened, I dusted with Massey dust to prevent trouble. I apply it low so that the powder will blow up on the underside of the leaves and fall on the ground, too. I did this late in the afternoon and will dust again in ten days.

March 12. It is damp and cloudy today; thinking of beauty for summer and autumn, I divided and set out many plants. The soil had been enriched and made ready, and the roots were not out of the ground long. The clumps of Michaelmas daisies and feverfew were separated with a knife before replanting, but I tore apart phlox and *Salvia farinacea* to the size wanted. After dividing chrysanthemums to single shoots, I planted them in a sunny location away from other plants. Also I planted some bulbs that were given me with dead flowers and foliage still clinging to them; I did not cut the foliage.

Tender green is showing on the fig bushes; corn planted "two days before the full of the moon" in February is up; and bleeding-heart, peonies and regal lilies are above ground.

March 15. We fertilized roses and had the winter mulch turned under. It is best not to wait too late to uncover them. If new growth has time to harden it will not be hurt by a late cold spell, but if uncovered too early the wind and sun may do damage.

A friend sent us a sack of bonemeal "to use on grass." We mixed it with wood ashes, half and half, and broadcast it on part of the lawn. Grass must have phosphorus and potash, though in smaller quantities than nitrogen. The vegetable as well as animal kingdom needs a well-balanced diet. Every lawn needs special care in spring; 10-6-4 will give good results if scattered thinly and watered in. If a vigorous turf is maintained by fertilizing and frequent mowing, weeds will be kept down. However, the lawn of one of our neighbors is quite attractive—a sheet of dainty little bluets (*Houstonia cærulea*).

The vegetable garden was plowed and an application of liquid manure was put around the sweet peas. We grow these flowers in rows among the vegetables. The roots of sweet peas demand moisture; an irrigation trench parallel with the row is a help.

March 18. The winds of yesterday dried the ground enough to allow cultivating in the perennial garden to conserve moisture, make soil mellow and kill small weeds.

A rock garden and rock-edged pool were started in the back yard.

The new pool will give us a place for baby fish. Yesterday morning when the fish were spawning in the old pool we placed cedar branches in the lily tubs; about two hours later we took the branches out covered with little jelly-like substances, the fish eggs. These branches were placed in a tub of water on the screened back porch. The old fish eat not only the eggs but also the baby fish. We have a lip on our present pool with a wire drop, which takes care of some baby fish, but we have been losing more than half our "crop."

Late in the afternoon I powdered the roses with Massey dust for the second time this month.

March 19. I was out early, for the ground is in good condition. Later I went in for breakfast, and when I got back to the garden I found that the hired man had dug up Siberian and Japanese irises. He thought the tops were wild onions and had cut up roots and all!

I planted Golden Gleam and Scarlet Gleam nasturtium seed. These plants are semi-dwarf, with short runners and double, sweet-scented flowers. They should be in a sunny place in only fairly rich soil. If given too much water or food, they will have luxuriant foliage but not many flowers.

All that I want to do now is to watch the men lay each rock for the naturalistic pool!

March 20. The wisteria vines are so full of bloom that they look like grayish lavender veils extending from tree to tree. Double jasmine and kerria lend a golden touch; pansies, English daisies and baby blue-eyes (Nemophila) are borders of color; and *Spiræa cantoniensis* (*Reevesiana*), Osage-orange, and pearl-bush (Exochorda) make white accents. Flowering plum (*Prunus Pissardii*) is a bronze glory with pink flowers and crimson leaves; later the foliage will be deep maroon. Double crab-apples are showy, and red maples with flaming crimson and scarlet flowers create a delightful picture. This is one of the prettiest times in the garden.

March 21. It was pleasant to ramble in the woods and see "heart leaves with pitchers" and birds-foot violets. Hawthorns and woodbines are in full bloom, and dogwoods are creamy colored. In another week they will be white. The woods and hillsides are responding to spring. We pulled up roots of yellow jessamine where they were quite thick in the soft leaf mold. A good time to plant this is while the flowers are still on the stems.

March 24. This dewy morning everything looked lovely. I sowed annual seeds—zinnias, spider-flower (Cleome) and candytuft. Annuals can make the vacancies decorative where bulbs and other perennials die down. In the vegetable garden I sowed seed of beans, lima beans, squash, cucumbers and okra. The ground is warm and apples are blossoming, which is the right time, "they say," to sow these warm-weather things.

The rock-bordered pool was completed today. I am having work done on a rock garden, placing the rocks carefully so they will look natural as well as make pockets to hold the soil and moisture. Water is to gush from the side of the rock garden, making a stream that flows down to the pool. To have the bed of the stream look natural, I sprinkled sand and pebbles on the concrete run while it was soft, and pressed them into the hardening cement.

March 27. With garden club members I went to a city in Georgia and saw six beautiful gardens. We started from the Garden Center where we noticed a yellow-flowered *Magnolia cordata* in bloom.

In several gardens climbing roses were flowering; Spanish Beauty (Mme. Grégoire Staechelin) gave a charming effect with pearl-pink, fragrant bloom. There was an approach to a winding azalea-bordered path under pine trees, through one bulb garden. In another garden the family coat of arms was carried out in pansies and moss phlox; and hybrid tea roses were in full bloom on big bushes. The gardener said he had not cut the roses back, for the warm weather had made them put out growth so quickly. Something that appealed to me was a semi-circle of old-fashioned pink roses, Old Blush China, edging a green turf sitting room and facing a tea house and wide border of white "flags." In one garden our attention was called to quaint cypress seats, with handles and rollers, that could be pushed about. We saw examples of the beauty of formal landscaping as well as informal gardens, and some were designed by the owners.

ANOTHER MARCH

God made the flowers to beautify
The earth, and cheer man's careful mood;
And he is happiest who has power
To gather wisdom from a flower,
And wake his heart in every hour
To pleasant gratitude.
—*Wordsworth*

March 1. A spring-like day. It doesn't look as if vegetation was much injured by the recent freezes. On a day like this, one is urged to active work. I am raking and digging but have to be careful not to harm plants that have not shown their tops yet. Hired help has to be cautioned, for there is much loss of plants with early digging.

184

I found the top dead in a cedar. This might have been caused by a beetle. After cutting out the dead portion, I treated with arsenic of lead, and tied a branch to a stake that was fastened to the trunk, to form a new leader.

March 7. We (I mean first my husband, then other helpers in the garden) set out azaleas that came this morning, in a partly shaded place protected from afternoon sun and already prepared with well-decayed leaf mold. The plants were burlapped; we cut the strings so that the burlap could lie back and leave no open spaces under the ball when watered. We could see the colors in the buds, which was a help in placing the bushes. The catalogs tell how tall the varieties will grow, and that helps, too.

Our plants of *Rosa Hugonis* have not done well. We think it is because of too rich soil; consequently, we are putting them in a more exposed place in poorer soil. They do not need as rich a soil as do hybrid teas.

March 10. Cultivation was done in the vegetable garden and corn was planted. From the orchard comes the perfume of plum blossoms; peach trees are laden with pink or white bloom. Pussy willow and silver poplars are putting out catkins.

Sifted hardwood ashes were scattered about the rose bushes, and the soil was lightly loosened between them with a spading fork. They must not be allowed to get tender under the slight mulch. I was careful not to let the labels get misplaced.

I was looking at the peonies well above ground when two friends walked through the garden. The man said he used to think men "sissies" when they worked with flowers but that he had changed his mind since acquiring a home and garden of his own. Later, Sidney and I sauntered about with an eye to future plantings and talked of how greedy a garden is, for it takes what we've saved to buy something else; so instead of going places, we look around and see our "trip" growing.

March 17. Though it's a real March day with drying winds, we're cultivating the borders of pansies, English daisies and Siberian wallflowers. These are necessities for colorful spring borders.

The garden changes constantly; right now blooms of bulbs are dominant. There was the delicious fragrance of narcissi and hyacinths over the place as I gave away bamboo, ivy, crape-myrtle, althea, chrysanthemum and other plants. One cannot afford to be stingy; plants do better when divided. Whenever one gets enough plants, he should share the surplus with others. Nature sets the example by scattering seed from one garden to another. Numerous garden clubs are undertaking projects where plant donations can be used.

While in the garden I took note that drying winds are hard on tender roses. And this is a difficult month for evergreens on account of the hot sun.

March 21. I noticed that the buds of pearl-bush (Exochorda) look like waxy pearls. This shrub grows best in a sunny place in well-drained soil. Redbud trees (Cercis) have pinkish lavender flowers clinging to the leafless branches along with a few red buds that have not opened. The flowers are deceptive, following the reddish buds. The white variety is very attractive, too.

I keep watch over our lupines. So far we have not lost a plant. The seeds were sown in August, and the plants were put in the garden in November.

March 24. Dead branches were taken out of some shrubs. One old spirea had termites in its roots. The soil was piled high around the branches; new roots had formed and the old ones had rotted. We had to take up the whole bush, divide it, go through it to select clean roots, and plant it elsewhere.

I can see now where certain colors are needed to bring out others. In every direction I look spring is responding: ferns and wild plants are peeping from the mold; regal lilies are showing their tops; and moss phlox and basket-of-gold alyssum make bright spots.

March 26. With friends I motored to another city to a daffodil show. It was a lovely as well as an educational sight. There were many kinds of narcissi—trumpets of different lengths, doubles, and cluster-flowered. We decided we must plant more of them.

Invited into a charming garden, we saw different colors of flowering quince—white, pale pink, orange-flame and bright red. Several large flowering peach trees were laden with double white and others with rose-colored blossoms. What a pity that flowering peaches are so short-lived! There were enchanting low borders of blue, pink and white moss pinks (dwarf phlox). Among the most showy mats of these phlox were G. F. Wilson, lavender-blue, and Brilliant and Vivid, a bright rosy pink and a warm rosy salmon. In shade under a pergola we saw a decorative wide border of aspidistra grown tall. I understand this plant harbors no pests, requires no special soil, withstands heat, cold, drought, rough usage and needs little light.

March 27. Today the gardener cleaned up in the vegetable garden and burned stalks that might harbor disease. Since the ground works easily, he plowed and worked fertilizer into the rows where the roots will get it. We sowed beans and other vegetable seeds.

Someone telephoned to ask if I could tell her why her bulbs did not come up the second year. She said she fertilized them after they bloomed last year, but they never came up again. Perhaps her bulbs decayed from poor drainage and standing water. Petunias had been planted over them and kept watered all summer; evidently the bulbs must have rotted. We plant annuals that are not deep rooting over ours, and the little watering necessary for them does not seem to harm the bulbs. Or moles may be present in her garden, providing runways for the rodents that do the damage.

March 31. Apples are beginning to blossom and early tulips are making a display. We do not take up our tulip bulbs every year. We cut the old blooms as they fade so that the bulbs do not become exhausted from ripening seed pods.

It is pleasant out-of-doors, and in the face of so many things to do one feels a little bewildered. This spring gardening exercise makes muscles pull. The remedy is to go at it again!

We note on this last day of the month that wisterias and dogwoods are only in bud. It will be at least two weeks before they bloom. Some years they are at their height at this time, with wisteria a little ahead of dogwood. In 1948, in the Carolinas, Florida, Georgia, Maryland, West Virginia and Virginia a fungus was found to be attacking dogwood, splotching and withering the blooms. This can be controlled by spraying the trees with Bordeaux mixture just before they bloom; but who is going to spray the wild trees? It is recommended that later in the season a spray of equal parts of Fermate and Deenate be used weekly. The spot fungus damages dogwood stems, leaves, flowers and fruits.

SECOND QUARTER

APRIL

Earth green with spring and fresh with dew
And bright with morn, before me stood;
And airs just wakened softly blew
On the young blossoms of the wood.
—*Bryant*

April 1. We enjoy walking through the garden at this season. The borders of iris, *Spiræa Vanhouttei* and *S. cantoniensis* (*Reevesiana*), with wisterias climbing over the pergola make a pleasing picture.

Much depends on the garden work done this month. I had the perennial beds cultivated. I am trying to keep our garden soil in good condition. Three necessary chemicals are nitrogen, phosphoric acid and potash. It is best to get these in a balanced, prepared plant food and use as mixed.

To keep the garden always in bloom, we plant annuals; today I sowed petunia and zinnia seeds. Often petunias act like perennials here. Portulaca seeds were raked between flagstones in some of the walks; it likes sandy soil and full sun, and stands dry weather.

April 5. I'm planting the new rock garden today. We want plenty of colors, with white to harmonize them. I used pink *Saponaria ocymoides*, yellow *Achillea tomentosa* and white arabis. Snow-in-summer (*Cerastium tomentosum*), with its silvery foliage and white flowers, will be lovely between the rocks.

To grow on the cedar pergola, I planted moonvine for fragrance in the evening and Heavenly Blue morning-glory for day bloom.

In the afternoon we went to the woods to get moss for the crevices of the rocks around the pool. Afterward we set out plants in the woodsy garden—trillium, wild columbine, *Phlox divaricata* and wild geranium.

April 7. After April showers it is nice to be out in the garden again. I thinned false dragonhead (Physostegia) and rudbeckia. We are still fighting chickweed and Bermuda grass, which persists in getting among the flowers, and wisteria, which runs and roots where not wanted. Wisteria thrives in an acid soil. Feeding with superphosphate exclusively for a time may induce bloom.

April 9. When I looked out this morning I saw Ajax, the peacock, preening before the gazing globe. Since all nature is putting on a show, I couldn't blame him for wanting to look his best. Flowers seemed to be nodding gaily around him while he pranced on the pansies and English daisies. The birds were singing sweetly; many have nests in the box trees and euonymus bushes.

Of course, we must take the bad with the good. Moles are in our garden. To catch a skunk that has been eating the eggs of setting hens, we put out a poisoned egg but caught a goose instead. Now the lonesome gander follows Uncle Jake, our hired man, all around.

April 11. My garden club went on a pilgrimage today. We saw many beautiful gardens and got new ideas and fresh inspiration. One large garden was enchanting with box-bordered walks and old-time summer houses. In another, azaleas and lovely azure-blue columbines were flowering. Scillas, blue and white, and yellow

Tall bearded iris is easy to grow and not subject to disease.
Iris is the state flower of Tennessee. (See page 127.)

Like forsythia, spirea does best when left unpruned, so that the branches may form long arches. Pictured is *Spiræa cantoniensis*, with double white flowers in early spring on a compact plant.

primroses were in an attractive setting; and there was a broad expanse of valley lilies. Pink dogwoods and weigelas shaded into each other with a footing of pink and white tulips. Tall irises were beginning to bloom, and dark red tulips made a dashing display. Climbing roses were a background and the beautifully kept green lawn a foreground for the shrubs and flowers.

April 16. After heavy rain and hail last night, beaten leaves and branches are around everywhere. I had to get them cleaned up, for a garden club asked to see our garden in the morning. Inspection makes one feel that nothing looks right. It is very different from having understanding friends on informal visits. At any rate, this rambling garden has grown the plants that will be presented to each of the club members—chrysanthemums, tiger lilies and day-lilies (Hemerocallis).

April 17. The tub of water on the screened back porch is alive with baby fish this morning! In the middle of March we placed in this tub evergreen branches covered with fish eggs that we had taken from the pool. In two weeks our new pool will have been filled and drained enough to put them in it.

The top-dressing put on the lawn last month has taken effect and the grass is a rich green. It is a continuous job to keep it mowed. We are trimming new growth on arborvitæs but not cutting back too much. We are also pruning some shrubs to keep them in bounds. Tomorrow the strawberry bed must be cultivated and mulched with pine straw.

April 20. From our woods we got sweet shrub (Calycanthus) plants where they were growing very thick. It is late to transplant them, but we took a ball of earth with the roots. Often wild things are overlooked in catalogs. A tall blue phlox that came from the woods is blooming beautifully in our wild garden. This is a perennial with lighter blue and smaller blooms than *Phlox divaricata*. (I think this must be a blue variety of *Phlox pilosa*.) *P. divaricata* likes shade and moisture; *P. subulata* will stand drought and does well in sunny spots among rocks, while tall summer perennial phloxes like a deep rich soil and lots of moisture. The annual phloxes, varieties of *P. Drummondii*, want a sunny, warm location and preferably sandy soil.

April 24. I went on a prilgrimage to visit iris gardens. Some of the newer irises were wonderful, but one can have beauty without the expensive varieties. The best time to select irises is when they are blooming, for not only the color but the height, kind of stem and quality of foliage may then be observed. There are low-growing, intermediate and tall bearded irises. Some bloom in early spring and others in May. There are also some that flower in late summer and autumn. The individual blooms live from three to six days; the buds will open in water.

April 29. I was frightened this morning when I went into a guest room to look out at the sweet peas. Something flew in my face; a chimney swift had come down the chimney.

Gaillardias are blooming and will continue to do so if the flowers are kept cut. Polyantha roses are ideal for borders; they and the large-flowering floribunda roses look attractive in front of shrubbery for color accent. They bloom throughout the season.

Clearing up fallen "tassels" of trees reminds me of how we raked and raked leaves in the fall. The afternoon was cool and windy, and the fire felt good in our outdoor fireplace.

ANOTHER APRIL
Gentle Spring! in sunshine clad,
Well dost thou thy power display!
—*Longfellow*

April 1. A real April Fool day, for it is cool and sunny this afternoon, after warm winds, dark clouds, lightning, thunder and hail this morning. I rushed out as soon as it was calm to see whether any harm had been done. A few blooms and a little foliage had been beaten off, but otherwise there was no damage. Scotch broom, crab-apples, spireas, Siberian wallflowers, calendulas, basket-of-gold alyssum, candytuft and violas are making the landscape colorful.

Looking toward the grove, I am reminded of autumn coloring, for there is tender brown and reddish new growth with the green.

April 4. I pinched off some weak shoots and small side buds on peonies to throw strength into the remaining shoots and buds. This makes larger show blooms. I sometimes see ants on peony buds; they are feeding on a sticky secretion and do not hurt the buds. However, they could carry disease spores.

Today we began the job of tying down foliage of bulbs that have bloomed, to make it less conspicuous and to give nearby plants more room. This is best done after the flowers have died and the tips of leaves are yellowing. I bend them down and use two or three of the leaves to tie the rest of the clump. In a long border I plait the foliage on the ground and tie it down with several leaves. Bulb foliage must not be removed until completely mature and yellowed; otherwise bloom is lost for several years.

I noticed the hemerocallis Apricot beginning to bloom; the apricot-orange flowers are borne on good stems. Although one of the oldest early-blooming hybrids, this is a favorite of ours. The double Queen Anne's jonquils of our grandmother's time have extremely fragrant, inch-across flowers. The foliage is round and small, and I have to caution helpers not to pull it up for wild onion.

It's such grand weather that I see neighbors out with hoes and spades, too. I heard the cook of one ask if they were to have the spinach without boiled eggs sliced over it. The charming lady was so busy in her garden that she had forgotten to order groceries! Wasn't I glad I could send her some new-laid eggs?

April 5. Atamasco lilies are flowering in clumps. These are native wood lilies of the amaryllis family, which thrive in leaf mold and partial shade. I note that the flowers of empress trees (Paulownia) are the same color as lilacs and are pleasing neighbors of yellow kerrias. While looking up at the interesting, sweet-smelling paulownia blooms, I stepped on some lemon lilies and broke the buds that would have been pretty next to lavender honesty (Lunaria).

April 7. It is rather cold, but we're glad for the freshness of the garden after last night's light showers. There was just enough moisture to put the ground in good shape for planting. We cultivated the soil about established plants.

We love our garden; we watch all the plants and enjoy particularly the ones we rooted from cuttings or grew from seed. But when visitors come, we feel that we haven't anything special to show them. Do other gardeners have this experience?

April 9. Darwin and cottage tulips are coming into their own. If we could have only two varieties, our family would vote for the brilliant darwin, City of Haarlem and the showy cottage, Dido. Personally, I like delicate tints.

Baby blue-eyes (*Nemophila Menziesii* (*insignis*)) are making stretches of blue; we also have early bearded irises, as well as the scented clusters of Maiden's Blush rose. This dear old rose seems to thrive anywhere. French lilacs are displaying their beauty, and the blue flower spikes of camassias blend with the blue of flax and *Phlox divaricata*.

Yesterday a true gardener was here. She jotted down notes in a little book and talked about sprays. She was interested in foliage, height of plants, etc., as well as flowers. I just know that the soil in her garden is always well prepared at the proper time for planting, and that her plants get all the water and attention they need.

April 14. A steady task now is to keep wilted blooms removed

191

from pansies, English daisies, columbines and other things, in order that the plants will continue to flower and not become exhausted from forming seed. We put out more hemerocallis; we want more and more of these easily grown perennials. With the hybrids we can have a succession of bloom from early spring to autumn. They need no protection; they stand drought and heat; they flower in partial shade or sun and are free from insects. I noticed beauty-bushes (Kolkwitzia) beginning to show creamy pink flowers with a delicate perfume. In the wild garden various ferns are unrolling their fronds.

Hardy carnation plants were set out 18 inches apart in a place that has good drainage. To make them bushy, I will pinch off the tips when they are 6 inches high. These are hybrids of the hardy old-fashioned pinks and the old Malmaison carnations.

April 23. The Crape Myrtle Garden Club visited our garden today. They admired the biennial honesty (Lunaria), which now has flat green "dollar" seed pods along with the stock-like flowers. They were particularly interested in the time to plant perennial seed. It is well to do it now, especially in outdoor beds, for they will come up and grow quickly in moist soil. June or later is much drier. If planted now, perennials can be transplanted in July. Seeds sown in summer should be about twice as deep as in early spring; the seedlings can be transplanted in the fall.

April 24. It was my privilege to attend an iris show in a city a hundred miles away. One can learn a great deal at flower shows. At this one, a tall green background, rock gardens and a field of iris in the middle of the building made an effective setting. Among the tall bearded irises that made a fine showing (all of them tested and tried older varieties) were Copper Luster, definitely copper in tone; Sierra Blue and Missouri, medium blue (these three were Dykes Medal winners); Cyrus the Great, a distinctive purplish blue self; China Maid, a pink blend; and Chosen, yellow. Three newer Dykes Medal winners were also outstanding: magnificent blue Great Lakes, large wine-red Elmohr and blended Prairie Sunset.

While in that city I visited several gardens. In one I was fascinated with the colors of large-flowered clematis—shades of blue, purple, reddish and pale tints. I was told that the individual flowers will last over a week. The curious seed pods as well as the blooms are attractive in arrangements. Clematis likes moist, rich deep loam, lime and rather deep planting. The crowns should be well below the surface of the soil.

192

Hyperion is a splendid hemerocallis with huge, fragrant flowers. These perennials are easy to grow for several reasons—easy, too, to grow with other things.

The rose has a distinguished history, and when one sees a garden of modern varieties one cannot help feeling that hybridizers are adding to the prestige it enjoys. (See page 122.)

April 27. My husband races me to the rose garden and gets there before I do every morning. I must loiter to see what irises have opened since yesterday. The tall bearded ones are worthy of notice.

Peonies are beginning to open, but old-fashioned pinks steal the show. The early hemerocallis Estmere, Gold Dust, Sovereign and dwarf lemon-yellow Gracilis are effective. Visitors always notice the odd three-petaled blue and lavender flowers of spiderwort (*Tradescantia virginiana*). Each bloom lasts only a day.

April 29. We transplanted cabbage, taking care not to cover their crowns. Tomato plants were set deep enough to make sure of a good root system, which will enable them to stand drought better.

Various plants were taken from the frames and put out in their permanent locations. These were healthy looking, for the glass has been raised each day, and lately all day.

I picked off and burned some blackspotted leaves found on rose bushes. The weather has a great deal to do with diseases and pests of roses, but I will continue to use Massey dust every ten days, or a good spray. Certain rose varieties are more susceptible to blackspot than others, but in general, strong plants can best resist trouble. Feeding with potash is helpful in controlling blackspot; use a tablespoonful per plant twice a year.

MAY

Now the bright morning star, day's harbinger,
Comes dancing from the east, and leads with her
The flowery May, who from her green lap throws
The yellow Cowslip and the pale Primrose.
—*Milton*

May 1. A glorious time of year, with the sun getting warmer and breezes blowing through the garden! Boxwood cuttings put out in November have tender shoots. They received winter moisture but not too hot sunshine. Some gladiolus corms were planted. They like good sandy loam and full sunshine, but a little afternoon shade is good for them here. Planting them 5 or 6 inches deep prevents the stalks from being blown over and lessens the need for staking.

May 2. We were out early to see what new roses had opened. I cut off withered flowers and removed dead leaves and weak stems. We want our plants to bloom a long time, and it takes more strength to produce seed than flowers. Dead flower heads on columbines were pinched off for the same reason. Sulphur and lime were put around tall perennial phloxes that have bottom leaves turning yellow.

193

I noticed that oxalis borders, white and pink, and blue linum are masses of bloom; both have flowers that close in the afternoon. Veronica, *Brunnera macrophylla* (*Anchusa myosotidiflora*) and anchusa Dropmore are sending out spikes of blue. There is yellow supplied by calendulas, wallflowers, hemerocallis, columbines, snapdragons, gaillardias, primroses and irises; and rose-pink by verbena, painted daisies, pinks and peonies.

May 3. The garden clubs of this city had a flower show today. The weather was fine, but hard rains last night mangled many flowers. However, most of those exhibited had been cut yesterday and the stems placed in deep water. The decorating committee created a background for the display that was lovely even before the flowers were placed. But after every available nook and cranny had been filled with beautiful specimen blooms and arrangements, the scene was exquisite. Garden clubs and flower shows certainly stimulate interest in gardening.

May 4. Noticing aphids on rose buds, I sprayed with nicotine sulphate. I am feeding roses once a week with liquid manure.

Several days ago we decided to make frog-stool seats to have near the naturalistic pool in our back yard. Using stove-pipes and old dish pans for forms, we poured the concrete. Today we removed the forms, inserted the "stems" in the ground and cemented the tops upside down upon them.

May 5. Uncle Jake, the hired man, found twin baby deer in the deer enclosure this morning. We have South American deer. They are more taupe in color than our native kind. These little fellows are covered with spots and are quite spindle-legged.

I motored with others to a city where we judged a flower show. The theme was "Gardens of Yesterday, Today and Tomorrow." I helped in the judging of annuals and perennials. One person entered forty-one different perennials, labeled and well grown.

I had tea with a college friend. The thing I admired most in her lovely garden was a large ornamental maidenhair-tree (*Ginkgo biloba*), with tropical-looking, ferny foliage.

May 7. These days a chorus of birds can be heard at dawn. Foxgloves are sending up tall spikes of bloom, and moss roses have attractive crested buds. Crested Moss is an old favorite; Golden Moss, of recent origin, has pinkish buds, which open yellow.

Bees are busy, and bright butterflies are active. We pull up inferior plants when they begin to bloom, lest bees carry the pollen to better varieties.

May 10. We moved some painted daisies, taking care to get soil with the roots. The open flowers were cut off but not the foliage. I will keep the plants watered.

Some of the earliest-blooming shrubs are about to get out of bounds, and we started pruning them. We remove all dead or diseased wood and some of the oldest stems. The pruning is done by shortening branches and not by shearing to formal shape or by cutting the tops flat. We avoid leaving stubs by cutting just above an eye. Many shrubs do well in partial shade. Most failures under trees are caused by lack of food and water. If the branches of trees are high enough for the sunlight to enter, we find many plants will flourish underneath.

From the vegetable garden we are having carrots, onions, turnip greens and Irish potatoes. Today we set out plants of Bell pepper and eggplant and began the pruning of tomatoes.

May 12. I wish choice plants had the persistence of weeds! Good soil makes them both grow. We had to pull out weeds and grass from between flagstones where portulaca is coming up. Many birds are enjoying the mulberries. Brown thrashers have their whole families on the ground. Our cow got out and in just a bite or two took the lily buds for which we had been waiting a year.

May 13. Climbing roses are making arbors and fences glow. As I was cutting some Dr. W. Van Fleet roses, which arrange beautifully, I noticed young catbirds in a nest in the arbor. Birds like thorny places for protection.

Old-fashioned roses are sending their fragrance through shrub borders, and mock-oranges (Philadelphus) are blooming. Rose acacias are conspicuous among the shrubbery, with clusters of flowers that look like rose-colored wisteria. The leaves resemble the locust. These increase rapidly by suckers and thrive even in poor soil or dry, sandy spots.

May 14. It rained in the night, and newly set plants are looking fine. The painted daisies put out the other day in large clumps have not wilted. The ground is not too wet, and one wants to plant bare spots while it is cloudy, with occasional showers. We find there are many plants that will bloom in semi-shade, such as snapdragons and forget-me-nots.

My husband and I like to view the garden as others see it. We get discouraged at times, but the joys outnumber the disappointments. Today, for instance, just to gaze at the blue-eyed African daisies and gaillardias made us think how worthwhile our efforts are.

195

The hollyhocks standing next to hedges and fences lend such an old-fashioned air, and the delphiniums are very pretty. Powdered lime and coal ashes kept slugs away from them.

In the vegetable garden we commented on the neat appearance of the herb corner. The bluish lavender flower spikes of sage (one clump was pink) and yellow clusters of rue with its grayish feathery foliage, makes a picture as pretty as any flower combination.

May 18. I wish I could be in three places at the same time. I had hired two extra men for garden work today. I told one to rake dead foliage from daffodils in front of the lilies. He took so long about it that I investigated and found he had taken up bulbs in another place where the foliage was still green. The other man fertilized ivy with rich loam, and I showed him how to pull up honeysuckle from near the ivy. When I went to see how he was doing his task, I found he had dug up all the ivy and left the honeysuckle! Maybe I don't know how to instruct helpers, so I let them go.

I got busy cutting back the dead flower stems of pinks so that the foliage will make a grayish border. I also cut seed pods from *Phlox divaricata;* this does best in semi-shade. It cannot be cultivated to any extent, for the plants are very thick. If the flower stems of this phlox are left, the plants disappear after blooming and the beds fill with weeds. Some gardeners allow the seed to ripen; then small plants are to be found in various places around the garden. When this is done, the stems should be cut as soon as the seeds have ripened. One can get a good supply of plants with divisions.

May 26. It is nice to pick raspberries in the morning in all their dewy sweetness! It gets hot during the day and is so dry that we are trying to keep plants alive by soaking them with water. I am beginning to cut honesty stalks. Where the seed pods are ripe enough, I rub off the outside covering on each side of the septum and hang them in the basement to dry. Large buds of regal lilies were cut yesterday and placed in purple and red ink and other coloring matter. Today we have pink, red and lavender lilies!

I nipped off faded tulips to give strength to the bulbs. The falling and decaying of the petals can cause "fire," which makes the leaves spotted and twisted. Sweet alyssum and portulaca plants were set out near the tulips. The shade does the bulbs good and does not harm the roots. Annuals planted over bulbs should be shallow-rooted ones that will not disturb dormant bulbs.

We gathered the first beans and squash from the garden—always an event! Beetles are a menace to beans, for they perforate and

Wisteria is a very vigorous, long-lived vine that often
is a sort of inheritance from one generation to the next.
Its long clusters of bloom seem to "belong" in the South.

Pansies are a very good edging for spring bulb borders, as well as a charming flower to bring indoors. They need to be picked often, for if allowed to go to seed they will stop blooming.

kill the leaves. I sprinkle tobacco dust under the plants every few days to combat them.

May 30. We went in the evening to look at the mimosa leaves "asleep" and noticed scale on a blooming euonymus nearby. We have many euonymus bushes and will not run the risk of its spreading. It is late to use miscible oil, so in the morning I shall have the shrub sawed to the ground and all leaves raked up and burned. Then I will scatter lime-sulphur on the ground. Or a nicotine sulphate solution could now be used as a spray.

ANOTHER MAY
Profusion bright! and every flower assuming
A more than natural vividness of hue
From unaffected contrast with the gloom
Of sober cypress, and the darker foil of yew.
—*Wordsworth*

May 1. The ground is easily worked and we enjoy getting outdoors and digging lightly about plants. Winds have almost ruined the blooms of tall bearded irises, but they seem to blow many other flowers open. The Dutch iris season is about over here. Siberian irises are beginning to open their dainty blue, white and purple flowers on tall stems. These need a moist, acid soil, well drained.

Sage (*Salvia Greggii*) is a joy as it continues to send forth its carmine flower spikes throughout summer. This little shrub withstands drought well. It can be propagated by divisions, by layering or by cuttings and is quite effective in massed plantings. The rosy flowers and whitish foliage of mullein-pinks (*Lychnis Coronaria*) are giving a dash of color, and pittosporum is wafting orange-blossom fragrance over the garden.

May 4. Volunteer vetch (Vicia) makes a pretty picture on the vegetable garden fence. It is used extensively for a cover crop and for forage. We will have it cut down soon, before it throws too many seeds, and will plant pole lima beans there.

It is so cold that a fire is needed indoors and a coat outdoors. Motoring with friends to a neighboring city to visit a flower show, I was interested to see the attractive farmyards along the way. There were many old-fashioned roses. We saw terraces in fields white with daisies and admired the Scotch broom (Cytisus) at one old place. The owner told us that the first plants in this country were brought to Virginia. The life of the plant is only a few years, but there are always seedlings to replace the old ones.

Carillon, the orange and coral floribunda rose, was greatly admired at the show. It was beautiful, indeed, either half-open or in full bloom, with good foliage and stems. As many preparations as possible had been made for the exhibit the day before, such as getting tags ready and conditioning the flowers.

May 8. Last night's showers made the ground just right to receive petunias from the frames and the pot-grown plants that came by mail.

We are not bothered much with blackspot on our roses, for we have kept up the ten-day dusting with Massey dust, but stem canker is bothering us now. We prune back the infected stems and burn them, and we keep on the lookout for spots on the stems.

Our "field" of poppies is a delightful sight, with larkspurs scattered about it and honeysuckle growing on a fence as a background. We don't mind seeing "something going," such as bulb foliage dying, for there is much "coming on," including swan river daisies (Brachycome), painted daisies (Pyrethrum) and coreopsis. Our idea of a real garden is something going, something coming and something at its best all the time.

May 11. Verbenas, species iris, snapdragons and gerberas make the garden colorful. When I transplanted early hemerocallis that had finished blooming, I was surprised to find one azaleamum in full flower; others have many buds. These look and smell like chrysanthemums, and I wouldn't have cared if they had waited until a little later to bloom, when they would seem more in season.

May 14. It was cold and windy after an all-night rain, and I rambled about the flagstone walks to see if the garden could cheer me. Flowers like linum were beaten down, but Golden Salmon polyantha roses bordered by Yellow Master pansies, and the dainty white polyantha Katharina Zeimet with a footing of blue Lake of Thun pansies were pleasing to the eye. Violas, English daisies and saponarias are sending out myriads of flowers in the rock garden, and there are pockets of violet and white sweet alyssum (Violet Queen and Little Dorrit). At a distance I could see a mass of double cornflowers, and the hardy annual calendulas are showy tones of yellow. The calendula seeds were sown in August and the plants set out in November. The earliest blooms were killed by cold in February. Climbing roses are blooming—Jacotte, Paul's Scarlet, Spanish Beauty and others.

The Korean chrysanthemums, placed just behind some bulbs last month, are coming on nicely. Chrysanthemums will grow in good average soil. When the first shoots are about 8 inches high, we pinch them back and keep on with this treatment until early July. We have to plan ahead. Chrysanthemums must be planted when the tulips are about over, and tulip bulbs are planted in November when the chrysanthemums have finished.

May 18. With the soil so porous, grass and weeds are easily uprooted, and it is hard to tear oneself away from the garden even when it is time to eat!

I was at a friend's home in the late afternoon, and every time I admired something in her garden she would say, "Isn't it pretty!" She appreciates flowers because she works with them. Her delphinium spikes on vigorous plants are indeed beautiful. She said she set out the plants the last of August and dusted them with Bordeaux mixture from the time they were small. Noticeable in her garden are two tung-oil trees. She planted two seeds several years ago. It took about five months for them to germinate, and she almost pulled them up in mistake for cotton. The blossoms have an Oriental appearance; the centers are reddish brown and the petals creamy. She said there would be three to five nuts in each husk. Tung plantings have made a new industry for the deep South. Tung-nut production extends over the north of Florida, southern portions of Louisiana, Mississippi and Alabama, and southwest Georgia.

May 26. Every morning we are outdoors, doing the things necessary for the upkeep of the garden—cultivating shallowly so that feeding roots will not be disturbed, edging, snipping dead blooms, having grass mowed, spraying or dusting as needed, tying tomatoes higher on stakes, and watering newly set plants.

In the orchard are ripe currants and cherries, and peaches are just right for pies. There are strawberries to pick, and for lunch we are to have raspberries over ice cream. For a little trouble fruits give us big returns.

May 31. Pansies are still blooming; they started in January. Regal lilies are opening, and it is a pleasure to see the different hemerocallis unfolding. Old Fulva day-lilies are an attractive sight with a background of arborvitæ and a foreground of periwinkle. Near them are butterfly-weeds (*Asclepias tuberosa*) of the same orange shade as the lilies. In the orchard the flowers of pomegranates add a bright touch. We enjoy the fragrance of magnolias, the whistling of partridges and the cooing of doves. This is a delightful time of year, even if there is much to be done.

JUNE

And what is so rare as a day in June?
Then, if ever, come perfect days;
Then heaven tries the earth if it be in tune,
And over it softly her warm ear lays;
Whether we look, or whether we listen,
We hear life murmur, or see it glisten.

—*Lowell*

June 1. It is delightfully cool after rain, and I was able to get three field hands to help with pruning, mowing grass and edging. It was a hard job to oversee them; one of them was always leaving his task to do something I didn't want done.

Some shrubs need severe pruning after flowering, but they frighten me when they look so "exposed." They will be prettier for having some of the old branches cut out in the center and thinned where necessary. No flowers will be sacrificed if pruning is done now; time is needed to make new wood for flowers next spring. We were careful when trimming climbing euonymus (*Euonymus radicans vegetus*) to cut the runners but not the spent blooms, for we want berries.

June 2. I like to keep the withered blooms of day-lilies (Hemerocallis) picked. Well-established clumps have flowers open each day for weeks, though the individual flower lasts only one day. Anyone can grow hemerocallis. They may be transplanted at any season if set at the level at which they grew. They multiply fast, and many of the older ones are inexpensive. The hybrids are lovely, in a range of color from lemon and orange to maroon, and some are fragrant. Right now Mandarin is effective, with its pointed lemon-yellow petals with green at the center. Golden trumpets of Ophir are standing high. Two other fine sorts are the rounded, orange-colored Cressida and the large, soft yellow Modesty with reflexed petals.

We had several Chinese parasol (Sterculia) seedlings taken up with soil on the roots to give away. It is late to plant them, but if they are kept moist they should live. We like this tree, which has pointed-lobed leaves and creamy flowers in panicles, followed by long seed pods. The trunk and branches are an attractive, smooth green all winter.

I'm having some spring-flowering bulbs reset now that the foliage has browned. Some are being stored in a cool, dry place till fall.

June 4. I walked out on the upstairs portico this morning, and as I glanced toward the pool I saw a goose and seven goslings. Now, goslings look pretty on water, but not in our pool! They had pulled

200

the plants up out of tubs, muddied the water and played havoc in general.

I cultivated the soil around dahlias. Several additional shoots were coming up and I pinched them off at the ground line to throw all the strength into the main stalk. Dahlias like a mellow soil; heavy clay produces foliage but few blossoms.

It is a joy to be able to pick flowers with a free hand and to know there will be more of them. I cut them early in the morning, taking off dead blooms and spindly stems, too, in order to keep the plants flowering. The roses are cut with stems long enough to encourage growth low down on the plant. If cut just above an eye that points outward, the new growth will also develop outward. New wood grows after the old bloom is gone, and if the new growth is strong the rose will be finer.

June 7. We are having Carolina cherry-laurels (Laurocerasus) pruned; there is a distinct almond odor when they are cut.

In the vegetable garden I superintended the placing of stakes to support tomatoes. We prune them as they grow, letting one or two main branches develop. There are tender beans and beets in our garden, and just over the fence I could see ripe cherries. June apples are getting ripe, too.

June 8. I cut faded flowers from peonies so that the formation of seed will not weaken the plants. I did not take off the foliage, for the plants need leaves through the growing months for future development. Dead flowers were removed from hollyhocks; the smaller buds should now mature. Children like to make dolls from hollyhock blossoms, horns from petunias and chains from larkspurs.

There are as many as a dozen blooms on the regal lily stalks. The borders are bright with mixed colors of scabiosa, canterbury bells and annual candytuft. Portulaca is blooming in the walks between flagstones, while shasta daisies bring a suggestion of the open field. Rudbeckia, flowering now, belongs to the same family as the familiar wild black-eyed susan.

While riding, we noticed wildflowers by the wayside and in the woods; conspicuous among them were daisies and Queen Anne's lace. Though the latter is a pest, it is admired by flower lovers. By dipping the flower heads in dyes, I have them in various colors.

June 14. It is pleasant outdoors after last night's showers. The ground is damp and I pulled up weeds and cinnamon-vines where not wanted. This plant, with heart-shaped leaves and fragrant flowers, drops little "potatoes" that cause new vines to come up in various places. It is troublesome to have to keep after them, but in special locations we like this vine that dies down in winter.

I pinched back the tips of azaleas to make more growth for next year's bloom and took the tops off cosmos so they will be compact and bunchy. We are trying to keep hardy phlox and other plants in a healthy condition, for then they will not be bothered much by insects and diseases.

Hardy water-lilies are blooming (Gloriosa, Paul Heriot and Sunrise). The leaves are beautiful as well as the flowers, but we keep the lily pads pulled back enough for the reflection of clouds to be seen in the water.

I had a barrel hammock made to swing between trees in the back yard. Holes were bored in the ends of staves of a hogshead and ropes threaded through. I'm going to paint it green; with cushions this will make an ideal "garden day-bed."

June 19. Perennial seeds planted a week ago in the frames are coming up! Folks who do not raise their own plants do not know the pleasure they are missing. I put laths over the frames, and each side gets sunshine and air during the day.

Frogs croaking near a pool are enjoying the murky weather! Gladioli look fresh since the rain, and altheas are beginning to bloom. The showy blooms of the Rugosa rose are very effective; the shining green foliage is oddly wrinkled. This hardy rose may serve as hedge or filler. The flowers are followed by clusters of orange-red fruits. The flowers of snowberry (Symphoricarpos) are inconspicuous, but the combination of flowers and berries on the same twigs is noticeable. The milk-white fruits grow larger and swing gracefully on the plants far into the winter.

June 22. I cut dead lilac blooms to induce flowering next year and pinched out the tops of border chrysanthemums to about 8 inches to make the plants bushier and freer blooming.

We began to prune climbing roses today. We cut the old canes back to the ground of the varieties that send up new canes each year, such as ramblers. Heavy pruning of ramblers will keep down mildew, to which they are susceptible. Some new shoots were pruned on climbers that send out laterals on older canes, like Dr. W. Van Fleet, but only the decayed old canes were cut out.

June 27. Another warm, dry Sunday. The perennial phlox clumps (Daily Sketch, salmon-pink with carmine eye, and Border Queen, watermelon-pink) are especially pretty. Hummingbirds are thrusting their bills deep into the flowers of bee-balm (Monarda) in search of nectar and insects. Plants with whitish foliage are cool looking, such as dusty miller, santolina and artemisia.

While sitting near a pool, listening to the trickling of water and sniffing the fragrance of various flowers, we felt a little breeze, but we do need rain. The vegetable garden is beginning to burn, but cultivation and soaking with the hose is keeping it alive.

A DRY JUNE

The summer morn is bright and fresh, the birds
are darting by,
As if they loved to breast the breeze that sweeps
the cool clear sky. — *Bryant*

June 1. This grand morning I was in the garden at an early hour cutting off wilted flowers. I had cornflowers, larkspurs and stock pulled up. It is best to buy new seed of these each year if special colors are wanted, but I am letting the poppies and a few of the finest sweet william and foxgloves go to seed.

More gladiolus corms were set out. We will try to keep them well cultivated and to hill up the soil around the plants.

A visitor today made no comment other than to say, "Well, your garden was pretty when the early bulbs were flowering."

June 4. Annuals that are not deep rooting were set out over some bulbs where the foliage had been raked off.

For tidiness I cut back coreopsis; painted daisies, too, were trimmed back to the tufted rosette of foliage. We do not cut leaves of perennials like columbine and bleeding-heart until they turn yellow.

Chrysanthemums were given a complete plant food—a tablespoonful worked into the soil around each plant. We are careful not to let peonies get too dry. They need to grow vigorously for next year's bloom. A food with plenty of phosphoric acid may be put around them now; I used bonemeal. Leafhoppers were observed on phlox and tiger lilies. Regular applications of a contact insecticide, like nicotine sulphate, must be used to destroy them.

June 5. The rose beds were soaked with water this morning. I am glad to say we have very little blackspot. We are not dusting roses now, for when the temperature gets above 90 degrees dusting might burn the leaves. If I should discover signs of blackspot in hot weather, I would spray with copper sulphate. Sometimes the loss of rose bushes in winter is caused by blackspot in summer and autumn; through the dropping of leaves occasioned by this disease, the plants lose their vitality and are unable to resist cold weather.

Many shrubs need water and a mulch now, especially those set out in the spring, such as dogwoods, magnolias, azaleas and camellias. We are not feeding camellias and azaleas at this time, for fertilizer would cause them to put out new growth at the expense of bloom. The flower buds will be setting soon.

June 8. It is very dry, and we are trying to give plants enough water to keep them alive. Vegetables must be gathered often so that they will continue to bear. Various creeping plants, like *Ranunculus repens,* had to be thinned out. Many plants can get to be a nuisance from careless gardening. Faded stalks of bearded irises were cut, to admit light and air to the clumps.

I took note of the telling display of shasta daisies, rose-colored yarrow (Achillea) and blue linums. Hypericums make a partly shaded place bright with yellow blossoms; and the hardy perennial grass, *Uniola latifolia,* with ornamental green heads, lends interest to several borders. The panicles of this grass make nice dried bouquets for winter.

June 19. We need rain! Light showers are not enough to do vegetation much good. Such standbys as veronica, gaillardias, petunias, polyantha roses, blue salvia and verbenas are blooming and will continue if withered flowers are kept cut. A little food and cultivation helps them. We want more roots of verbena, so we pegged down and covered some stems with soil. If we keep them moist, it will not take them long to send out rootlets.

This cloudy day is ideal for preparing a place for new bearded irises that are to come from Oregon. They can be transplanted any time after they bloom and on into autumn; however, if the job is done too late, they do not get established in time to bloom the following spring. We had to remove other plants from an open-sun border to make room for the iris. The earth was dug out 18 inches or more, clinkers were put in for drainage, and the soil was thoroughly mixed with hardwood ashes and bonemeal.

June 21. Friends of ours have a wisteria tree in their garden, and we have been wanting one, too. So today we started training to tree form a wisteria that we have had for several years. We chose a strong branch for the trunk, removed all branches up to the height desired, topped it and cut the upper branches short. Then we drove down a stake to support the main stem. We must keep growth rubbed off the stem and must cut back new growth in the top. In a year or two we should have a flowering tree. *Wisteria floribunda præcox* is not rank in growth and would be fine as a tree wisteria.

The mountain-laurel is a valuable broad-leaved evergreen that likes the acid leaf mold and part shade of
woodland areas. It is a native of mountainous regions.

The pampas grass in the foreground makes huge clumps of fine foliage and long feathery plumes. It is especially cool and restful-looking in midsummer and it combines well with other grasses.

We are still fighting weeds. Crabgrass, an annual that thrives in hot weather, should be eliminated from the lawn before it seeds. We uproot it, or rake it before mowing to raise the seed heads so they can be cut by the mower. Another grass to get rid of is quack-grass, a perennial with thick roots creeping in all directions. This has to be smothered or grubbed out.

June 23. Last night was insufferably warm, and I was up before the sun so as to enjoy the freshness of the morning. I gave various plants a soaking to encourage deep roots. Seed beds must not be allowed to dry out. In our rose garden we are trying light cultivation for a dust mulch instead of a straw mulch.

The dryness and heat are exhausting, and it is discouraging to see cucumber vines scorched and tall corn burned. Corn planted in deep trenches stands the drought best. We enjoy our shade trees now as we relax in the middle of the day.

June 29. Many perennials are dying down. I put stakes beside Oriental poppies and doronicums that are disappearing. As I was cutting the deep red foliage of the ornamental purple-leaf plum (*Prunus Pissardii*) to arrange with grasses, tamarix and vines, I noticed purple plums on the branches. So these trees have fruit, as well as dainty pink blooms early in spring and highly colored foliage until late fall!

Grasses do not seem to mind the warm weather. Low blue-green fescue (*Festuca ovina glauca*) is attractive in clumps at the foot of a rock garden. Feather-grass (*Stipa pennata*) makes a nice border plant and bouquet grass. Others giving a pleasing effect in our garden are cat-tail grass (*Phleum pratense*) and tall ribbon grass. A miniature white and green striped ribbon grass makes a dainty low edging for a flower border.

THIRD QUARTER

July

To me the meanest flower that grows can give
Thoughts that do often lie too deep for tears.
—*Wordsworth*

July 1. This is a real summer month! I cut back verbenas that are growing too rank; now they will probably bloom again. Seed pods were taken off other plants to make them flower longer. We are cutting back many perennials, but just a little at a time as the tops die, for the leaves restore vitality to the roots.

205

July 4. I fed rolled oats to fish in the pools and shook the little insects off the leaves of water plants. We saw a dead fish floating on the water yesterday, and today there was a cat on the brink of the pool. She had clawed another fish so badly it will die. Water cannas (Thalia) have arching spikes of queer purple flowers on the margins of the pool. Fancy-leaved caladiums look as if they belonged nearby; after the leaves develop, we never let them get dry.

It's impossible to keep everything watered. How we would enjoy underground and overhead irrigation! Portulaca does not mind the dryness, however, and gives a cheerful touch to the garden. Oxalis continues to bloom, too.

July 9. Today is another scorcher! I had the man mow the grass, but not shorter than 1½ inches. Lawns should not be cut close in hot weather, and it is better to water the grass thoroughly once or twice a week than to sprinkle lightly. When grass rakings are dried, we use them as a mulch for roses, after giving the rose beds a good soaking from the hose with the nozzle off. Polyantha roses are a great satisfaction. They bloom all summer when the old flower clusters are kept cut back.

Vegetation looked a little wilted today. One woman glanced at our garden in the middle of the day and remarked, "I see you are doing no gardening at all."

July 11. I was out early to cut flowers for the house. Blooming in spite of dryness and for the most part depending on cultivation or mulch for moisture, are gaillardia, anthemis, veronica, blue sage (*Salvia azurea grandiflora*), buddleia, abelia and althea. Spider-flowers (Cleome) are showy, with spidery stamens and rose-lavender petals. This annual likes a sunny location and sandy soil. The old-fashioned four-o'clocks (Mirabilis) open in the afternoon and in cloudy weather.

I plunged the stems of cut flowers in cool water for an hour before arranging them. Water takes the place of the sap that was lost after the flowers were cut. Large buds of Egyptian lotus were taken to my brother in the hospital; he can watch the flowers unfold tomorrow.

July 15. Everything looks refreshed after the much-needed rain. During the dry weather the vegetable garden was kept alive mostly by cultivation, though water was given to tomatoes, cucumbers and squash by means of a trench. Now we have corn, beans, lima beans, cabbage, beets, carrots and peppers; and from the orchard peaches, apples, figs and grapes. We're glad to live in the suburbs where we can have our own butter, milk, cream, ham, chickens and eggs. When July comes I wonder if many people wouldn't like to move "back to the country" where there is plenty of room for outdoor living under the shade trees.

A glance at the garden will show what flowers clash in color, such as deep pink althea, carmine salvia and orange-red montbretia. Now is the time to plan changes.

Numerous mimosa seedlings are coming up; we give them away but will reserve some for places where they seem to want to grow. After awhile I suppose our home will be known as "Mimosa Lodge" or "Crape-Myrtle Rendezvous." We can't resist the charming colors of crape-myrtles.

July 18. The weather is hot, and a visitor commented on the cool restfulness under our pergola covered with scuppernong vines. We have shade there in summer and sunshine when the leaves have fallen in winter. The only disadvantage is having to gather the fruit from stepladders in September.

Many perennials are dying down; others, like painted daisies, are putting out new growth. I had ivy borders edged; where ivy grows on tree trunks, I had it cut back enough to keep it from killing the trees.

We are not doing much in the garden now—just watering, cultivating, snipping faded flowers and spraying as needed.

July 20. Our gladioli are a pleasure; when one gets started with them, they become very interesting.

The summer-flowering annuals and perennials have been given a light feeding at intervals since early spring. We prefer giving them a little food often, and are careful to get the fertilizer around the plants and not on the foliage. Some plants, like the annual cockscomb (Celosia), do not do well if the soil is too rich. Cockscombs like to be started in a rather rich, moist, light soil. If their roots get too dry, the leaves will drop.

We had a man rob the beehives today. My boast is "I'm not afraid of bees," but our man said that with all his veiling and gloves "the bees were popping him."

July 23. Today we discussed with guests various methods of transplanting. Some gardeners transplant whenever it seems good to do so; others prefer to follow rules.

Fragrance from tuberoses floated over us, and we could glimpse the brightness of zinnias. Lantanas in soft tones were nearby, and tiger lilies at a distance made tall orange accents.

Hydrangeas, blue and pink, are flowering. They need good loam and plenty of water; soil conditions are responsible for the colors in many instances. Acid soil produces blue flowers. One can change pink to blue by adding a handful of cottonseed meal or iron filings to the soil, or a few spoonfuls of Epsom salts or tannic acid, or a teaspoonful of alum. Oak leaves or sawdust mixed with the soil will also make it acid. To change blue to pink, put a cupful or two of soot around the plant. This will need to be renewed every few weeks. Crushed lime rock will keep flowers pink.

July 28. I was out cultivating early this morning. I cultivate rather than water, to allow air to penetrate and a deep root system to be developed. We do not like to use water sprays in the late afternoon, for leaves that are wet overnight invite mildew. One should apply dusting sulphur, Bordeaux mixture or some good fungicide to plants suffering from rust or mildew.

A man pruning our shrubbery ran into wasps. Sprinkling the shrubs with water kept the pests from flying out of the shrubs, and he could go on with his work.

The afternoons are too hot for any gardening, and one only wants to be in the shade. We are enjoying salvias now. Some are annuals, some biennials, others are hardy or half-hardy perennials or shrubs. They grow in common soil and sunshine.

ANOTHER JULY

O gift of God! O perfect day
Whereon shall no man work, but play;
Whereon it is enough for me,
Not to be doing but to be!
—*Longfellow*

July 1. This morning I noticed the first blooms on Scarlett O'Hara morning-glories. I am not surprised that some years ago this was an All-America Gold Medal winner. The large flowers are rosy red, with scarlet veins in the shape of a star going down into the white throat. The leaves are three-lobed.

In the evening we ate supper in the garden, where we could hear water trickling into a pool and admire fancy-leaved caladiums and different shades of phlox—white Miss Lingard and soft pink Lillian, among others. These tall perennials bloom intermittently all summer if the dead flower heads are kept cut. Columbia phlox and Salmon Supreme petunias are the same lovely tone of pink.

July 4. We expected only nine guests, but twelve came yesterday to spend the night. Even if we had to borrow rooms from neighbors,

The Northerner traveling toward the South gets perhaps his first touch of old Dixie when he sees the crape-myrtle blooming so profusely from Virginia on. Planted alone, the bright-colored sorts make very fine displays but are even lovelier when combined with white varieties. If the flowers are cut off just before they fade, the plant will keep blooming until late fall. Crape-myrtle is especially good for roadside planting. (See page 211.)

Gardenia or cape-jasmine

The fragrant, lacy-foliaged mimosa

we could at least give them food we had raised ourselves. For supper there was hominy-grits fresh from our own corn, cooked practically all day in a double boiler, with cream beaten in just before serving. The two-year-old applewood-smoked ham was fried in thick slices so there was red-brown gravy; the corn pie had green Bell peppers chopped fine in it. We had French fried potatoes, sliced tomatoes, home-made rolls, our own butter, preserved figs and real made-at-home pound cake. The night was warm, but there was a breeze on the terrace when ice-cold watermelons, vine ripened, were served at a late hour.

For breakfast we had chilled cantaloupes and plums from our garden, as well as apples fried in butter. The young tender chickens were fried a golden brown (the cook's mistake, for I had told her to have broiled chicken on toast; however, one guest said she was tired of "things on toast"), and we had milk gravy and popovers.

The guests stayed for the mid-day meal (we speak of it as dinner), at which we served ice-cold fresh apple cider. Then we had South Carolina rice, each grain standing alone. The ducks were stuffed with potato dressing seasoned with dried sage, and since this is the Fourth we had barbecued hash cooked in an iron pot. There were home-made pickles and cottage cheese. Though the vegetable garden is burning and depending mostly on cultivation for moisture, we were able to have string beans, tender lima beans and okra; beets, cucumbers and tomatoes with pure apple vinegar over them were served as a salad. For dessert there was peach pie with flaky crust made from our wheat flour, topped with custard ice cream. The guests seemed to like the home-grown and home-prepared food, but the next time we have company on the Fourth of July, here's hoping it won't be so "dripping" hot!

July 6. There was wind and a little rain last night, and it was cloudy this morning when we set out collard plants. I dug about roses lightly to conserve moisture, for we did not put mulch about them this year. We are making use of a dust mulch instead.

We are behind schedule with the clean-up in the garden, but it is so hot one loses all pep and we are doing only the necessary things early in the morning and late in the afternoon. But we are taking care that shrubs do not die when watering now will save them.

The Spanish daggers (*Yucca aloifolia*) have handsome spikes of creamy, bell-shaped flowers. We admire them from a distance but do not like to get near them on account of the lance-like leaves. Years ago I asked a relative to give us a start of Spanish bayonets.

He got stem offsets and rhizome cuttings reluctantly, saying he would be "safer near a kicking mule."

July 15. Flowers for the house were cut this morning. Both blooms and plants are apt to be injured if cutting is done in full sun.

There is not much blackspot on our rose foliage, but each morning I pick off any infected leaves on the hybrid teas. Today I cut long branches from hybrid perpetuals that were getting out of bounds. To keep standard roses in shape, the flowering shoots were trimmed back to about five eyes, to an outward-pointing bud. The new shoots should point away from the middle of the tree so as to keep the center from being choked and to allow air and light to enter.

We find it best to gather herb leaves in the morning, just as the dew is gone, and to dry them in the shade as quickly as possible. The tender tips give the best flavor. We gathered sage leaves this morning to dry for seasoning. Seeds of other herbs, like caraway and anise, were collected also, for they are now mature. Lavender stalks are cut as the blooms begin to open, tied in bundles and hung up to dry. Later they are tucked among linens.

Tiger lilies, with brilliant orange-red flowers, are noticeable at this time. They are easily grown. If the little black bulbils are sown soon after ripening, in part shade in leaf mold, the plants will be ready to set out the next season. The false tiger lily (*Lilium Leichtlinii Maximowiczii*) is similar but is without bulbils; *L. tigrinum florepleno* has double flowers.

July 20. Since it is so warm, pale colors in masses are restful and foliage is important for providing a cool atmosphere. The pale pink flowers of annual balsam are an arresting sight. The plants become bushy when given at least 2 feet of space.

In the evenings we delight in the fragrance of white nicotianas, the beauty and the lemon odor of night-blooming tropical Missouri water-lilies, the exotic scent of heliotropes and the gratifying perfume of moonflowers.

July 21. We're taking it easy and enjoying vacation at home. One can be comfortable right here, and vegetables and fruits from our own labor taste good! We have an appetite for breakfast when it is served on the screened porch, the terrace or in the garden; a cold-plate meal or a supper cooked outdoors is delightful.

July 28. I cultivated about the chrysanthemums but gnats that seemed to "make a beeline" for my eyes made me uncomfortable. Plants look refreshed after the rain, but small weeds are coming up and we are trying to eradicate them. Grass between flagstones is easily pulled out now. Portulaca should thrive there in the open sun, in the rather dry, hot soil. In other walks where we want to exterminate weeds and grass, we are using crank-case oil.

We pulled out dead calendulas today, and seeing seedlings around them, decided this would be a good time to sow seeds in beds. These seeds were saved from our best selected blooms of calendula, columbine, pansy, sweet william, linum, delphinium and snapdragon.

July 29. Three Celeste fig bushes give us an abundance of figs for preserves, for the neighbors and for birds. The bushes have grown so large that some of the limbs have to be reached from stepladders. This particular small brownish fig is my favorite. We have two or more crops from it every year; often the first one is killed by cold. Hardwood cuttings of the fig bushes root readily, and the plants bear in three or four years.

Crape-myrtles (*Lagerstrœmia indica*) are showy with crapy fringed panicles of flowers. Someone called them the "darlings of the South," for here these shrubs or small trees from the Orient are completely at home. When motoring through Virginia, one is impressed with the crape-myrtle plantings along the roadsides. If the plants are pruned severely and fertilized in winter, they send out fresh growth and larger clusters of flowers. They bloom for over three months. The shades of pink and lavender are lovely with white-flowering ones interspersed.

AUGUST

Yes, in the poor man's garden grow
Far more than herbs and flowers—
Kind thoughts, contentment, peace of mind,
And joy for weary hours.
—*Mary Howitt*

August 1. As we sat on the porch after church services, we watched hundreds of June bugs swarming like bees and saw many kinds of butterflies hovering over the buddleias, while we listened to the noise of insects and the chirping of birds. Mallows (Hibiscus) are putting on a show and altheas in several shades are blooming.

Ausust 3. We can take things easy this month, but we must not give up the garden. Seed pods ought to be cut before they scatter seed. (If seed is to be saved, it should not be gathered while it is damp from rain or dew, and it should always be mature.) Blossoms should be removed from annuals to extend their blooming. Some spraying, cultivating, weeding, watering and grass cutting must be done.

211

A decayed stump that had been a bird bath was dug up and the ground well prepared for hemerocallis and columbine. It is partly shaded. The winter jasmine (*Jasminum nudiflorum*) that was taken up was given to someone who had recently built a home. This jasmine blooms very early and will grow under trees. The flowers are gone before the leaves appear. The half-climbing habit of these twiggy shrubs causes them to make new plants by self-layering.

August 4. Ripe figs have to be picked early in the morning before the birds eat so many of them. Grapes are bearing luscious fruit.

The hedges are being trimmed again to keep them in shape. We have this done three or four times a year. This is a good time to shear conifers. With the family protesting, I clipped the dwarf box-woods (*Buxus sempervirens suffruticosa*) to keep them shapely but soft and fluffy. This box is useful as an edging; it can be pruned and kept as low as desired. I had to let the hired man trim the box trees (*B. sempervirens arborescens*) to keep them dense. He needed a bench to reach them.

August 6. A rain came this morning, just in time to save some perennials. We had a man from the farm working in the garden, and when it began to rain I went out to see if he had finished his job of edging the walks. I found him digging up perennials and throwing them in a pile! He thought that since the tops were getting yellow, the plants ought to be taken out of the beds.

August 10. This "rest" month is a busy one right now, for with so much rain the grass needs mowing often and more pruning has to be done. Shrubs that flower in early spring must not be pruned again, for they are getting ready to form flower buds for next year. We fertilized chrysanthemums and asters. We find that asters like to have their roots kept cool with a mulch. They do well in semi-shade, while "mums" prefer full sun.

There is a border in the garden that looks rather interesting now. The old-fashioned roses have colorful orange and red hips that tone with the star-shaped white flowers of Jerusalem cherries and their green, yellow and red fruits, the flower spikes of montbretias, and the round orange and scarlet heads of marigolds.

Last night I cut Heavenly Blue morning-glory buds and carried them to a sick friend to let her see them unfold their beauty this morning.

August 11. The rains skipped us for two days, and though the afternoons are too hot for gardening we are trying in the mornings to keep the plants healthy. We are giving the soil a light cultivation

212

Tuberous begonias will put on a great show if they are
planted in a shaded spot, with mulch over their roots,
and given an abundant supply of water. (See page 50.)

In shade where grass will not grow, pachysandra is a good ground cover. (See page 100.)

to hold the moisture; to prevent the garden from looking ragged, we do some edging. The lawns are a mossy green, and flowers are taking on new life. The more I cut back the roses, the more they grow. We are enjoying these long-stemmed blooms of August.

August 17. I was outdoors early, to soak the rose beds. I sprinkled the leaves, too, for they looked thirsty; the sun will dry them. The hired man said, "It seems cooler to keep stirring than to stop." I agreed with him and made a dust mulch about some plants. While cutting down dead stalks of tiger lilies, I saw pretty green ferns in the woodsy garden. A refreshing sight was the fountain spray in a pool and six wet green frogs on lily pads. One appreciates green ground covers at this time, such as periwinkle (*Vinca minor*) and spurge (*Pachysandra terminalis*). Lavender and white flowers look restful.

Everyone should have the old tea rose Duchesse de Brabant, which is a mass of delicate pink blooms with delightful fragrance on vigorous bushes. The climate of the South suits tea roses.

August 19. Such a breeze sprang up in the night that today is the proverbial "cold day in August." I picked dead leaves off water plants but left some lotus seed pods, for they are decorative.

Black Ischia figs are ripe, and crab-apples are hanging yellow. Preserves and jellies must be made. But with the windows open, there will be fragrance of phlox, heliotrope, petunias and abelia.

August 24. The night-blooming cereus, pot grown, had blooms that were lovely and fragrant last night, but they are drooping this morning. With friends we enjoyed watching the exquisite flowers opening.

All of us are droopy this hot dry weather and feel the need of rest in the shade. We water thoroughly once or twice a week and cultivate as soon as the ground can be worked; and we don't forget to see that the bird baths are filled every morning.

August 27. This morning was hot, and everything looked wilted. However, the plantain-lily (*Hosta plantaginea*) is bearing fragrant white flowers. This plant revels in rich moist soil and shade but does not like a wet crown. Zinnias bloom on, even with white mildew on their leaves. We dust with fine sulphur to prevent the mildew from spreading. Crape-myrtles are getting sooty mildew. We will spray them with 6 teaspoonfuls of Black-leaf 40 and ½ pound of Bordeaux mixture to 3 gallons of water.

We are trying to keep evergreens watered. We want to guard against red spider, the small mite that sucks sap from the foliage and causes the green to have a rusty look. When water spray does not get rid of red spiders, a glue spray can be used: ½ pound of carpenter's glue dissolved in ½ gallon of hot water, and mixed with 4½ gallons of water. Spray again in a week. (See Chapter III, Spraying and Dusting.)

August 31. The month, which began with plenty of rain, ends dry and hot. But the garden does not require much attention now. The little that is done is a pleasure for the early mornings.

While out riding this morning, we saw Heavenly Blue morning-glories in full bloom over a fence and arched gateway, and white *Clematis paniculata* was draping a lacy veil over a large, rose-colored crape-myrtle. Pictures like these are remembered.

A RAINY AUGUST
Nature never did betray
The heart that loved her.
—*Wordsworth*

August 2. Decayed stems were taken from rose bushes and the weak growth cut out. We had a trench dug between the bushes and manure put in it, to encourage fine fall blooms.

Scabiosas are noticeable now. The variety Blue Moon has quite double blue flowers on long stems, while Loveliness is salmon-rose.

A friend invited me to see her field of zinnias, and they were indeed a picture. She had many varieties and colors, each planted separately and blended into the next. Many of the blooms were larger than a saucer; some looked like scabiosas, others like dahlias. There were odd Fantasy zinnias and enchanting flowers of the baby or lilliput type. All the plants were vigorous. She said she had seen to it that they did not lack water during the dry spell last month, but that the hose was not turned on them in full sunshine. Seeing her zinnias made me resolve to have more of them another year.

Her plantain-lilies, with white-margined leaves and spikes of bluish lavender flower bells, fascinated me. These grow rapidly in sun or shade if they are planted in good humus. The clumps can be separated in autumn or spring.

August 5. There has been rain enough to really penetrate the ground. Lupines, which had looked dead, are sending out new growth. I noticed also that dandelions and plantains are coming up on the lawns. These are a nuisance, for their big leaves crowd out the grass. It is not an easy job to grub them out, but there are tools that drop a destroying chemical in the middle of each plant. Or an oil-can with a slender spout can be used.

August 7. During this lazy month, spent flowers are clipped here and there, and shallow cultivation is continued where there is no mulch. We spray and dust when necessary. We notice the many different butterflies, such as monarch, tiger swallow-tail, viceroy, cloudless sulphur, buckeye and others. They are as colorful as the flowers. I understand that they are attracted by the color of flowers and not by the odor.

Marigolds are making a display at this time. Crown of Gold has slightly sweet-scented flowers but the foliage is odorless, as is the case with Silver Crown. Dwarf Little Giant, growing about 6 inches high, makes an effective edging for a border. There are many kinds of marigolds, including African and French and their tall and dwarf hybrids. Some have odorless foliage. Colors range from reddish to gold to primrose-yellow. Everyone should have a place for the showy marigolds; they are easily grown, not choosy about soil and have a long flowering season.

August 8. It is possible to have many flowers blooming this month. I was in a neighbor's garden this afternoon and saw shrubs, perennials, annuals and bulbous plants in bloom: crape-myrtles, white and shades of pink and lavender; double altheas, pink and rose; kerrias, abelias, roses, dahlias, verbenas, yarrow, physostegia and four-o'clocks, as well as salvia, marigolds, zinnias, periwinkles, tuberoses, plantain-lilies and gladioli. Snow-on-the-mountain (*Euphorbia marginata*) with white-edged green leaves was cool-looking in sunny places. In the orchard were ripe peaches, apples and grapes. A wood and tool house and a scuppernong arbor were made attractive with vines and other plants. These could have been concealed with tall shrubbery, but in this garden they are cool retreats in which to rest or work.

August 10. It didn't take much persuasion from friend husband to make me seek shelter from the hot sun at ten o'clock! We are in the midst of another heat wave, but on this dewy morning the garden looked enchanting. Near an herb corner I got whiffs of the clove-like odor of basil and the aromatic fragrance of savory and thyme.

Hearing a noise on top of the house in the afternoon, I investigated and found several peafowls perched on a chimney. I "shooed" at them, but they only cocked their heads. The tail plumage was plucked from the cocks in May and the new feathers are coming out; black spots can be seen bordered with brilliant green, blue and gold. It is puzzling how anything so beautiful can give such screams!

August 17. Heavy rains have soaked the ground. It is too wet to have the lawns mowed, and the grass has grown high. By keeping on the stepping-stones, I was able to cut an armful of beautiful roses. Zephyranthes are blooming profusely; we call them rain-lilies, and they really do come after rains. *Liriope Muscari* has spikes of blue flowers that look like grape-hyacinths, and hardy phlox and verbenas that were cut back are a mass of bloom again.

Cannas with tropical-looking leaves have large heads of flowers. They are quite dependable, reveling in full sun and lots of humus. King Midas has rich yellow flowers among the green foliage. There are also showy red ones like President, but my favorites are rose-pink Rosea Gigantea and salmon-pink Mrs. Conard. When cannas are planted so that the colors do not clash or are grouped in borders of separate colors, they are very effective. They bloom all summer.

We are enjoying the beauty of petunias like Violet Beauty, Silver Lilac, Rose Gem and Apple Blossom not only during the day but also at night, when their sweetness is all over the garden. It is nice to have flowers with names that are pretty as well as descriptive.

August 19. Today we are motoring to New York, and from there to New Hampshire. This will be my first trip to the New England States. I shall take special notice of the difference in flowering time between plants there and here.

SEPTEMBER

Look on this beautiful world, and read the truth
In her fair page; see, every season brings
New change, to her, of everlasting youth.
—*Bryant*

September 4. Last night we returned from a motor trip up north. All the way into the New England States the flowers blooming were not unlike ours at home, though the season is later. Our favorite crape-myrtle disappeared after we left Virginia. In some states the roadsides are planted with native material, which thrives with a minimum of care. In Connecticut, roadside beautification is particularly noticeable. In Vermont and New Hampshire we commented on the clean, well-kept highways with trash containers and no disfiguring billboards. Continuous plantings of lilacs were striking in New Hampshire, where the lilac is the state flower. How lovely it must be when they are flowering mile after mile, in groups or as specimens. We were told the state highway department gives lilac bushes to clubs to be planted along the roads. I shall always remember this part of the country with its mountains, birch trees and picturesque homes.

216

One likes to take trips but appreciates home afterward. It is cool here, and we are told it rained almost daily while we were away. And how the weeds and grass have grown! The damp weather made the lichens and tree moss green, and toadstools showing on lawns are vari-colored little umbrellas.

September 6. It hurt to have a large oak cut down this morning, but we needed more sunshine. The roots were going too far under a shrubbery border, and the shade was not necessary. We have to sacrifice trees sometimes for flowers, but I felt better when the stump showed a little decay. The new rose garden is to be nearby.

Dahlias were given shallow cultivation in the afternoon.

September 8. Cypress-vines are dashes of color now. This dainty annual vine with red or white star-flowers is my husband's delight.

We sowed turnip and mustard seed and had the vegetable garden cultivated. September is a rather trying month, with cool mornings and nights, hot mid-days and usually plenty of dust. But necessary things done in the garden now give great satisfaction. We did some cleaning up and removed dying and dead plants. The diseased ones were burned and the others were put on the compost heap.

All families are trying to get as much pleasure as possible from these last vacation days. Outdoor suppers are in order. I know one family that has a supper table under a pergola covered with the foamy white flowers of the silver lace-vine (*Polygonum Aubertii*). This decorative perennial vine is vigorous and fast growing. It blooms in the spring and again in the fall.

September 11. It was cool enough for a coat today. I disbudded some chrysanthemums and cut dead tops off phlox. We expect fall bloom from these, so I cultivated about the plants, watered them and applied liquid manure.

We are having to soak the ground around many plants to keep them alive. In the frames, which I keep moist but not soaked, columbines, calendulas and Siberian wallflowers are fine plants, and pansies are coming up. In the herb borders I noticed seedlings of dill, borage and other plants. There are enough to transplant and to give to friends.

September 20. My sister tells me she was having bearded irises dug this morning to divide and replant. She told the laborer to place the labels by each clump as he dug them. When she went back in the garden, he had all the irises in a heap and had stacked the labels neatly in a pile.

This afternoon I heard a lecturer on landscaping say, "Two things most needed in a garden are elbow grease and humus." I thoroughly agree. Conditions everywhere are different, and it is fine to have the owner's personality expressed in his garden. We can observe other gardens and study landscaping, and then experiment in our own grounds. A gardener need not get discouraged, for the right planting material can be found for every situation.

September 22. Spider-lilies (*Lycoris radiata*) surprise us by popping out of the ground. The narrow green leaves with a stripe through the center come later. They need winter sun. These plants bloom best when they are growing thick; they do not require dividing for years. These lilies from Japan and China are sometimes called Guernsey-lilies or nerines, but the true nerines from South Africa have broader, flat leaves and lily-like flowers and are hard to grow in this part of the country. However, many stand the winter in Arkansas and Louisiana.

Cockscombs (Celosia) are adding their bright colors to the landscape. *Genista tinctoria* is a mass of yellow bloom. Fragrant fruits of flowering quince (*Chænomeles lagenaria* (*Cydonia japonica*)) are on the ground. The cone-shaped seed pods of magnolias have burst, leaving clusters of red berries. The native American euonymus has strawberry-like fruits.

September 23. Staking off the new rose garden was started, after drawing it to scale on paper. The beds are to be 3 feet by 8½ feet; in them we will plant ten hybrid tea roses 18 inches apart. There are to be grass walks, a border of polyanthas and tree (standard) roses for accents. The hybrid perpetuals will have a place to themselves; they will be planted 24 inches apart or more.

September 25. The beds for the new roses are being prepared so that they may settle and be ready when the plants arrive. The beds are to be spaded out 2 feet deep; clinkers and gravel will be put in for drainage, followed by manure, bonemeal, wood ashes and red clay mixed thoroughly with the topsoil.

Boxwood has such an interesting appearance that I cannot blame the spiders for spinning lacy webs over it, but it keeps me busy wiping them off. These webs do no harm to the plants, but they look untidy.

I planted brodiæa corms in the rock garden. These thrive in partly shaded places in sandy soil, which should be firmed but not watered after planting.

September 20. In separating Japanese irises to replant, we cut off portions of root and stem with a sharp knife. We saw to it that the soil where they were planted contained moisture-holding material.

218

We used leaf mold and compost but no bonemeal or lime. The divisions were placed so the crowns would be 2 inches deep. Sunshine is necessary for these irises, but not all day.

September 30. This morning I found a pool had leaked and many large fantail, comet-tail and other beautiful fish were dead. It was pure carelessness on my part for not having discovered this leak before so much damage was done. I don't feed the fish oftener than twice a week and had not noticed what was happening. We got busy, caught the few live fish that were left, put them into another pool and got everything ready for recementing the sides.

ANOTHER SEPTEMBER
In all places, then, and in all seasons,
    Flowers expand their light and soul-like wings,
Teaching us, by most persuasive reasons,
    How akin they are to human souls.
                        —Longfellow

September 1. Summer flowers are still at their height of beauty, there is an abundance of vegetables and fruits, and weeds and pests are under control!

September 4. I cut faded flowers from annuals and saved some well-ripened seed taken from the best plants. I will put them in labeled envelopes in tin boxes.

We planted madonna lily bulbs (*Lilium candidum*) 2 or 3 inches deep in good, rather sweet soil. They require early planting and produce leaves in fall that stand winter. We placed sand around the bulbs to drain away moisture and to keep them from decaying. They can be grown in sun or partial shade. We put some in front of shrubbery and naturalized others. These lilies make effective display beds and are fine for indoor decoration. In cutting them, the foliage and lower stem must be left for future growth of the bulb.

September 6. Buddleias are full of graceful flowers. Butterfly-bush is a good name for them, because butterflies are always hovering around the plants. Michaelmas daisies are blooming, and snow-on-the-mountain (Euphorbia) is attractive with its white-edged green bracts. This morning we took particular note of a delicately beautiful spider's web jeweled with dew. Spiders' feet rest upon the threads of the web without breaking them or sticking to them. Spiders are real friends of the gardener.

While resting, I heard "darkies" singing in a cotton patch not far away. They were worth listening to!

September 8. From one point of view a garden is interesting because it is never finished. We're trying to put every plant in its place, eliminating undesirables and mistakes. Garden ornaments should supplement and not dominate the planting of the grounds. The gnome my sister gave us to cast his line over our rustic pool seems to belong there, as does the large green china frog donated by another sister for the other pool.

September 13. With friends in the garden this Sunday afternoon we talked of how to plan for color harmony, taking perfume into consideration, too. The first thing we do with a new bloom is to smell it. In many localities flowers with sweet scent can be enjoyed throughout the year. Sweet herbs as well as flowers should have a place. Our herbs have a border to themselves in the vegetable garden, but they are interesting and effective among flowers, too. The foliage of rue is particularly pretty. The seed pods are ready to be gathered now, and yellow blooms are showing again.

September 14. Mexican rose (Antigonon) vines are covering an arbor with sprays of pink flowers and heart-shaped, green leaves. These vines, which die down in winter, are a southern favorite. Mimosa trees are attractive, with sensitive ferny foliage and yellowish green seed pods. We like plants that look well even when they are not blooming. Seed pods of sterculia trees have already burst. Paulownia trees with catalpa-like leaves have old brown seed pods like cotton bolls and new green seed pods; buds for next spring are already in the making.

September 20. We're feeding chrysanthemums with liquid manure but will discontinue as soon as the buds show color and signs of opening. Black aphis are appearing on the asters and chrysanthemums. I sprayed them with a nicotine sulphate preparation. Where grasshoppers were eating the stems of plants, I drenched them with arsenate of lead solution and the hoppers disappeared.

The weather is so pleasant that the family decided to ramble in the woods this afternoon. There are many lovely things to see in September. Wild asters and goldenrod are blooming by the wayside, berries of dogwood (*Cornus florida*) are getting red and fruits of pokeweed are hanging in dark clusters. There is a tinge of red where sourwoods and black gums grow, and sumac berries are turning lavender. Many wildflowers are blooming, among them bouncing bet or soapwort (Saponaria), which long ago escaped from gardens and ran wild. Our ancestors ascribed healing virtues to this plant.

September 21. We divided and replanted painted daisies (Py-

220

Shadbush is a decorative large shrub or small tree at home at the edge of wooded regions. (See page 80.)

Here fine-leaved bamboo and plume grass have been combined as a low hedge.

rethrum). Sometimes double pyrethrums bear single flowers the first year; we must wait until the second year to know what we have.

We are still cultivating the vegetable garden. Good rutabagas must grow quickly, so we stimulated them with nitrate of soda. I picked red cayenne peppers and strung them. They should be mature before being gathered. I find if they are pulled green, they will turn yellow and reddish but will rot before they dry. Dried peppers give a tang to vegetables and meats. In our vegetable garden are lima beans, cowpeas, turnip greens and okra, tender and ready to be picked.

September 23. Today the peonies were divided. We left four to five good eyes to each division and set them 2 to 3 inches below the surface of the ground. Too shallow planting may hurt the buds, while too deep planting may fail to produce buds or may rot the roots. (See Chapter IV, Autumn.)

We gave the rose bushes plant food for fine autumn bloom. In our garden Margaret McGredy roses are making a show; they are more of an apricot color than in the spring. Ami Quinard is a lighter red now; shell-pink Warrawee has bloomed and bloomed.

September 27. The wind brings down pears and late apples. Pickles, preserves and apple sauce will be "in the making" tomorrow. In the garden we noticed how interesting the grasses are. They are such a natural part of the landscape. Pampas-grasses, *Cortaderia argentea* with silvery plumes and the variety Roi de Rosea with plume-like spikes of delicate rose, are very ornamental. These grasses are hardy, and the clumps grow in size and beauty each year. Marigolds are bright, and the perennial helenium is effective in the back of the borders; the glowing gold and maroon are expressive of the autumn mood.

September 28. Some plants were set out from the frames. A general rule is to transplant spring-blooming perennials in the autumn and vice versa. We're having borders prepared for more narcissi and hyacinths. They need well-drained, loamy soil. If we leave the border above the ground level to allow for settling, it should be in good condition to plant next month.

September 30. The gentle, all-night rain has refreshed plants and caused crimson berries on dogwoods (*Cornus florida*) and orange-colored fruits of *Pyracantha coccinea Lalandii* to glisten. An unusually pretty sight is a neighbor's field of golden lupine (Crotalaria) with its racemes of pale yellow, lupine-like flowers marked with reddish brown. This is an annual that blooms from July to frost. It does best in full sun but will stand some shade and will thrive even in dry soil. *Crotalaria spectabilis* is taller growing than *C. retusa*. These enrich the land and make showy cut flowers.

Tonight we tossed bugs to a toad that had hopped on the porch and were amused at the way he darted out his sticky tongue. Toads are helpers in a garden, for they catch slugs, worms and other pests.

FOURTH QUARTER

OCTOBER

O what a glory doth this world put on
For him who, with fervent heart, goes forth
Under the bright and glorious sky, and looks
On duties well performed, and days well spent!
—*Longfellow*

October 1. October is a popular fall planting month: "A garden for next year is beneath our finger tips." My fingers go down into the soil, and since gloves are in my way I find it best to rub soap over the ends of my fingers before working in the garden.

I divided and transplanted the tall perennial phlox plants, using the outer parts of the clumps and discarding the exhausted centers. They do not do well if they become too dense. They need breaking up and resetting every four or five years. These flower through a long season and succeed in almost any soil, though they prefer a moist, rich loam.

We went for a drive this afternoon and stopped at a home where many flowers are blooming. We asked the lady of the house and garden how she got her flowers to do so well. She said she planted them when the "woman in the almanac held a lily in her hand."

October 4. Canterbury bells and snapdragons were set out. Third-year blooms of snapdragons are superior to the first year. Shoots coming from the old roots make larger and healthier plants.

I had a large tree stump in the back yard hollowed out and cemented, and I pressed small pieces of tile into the concrete. We will plant ivy, periwinkle and winter jasmine around it, to make a rather attractive-looking bird bath. Wild primrose-pink roses are already growing there.

October 8. It was cool enough for a coat in the garden when I divided and reset some tall bearded irises. I trimmed the leaves back to 4 or 5 inches to prevent excessive evaporation while new roots are developing. There were enough rhizomes to give some to a garden club for a beauty project.

The new bearded irises that came this afternoon were set out according to height, color and time of bloom. These plants need good drainage and sunshine, though partial shade from the hot afternoon sun is desirable. The rhizomes should be planted just below the level of the soil, with the roots spread out and firmed well. We moved clumps of an older iris, William Mohr, and will replace it with taller varieties. We particularly like William Mohr; it has large, lilac-veined flowers on stems only 24 to 30 inches high. It does best for us with an eastern exposure in rather rich soil.

October 9. The first light frost was observed here this morning. There is a tang in the air, and in the house a wood fire is cheerful. We had the grass fertilized; this time we used half cottonseed meal and half wood ashes, from our own cotton and fires. In a few days winter grass seed will be raked in.

I heard a friend say she could not enjoy her garden for thinking how much needed to be done. A garden should not be a burden. We take such pleasure in ours that the danger is that we will neglect other things.

October 10. Our fairy-lilies (Zephyranthes) are a joy, and veronica is adding charm to borders. We noticed that even poison oak looks pretty on the edge of the woods, with colorful foliage and bunches of grayish white berries, but we will destroy these dangerous plants with a strong brine solution. The Virginia creeper (*Parthenocissus* (*Ampelopsis*) *quinquefolia*) is beautiful with its brilliant autumn coloring. It will grow in any good soil and can be planted close to walls, where it will cling.

The gorgeous coloring of foliage and berries is seen all around. Now is the time to plan and plant in order to have displays of nature's colors in our own gardens. There are many trees and shrubs valuable for their color; some bear bright fruits and foliage at the same time. Some berry-producing shrubs will grow in dry exposed places, such as dogwood (*Cornus racemosa*) with white berries and red-cedar (*Juniperus*) with bluish gray berries. In a shady, sheltered spot one can have the white fruits of snowberries (*Symphoricarpos albus*) and the scarlet fruits of red elder (*Sambucus racemosa*). For damp places there are such shrubs as winterberry (*Ilex verticillata*) with red fruits and withe-rod (*Viburnum cassinoides*) with pink fruits changing to blue-black. At the seashore red-fruited American holly (*Ilex opaca*) and shadbush (*Amelanchier ovalis* (*rotundifolia*)) can be grown.

October 12. Bulbs that came this morning were planted in well-prepared soil. Dutch irises were placed about 4 inches deep and 6 inches apart in a rich, sandy loam. They will be in shade part of the day. Crocuses were planted 2 inches deep and 4 inches apart. A safe rule for all bulbs is to plant them one and one-half times their own depth. They like rich, mellow, well-drained soil but dislike manure around the roots.

I worked about the rock garden, which is attractive now with sedums. *Sedum Sieboldii*, with round, gray-blue foliage on long stems and pink flowers, is particularly interesting. We have started another rock garden near trees in the back yard. Thus far we have not been able to get anything to grow there. Now we will see what we can do with rocks to hold the fertile soil and moisture.

October 14. We're having loquats (*Eriobotrya japonica*) set out. In the lower part of this state these have striking corrugated leaves and flowers in fragrant panicles in November and December. We want to see if they will set fruit here.

More lilacs were planted. They are adaptable shrubs that can be used singly or in masses; with good care, the older the bush, the better the yield of flowers. They are heavy feeders and give good results if well-decayed manure is dug into the ground. They thrive best in a sunny spot in alkaline soil but will grow in part shade. Though common lilacs require a number of years to bloom, most young plants of hybrid lilacs bloom the first season after transplanting. Our French lilacs flowered beautifully in April and May and are free from suckering.

Most shrubs and trees can be planted at this time but there are exceptions, such as magnolias and dogwoods, which prefer early spring planting. Holly does best for us defoliated and planted in the spring, but it can be set out in the fall before the young wood has fully ripened. We plan to put out some of the yellow-berried variety of holly (*Ilex opaca xanthocarpa*) in the early spring. I saw it with berries in the lower part of South Carolina.

October 21. Today is cold and windy after Jack Frost's visit, but the evergreen mixture of grass is showing green and eleagnus is beginning to bloom. Its fragrance is wafted over the garden. The Korean chrysanthemums are opening. Early Sappho has showy single yellow blooms and Daphne old-rose ones. The oldest varieties are still charming. Apollo is red and gold with a tinge of salmon, and semi-double Mars is an unusual deep red with a sheen. A little later Saturn will be a delight with single, bronze and gold flowers.

Chrysanthemums are the queen of autumn flowers. The many, many
types and varieties are a continuing joy for the gardener who likes to
bring them indoors and make her own bouquets. (See page 131.)

One of the most celebrated gardens of the South—Middleton Gardens, on the Ashley River near Charleston, S. C. The building is the only wing remaining of the original mansion house. Here azaleas, camellias and immense live oaks are especially notable. (See page 3.)

October 24. What could be pleasanter than being in the garden with friends to enjoy the glow of summer and the richness of autumn? We talked of fall as the garden's ultimate perfection, and of how gardeners want a succession of bloom, sweet odors and berries. The gorgeous leaves led to a discussion of autumn coloring. These colors are not brought on by frost but by natural ripening. The juices of the tree are drawn from the leaves to the branches, leaving the minerals that give the color.

October 31. I sowed poppy seeds in a place prepared for them. Then I had shrubbery moved to make beds for single hybrid tea roses, such as Dainty Bess, Cecil and Irish Fireflame. The shrubs were spaded with balls of earth and put in a place made ready for them ten days ago.

The last day of the month is here, and we are still planning and planting. We plan ahead for months and even years, and our garden always has room for changes. The ideal weather we enjoy now, in a world full of color, makes gardening a most pleasant recreation.

ANOTHER OCTOBER

Ay, thou are welcome, heaven's delicious breath!
When woods begin to wear the crimson leaf.
—*Bryant*

October 2. There is the feel of autumn in the air. Much foliage has taken on a brilliant tint.

I got a man's point of view today as I was cutting blooms in the rose garden, which can be glimpsed from the street. A man who is a flower lover stopped and asked me to suggest at the next garden club meeting that people plant more flowers in front of their homes for the public to enjoy. He pointed out that "People can't ramble in back yards to see flowers without an invitation." I agreed to do this, but said that the prevailing idea now is to use low shrubs and a green carpet of grass to frame a picture of the front of the house.

October 4. There are two kinds of flowers now—real autumn ones and summer flowers that linger on. Asters are important fall flowers; the new dwarf hardy kinds are easy to grow.

October 9. In the afternoon I motored with friends to a dahlia farm in the suburbs of a neighboring city. The many types of dahlias include semi-cactus, formal decorative and informal decorative. I like the miniatures, singles and pompons. At this farm they were planted in rows in full sun and mulched with hay and leaves. We were told that potash, bonemeal and manure are used as fertilizer.

October 13. Light showers are not enough to do vegetation much good, and it is too dry to start fall planting. Red euonymus berries with pinkish caps are showy now. Different varieties of euonymus are very decorative. They are not particular as to soil or location, and cuttings root easily. They are bothered, however, with disease and insect pests. The native euonymus or strawberry-bush (*Euonymus americanus*) has quite attractive fruits—scarlet burs opening to show crimson berries inside.

Groundsel-trees (Baccharis) are beginning to produce downy panicles of white; some are yellowish. These plants of shrubby growth greet one on the highways or at the edge of woods. They frequently spring up in gardens, even in dry, rocky places.

October 20. After showers yesterday, it is pleasant to work in the garden. We are getting places ready for tulips that are to be planted next month. Well-decayed manure and bonemeal were worked into the soil and turned under deep. Our new tulip bulbs came this morning, and we can hardly wait until the middle of next month to plant them. If these are put out too early in our mild climate, the leaves may come before the roots have time to develop.

Manure was turned under in the borders where we will set out pansy plants next month. It is best not to plant them here till then; the October sun is not good for them. As I passed near the flowering limes (citrange), I got whiffs of delectable fragrance and noticed that many of the small yellow fruits are on the ground.

In the vegetable garden, Jerusalem artichokes were dug. We want some while they are tender and fresh to cook with a cheese-cream dressing. Dry lima beans were picked for winter use. The vegetable garden still supplies us with eggplant, okra, peppers, tomatoes and turnip greens.

October 22. Korean chrysanthemums are making a display. The cut flowers last in water for two weeks or longer. A cheerful-looking one is Burgundy, a crimson-cerise. Pale Moon, primrose-yellow, is flowering next to Lavender Lady, which lives up to its name. These have double flowers and grow about 2½ feet high. The soil for these mums contains much organic matter. They like plenty of food and good drainage.

Today we transplanted hybrid perpetual and Radiance rose bushes from rows in the vegetable garden. Cuttings put out last December now have strong root systems. Later, we will take up the polyanthas and other hybrid teas produced from cuttings and put them in the rose garden. They have bloomed all summer.

Calendulas and columbines in the seed beds have grown quite large. We watered them well and then moved some to the flower borders. These are grown from our own seed from selected plants. We believe they will give fine flowers in the spring.

October 24. If our japonicas (camellias) and azaleas bloom well next spring, I shall feel repaid for the many times that I gave them water. They are forming leaf buds now and need plenty of moisture.

The weather is delightful, neither hot nor cold, but it is very dry. Everywhere in the city people are seen with watering hose or underground irrigation sprays, trying to encourage the winter lawn grass seed to germinate. We often wonder whether our spells of extreme weather are abnormal. The records show that in past years there were many very hot and very dry seasons. In spite of the dryness, when I cut off withered roses this morning I found a few black-spotted leaves to pick off.

We are not cutting our roses with very long stems just now, for the plants need the leaves. The roots depend on the leaves to store up food. Yesterday a friend told me our rose beds are porous but her soil is hard. We have maintained a dust mulch all summer, and our roses have done well.

Late this afternoon we kept hearing a smacking, popping sound. We thought it might be squirrels, or maybe a pig looking for acorns. But when I investigated, I found that the noise was caused by the bursting of wisteria seed pods. No wonder so many seedlings appear in the flower beds!

October 31. Evergreens are noticeable at this time in contrast with autumn coloring. Sprays of autumn foliage can be kept for a long time if they are put in containers filled with two-thirds water and one-third glycerine.

I must shear the old bloom stems of the lavender verbena (*Verbena bipinnatifida*). I don't want it to become exhausted from forming seed.

NOVEMBER

Ere, in the Northern gale,
The summer tresses of the trees are gone,
The woods of autumn, all around our vale
Have put their glory on.
—*Bryant*

November 1. This is a good planting month, though in this section plantings can be made all during the winter. And we have no more losses from doing the job in the fall than in the spring.

November 3. Some time ago rows were opened in the vegetable garden. The ground is moist now and we sowed carrot, spinach and beet seeds. Onion sets were put out, too. They should be planted in line and at the right depth. Usually this is almost as disagreeable a task as gathering okra. The little stickers of okra get in my fingers and irritate the skin. However, the pods should be kept cut so that there will be tender okra all summer and until frost. There is an abundance of tender turnip greens in the garden now. We like them seasoned with at least one pod of cayenne pepper.

November 5. Good-sized plants of calendula, wallflower and snapdragon were moved from the frames to the borders today. We planted them in well-prepared soil, poured plenty of water about them and raked dry soil on top after the water had soaked in.

While out riding this afternoon, we noticed the many goldenrods and wild asters. Rabbit tobacco (Gnaphalium) was a nice mixer with them. We took note that honey-locust pods are ripe. As soon as frosts ripen the persimmons, we'll have locust-persimmon beer! A friend has a Japanese persimmon in her garden that makes a beautiful specimen. The large fruits begin to color when half grown. She told me they gather them just before frost is expected and let them ripen in the house to improve the flavor.

November 8. This Sunday my husband and I looked over the ground with an eye for changes, for gardening is not just putting out plants but finding the real beauty of the garden and making it "speak for itself." Vistas not only show up trees and plants, but also the need for them. The garden actually consists of the whole surroundings of the house, and there should be a definite relation between house and garden. It pays to plan ahead for beautiful year-round pictures.

Transvaal daisies, gaillardias, ageratum and chrysanthemums are still blooming. Button chrysanthemums are in tight bud. They stand considerable cold and sometimes flower even after a killing frost has browned the foliage. Edible pomegranate (Punica) fruits are hanging reddish yellow, along with the yellowed leaves.

A neighbor has borders of Chinese forget-me-nots (Cynoglossum) blooming, and bittersweet vines (*Celastrus scandens*) on the fence have berries. The evergreen bittersweet (*Euonymus Fortunei radicans*) has somewhat similar berries.

November 9. Hardy water-lilies were replanted in tubs and the tubs put back in the pools. Now this will not have to be done next spring. Manure was scattered around shrubs and trees, lime about lilacs and coal ashes around delphiniums. Johnny-jump-ups (*Viola tricolor*) have volunteered to such an extent that we had to thin them. I put down pieces of clove pinks to root; I do this each year in order to have a steady supply of plants.

We watched a pretty sight—yellow butterflies hovering over the white and purple petunia border. When Bill, the spitz, dug up a mole we were as delighted as the puppy!

November 16. Today, in ground already prepared, I planted tulip bulbs, 6 inches deep and 6 inches apart, on ½ inch of sand. We like to see several bulbs of a variety planted in a group, of two or three tones of the same color. The bulbs do not have to be lifted annually but should be fed at least once a year, in early spring or fall.

Seedlings for an Osage-orange hedge were set out around the orchard. Birds like to nest in the thorny branches; the flowers are pretty in spring, the fruits are attractive, and the branches stay green all winter. However, this plant can get to be a nuisance on account of seedlings.

November 20. There were heavy frosts the last two nights. Today I planted scilla and glory-of-the-snow (Chionodoxa) bulbs. I had the strawberry beds mulched with well-rotted manure to protect the plants and prevent deterioration of the soil. We are careful not to have the mulch matted on the crowns of plants.

Crape-myrtles were pruned. This can be done any time from now into February. The fading of the blossoms is the signal to prune all shrubs, to encourage new growth and a better display of bloom.

Some rose bushes came from the nursery, and we set them out in the ground prepared for them. First, the tops of some had to be pruned a little and roots clipped. In planting, we spread the roots so that none crossed, worked soil among them and made the plants firm. After watering, we put soil around the stems, which will remain until the roots are established. They were planted according to color: first the yellows, then red, apricot, white, salmon and pink.

November 21. This is a cold day, with the ground frozen and plenty of ice. Ligustrums, coral-berry, snowberry, aucuba and Chinese firethorns have very attractive berries.

Lawns should go into winter with longer grass blades than usual. Most grasses are shallow-rooted, heavy feeders and should have plant food now.

November 25. The day before Thanksgiving, and unusually cold here. The whole neighborhood is having leaves raked, and at several places the workers have bonfires. We find a cheerful wood fire will make the family enjoy staying home at night. The crackling flames licking around the big back log make a deep fireplace appear even deeper. The embers are fine to pop corn of our own growing, and we roast "our make" sweet potatoes in the hot ashes.

November 27. Low spots in the lawn were filled with good soil; when not more than an inch or two deep, the grass blades come right through. We are mulching a few plants, but many perennials do not need extra covering in winter. The object is to protect them not from cold but from warm weather and thawing. Alternate freezing and thawing and consequent heaving out of the ground does the damage.

November 30. The weather has turned much warmer, and I had to remove my coat while raking and superintending the removal of fallen leaves. We like lots of leaves to turn under, to condition the soil, but there are so many now that we seem submerged as we rake them from perennials and lawns!

At this season we especially value the effects of green foliage. Greenery is a part of the garden which lasts when flowers are gone and autumn leaves have fallen.

ANOTHER NOVEMBER

For when spring is but a spendthrift's dream,
And summer wealth a wasted flower,
The fields are stripped, the groves are dumb,
Then blooms the bright chrysanthemum.
—*Holmes*

November 3. It is glorious weather but too dry for much work in the garden. At times it is better, anyway, not to curb our gardens but to let them have their way.

Jerusalem artichokes have been dug and peppers and green tomatoes gathered; the time has come to make pickles that will be relished for many months. For an entree we like artichokes pickled whole: after scraping the artichokes, we pack them in glass jars together with small onions, red peppers and sticks of cinnamon. Salt and spices are sprinkled over them, and boiling vinegar is added before sealing.

November 4. Today the clouds and wind make me think we will have rain soon, and perhaps cold weather. Ferns that I repotted were put in the sun porch. Then I took up small geranium cuttings that have rooted in the garden and potted them. I noticed many seedlings in a bed where we had Chinese forget-me-nots (Cynoglossum) and double rose-colored larkspurs. The forget-me-nots will make fine plants, and some of the larkspurs may come true to variety and color, although it is best to sow new seed of these.

November 5. This afternoon we went for a drive, and in every direction was a display of color. A pear orchard was a marvelous sight, and the maples were gorgeous. Gums and sassafras have rich colors, and many oaks mingle green touches with their bright foliage. Fruits and berries in gardens and woodlands add their brightness to the landscape, such as the orange and scarlet berries of pyracanthas, the pink-capped red berries of euonymus, the crimson fruits of nandinas, the blue-black berries of ligustrums, the reddish berries of cotoneasters and the small, bluish gray fruits of cedars.

Borders of chrysanthemums can be seen in many gardens; the flowers of various colors and sizes lend their glory to an Indian summer world.

November 7. To save time in spring I am sowing hardy annual seeds. Some like larkspur and cornflower can stand winter above ground; other annuals that are sown now will not germinate until spring but will bloom before those sown next spring.

We set out plants grown from seeds sown in August, placing them in groups according to height and color. Honesty (Lunaria) was transplanted. We find it best to treat this as an annual. It likes full sun but will also thrive in part shade.

Ivy runners were fastened down with hairpins, where a wide green border is wanted. Ivy can be clipped to keep it the right height and width. Pansies were set out according to color, in borders previously prepared for them. We're planning and planting for spring effects now!

November 9. Some bulbs were planted today—grape-hyacinths (Muscari), wood hyacinths (*Scilla campanulata*) and guinea-hen-flower (Fritillaria). Boxwood cuttings that had been placed in sand and kept moist had such good roots that I planted them in the garden.

I noticed dusty miller (*Senecio Cineraria (Cineraria maritima)*) with its deep-cut, white leaves. This gives a pleasing effect all summer but gets leggy if the stalks are not pinched back. It will grow 18 inches tall. The border of ground-cypress (Santolina) has feathery gray foliage and is looking pretty.

Vacant spots among the shrubbery were planted; we can see now where more shrubs are needed. It is well to view the garden from different angles and to use low-growing plants where open vistas are wanted. Tall-growing shrubs should be planted for screens.

November 12. I was one of twelve judges at a flower show in a city a hundred miles from here. This was a very beautiful spectacle. A tea-house with thatched roof was fenced with bamboo. There was a pool with growing cat-tails and a tall background of downy flowering baccharis. The chrysanthemums were exquisite. It seemed hard to have to disqualify several collections of chrysanthemums that had thirteen gorgeous blooms when only twelve were called for. But why have schedule regulations if they are not followed?

November 16. I looked after my Bell peppers and eggplants. If left in the garden they may be damaged by the cold. They will keep a long time in a cool place in the cellar.

Someone telephoned to ask what to plant as companions for tall bearded irises. There are any number of things she can choose. These irises start blooming here early in April. Early hemerocallis, such as Flava, Apricot, Gold Dust (bright yellow with brown petal reverses), the dwarf lemon-yellow Gracilis, with grass-like foliage, or Estmere, are good neighbors for iris. Then there are poet's narcissi and peonies, painted daisies and airy columbines, sweet william, pinks and forget-me-nots. Baby blue-eyes (Nemophila), if planted this month, will be showy mats at iris time, and pansies make very effective footings. Flowering shrubs, such as snowball, beauty-bush (Kolkwitzia), deutzia, weigela, mock-orange (Philadelphus), certain spireas and Persian lilacs, are pleasing backgrounds for iris. All these can be planted at this time.

November 18. Tea olives (*Osmanthus fragrans*) and holly-leaf tea olives (*O. Fortunei*) are shedding their fragrance. The blossoms of the holly-leaf tea olive are larger and purer white. Both kinds prefer shade from mid-day sun. Hybrid tea and polyantha roses continue to flower, and petunias and sweet alyssum are masses of bloom.

I was at the home of a friend who was expecting a cold wave. She had cut her roses and chrysanthemums. I noticed thirty containers of beautiful flowers in different rooms before I stopped counting. She said she had kept her flower and vegetable gardens watered and is now having cabbage, lima beans and honeydew melons. This is unusual at this time but shows the reward of labor and care.

November 22. I worked two hours in the garden setting out cuttings and rootlets of candytuft (*Iberis sempervirens*) and *Phlox divaricata*. Dead stalks were taken from regal lilies and brown leaves were cut off peonies. Fearing disease, I burned the spent foliage. Dutch iris and crocus planted in October are up now.

I passed a house today where pansy plants were being set out

Poinsettias spell Christmas all over the United States, but the low South is fortunate in having them as outdoor shrubs. There are pink and white varieties available, in addition to the familiar scarlet. The flowers are really the tiny yellow central clusters.

On the famous Mobile Azalea Trail there are countless spectacles to enrich the experience of the thousands of yearly visitors. Pictured is *Azalea elegans*, Pride of Mobile. (See page 5.)

in hard, unprepared ground; only small holes were dug, and the roots were packed in. I don't see how they can survive.

November 23. Thanksgiving Day is almost here, and the weather is quite warm. Last year at this time there was a cold spell. It is time to think about Christmas gifts. In place of Christmas cards for my garden acquaintances, I am painting illustrative flowers and greetings on cards to which I have pasted envelopes of seed saved from plants. On some I have honesty seed, on others snapdragon, flax or sweet william.

November 28. Our coldest day so far. All tender plants are killed, and the rose buds that we should have cut yesterday are brown. I had borders cultivated a bit. It helps to leave the earth roughened, and the digging may destroy some insects and their eggs. But I wish that the insects that devour plant lice would winter in our plantings and eat their fill next spring!

DECEMBER

Every pine and fir and hemlock
Wore ermine too dear for an earl,
And the poorest twig on the elm-tree
Was ridged inch deep with pearl.
—*Lowell*

December 1. We pruned hybrid tea and hybrid perpetual roses a little to keep the long branches from being whipped about by winds. Our main pruning of these is done in January or February. A little soil was hilled about each bush. Climbing roses and rugosas do not need hilling here, and it is not absolutely necessary for the others. In this climate most plants come through better without mulch, but azaleas and other shallow-rooted ones must be protected by mulch in both winter and summer.

We have a bed for rose cuttings in the vegetable garden. Today many cuttings were placed there, with at least two eyes under the ground. When root growth starts, the new roots must not have too much top to support. We covered the cuttings with glass fruit jars, pasting the name of the rose from which the cutting was taken in the bottom of the jar so that it can be read from above. (Zinc or tin labels can also be used, stuck into the ground.) Some roses grow well only when budded; others make fine bushes from cuttings. This bed is watched with interest, for we like to have plants of our own to replace those that die and to give to new adventurers in rose growing.

December 4. Plantings were mulched with manure to reduce

233

the penetration of frost and to increase soil fertility. The tops of phlox, rudbeckia and marigolds are dead; we cut down the stalks this morning. Many plants, such as pansies and English daisies, flourish in the cold. The tops of polyanthus primroses are showing, and bulb foliage is pushing out of the ground.

A garden is an ever-changing picture. Winter shows features not seen in summer. The glittering foliage of eleagnus is beautiful at this time, and fragrance from the flowers that still hang on is delightful; the lantern-like berries turn red in February. Barberry, which stands drought and cold, has red berries all winter; its green foliage has turned bronzy. Holly trees are full of berries; these do not like hot sun, but prefer morning sunshine and afternoon shade. (See Chapter IX, Holly.) Partridge-berry (Mitchella) is attractive in the woodsy garden, with little trailing shiny leaves and red berries. *Nandina domestica*, with dainty foliage and scarlet berries, is bright and airy. This plant likes a sandy soil. The leaves turn bronzy red if the ground is acid but remain green in a dry alkaline soil.

December 9. We rake leaves continually and place them about shrubbery, where they will be spaded into the soil in early spring.

Virginia bluebells (Mertensia), which like a moist, loamy soil and a partially shaded position for their roots, were divided and replanted. I meant to get around to this earlier. Usually these should not be disturbed for years.

December 16. Today was not too cold to make a visit to the garden. The Jerusalem cherry hedge that was so pretty all summer and fall looks sick now, but some of it will grow again in the spring and there will be numerous seedlings. Even with the past severe weather, breath-of-spring (*Lonicera fragrantissima*) is opening its fragrant blooms.

Friends came to get Osage-orange twigs to make gum-drop trees for Christmas decoration. They choose twigs that are tree-like, cover them with silver-gilt paint and sprinkle with glittery dust before the paint dries; then they stick gum-drops on the thorns.

December 19. There is a feeling of expectancy in the air, and one finds many hidden packages. Outdoors it is spring-like, with birds singing, and we went to the woods to get berries and greenery. I explained to the children how to break plants without hurting them. It would be a pity to deprive the children of the great pleasure of helping to get ready for Christmas. A covey of partridges flew up near us, exciting the two dogs and startling us.

Tonight we drove around to get a glimpse of "lit-up" homes.

Many are now attractively decorated, but there will be others in a few days. The Daffodil Garden Club is sponsoring a contest for the home that looks most beautifully decorated from the outside. The contest opens December 22; the homes must be lighted that evening and every evening for a week. The decorations are to be judged for originality, appropriateness and effectiveness, and each person in the city is asked to cast a vote.

December 20. After doing some decorating and wrapping a few packages, I went to the orchard and superintended the pruning of the grape vines. We try to do this by the latter part of December, but it can be done any time during the winter before the buds swell, so long as the wood is not frozen. We have an abundance of grapes in a small space with little labor, using the Kniffin system of training, in which four branches are trained to two wires and each branch allowed to produce five or six shoots. If grapes are not pruned until spring, the weather may turn warm and the vines bleed. Now is a good time to put out grape cuttings. One should use last season's growth about 10 inches long.

December 22. No tree is so full of meaning as a Christmas tree. Today we secured a live one to be planted in the garden later.

We made interesting wreaths of evergreen foliage and small fruits by using grapes, cranberries and kumquats. Mistletoe, covered with white berries, was taken from trees. This is supposed to bring about kindly feelings toward everyone who enters the house where it is. This parasite lives on deciduous trees in the South. The seeds are covered with a sticky substance that makes them adhere to the tree branches when birds drop them.

December 24. Today I delivered packages and had sniffs of fruits, turkey, mince pie and candy in the making. At one home I saw a distinctive arrangement of red-cedar and—of all things— smooth, old-ivory china-berries. My friend asked me to step into her charming garden, and there were wallflowers, narcissi and winter jasmine in bloom. It hardly seemed natural at this season. She showed me how she turns spotlights on her pyracanthas, loaded with berries. This made an effective outdoor decoration.

December 25. Christmas again, with friendliness everywhere! The hoped-for white Christmas did not materialize in this part of the country. Many of our packages were so artistically decorated that we could hardly bear to cut the wrappings. Among my presents were shears to cut and hold the stems of flowers. There were two bird feeding stations; we had pleasure in placing them where we could see them from windows. We'll enjoy the Cape Cod fire-lighter with an iron pot-holder and long-handled toasting forks for the outdoor fireplace.

December 28. My sister's house won first prize in the decorating contest. It had a large star high on the front of the second story, its points outlined with blue lights. On either side of the star were tall blue candles made from cardboard tubes, with yellow flame lights. Around the front door were garlands of magnolia leaves with white lights showing like flower buds. The low living trees in the foreground were lighted with yellow, white and blue lights. A blue floodlight on the lawn showed Santa Claus in a colorfully painted, gift-laden sleigh, driving eight reindeer single file through the air toward the top of the house. The window curtains were drawn back to show a white tree (an oak limb, whitewashed) with blue ornaments and lights, reflected in a mirror. In the library stood a white tree with crimson lights and ornaments. Concealed lights showed snow scenes on the dining-room windows. "Snowed" windows are painted with fluffed whites of eggs with artificial snow sprinkled on while still moist, or with a solution of Epsom salts.

December 30. I can hear laborers in an outhouse beating out cowpeas, so we are assured of "peas and hog jowl" for New Year's Day. In the garden I noticed a limb hanging from a rose tree. I placed a splint under the broken piece and tied it back in place. In the vegetable garden are collards, cabbage, beets and carrots. Spinach, turnips and onions are trying to grow as chickweed keeps coming on.

Tonight I am sending for seed and plant catalogs. I like to keep old numbers so that I can trace the development of certain flowers from year to year.

December 31. Friends thanked me for dried bouquets of honesty that I sent them with gifts. It helps to know there are people who appreciate little things, and it makes one glad to share the garden.

ANOTHER DECEMBER

Where, twisted 'round the barren oak,
The summer vine in beauty clung,
And summer winds the stillness broke,
The crystal icicle is hung.
—*Longfellow*

December 1. On a dismal, rainy day like this, one can view the garden from indoors only. I shall make out my Christmas list. I feel sure friends with gardens will like to receive burlapped shrubs,

Many towns in the low South have stately avenues of
royal palms. They grow very tall and like moist, rich soil.

Acacias are popular for street plantings in warmer parts of the South. These spreading trees with fine feathery foliage and sprays of small yellow flowers are quick growing but short lived.

bulbs and garden books or magazines that will be a helpful reminder each month of the year. I have some Jerusalem cherries, begonias and geraniums potted, which I hope will bring cheer to shut-ins. The pots of poinsettias give a showy effect. We think of them as bright-colored flowers, but actually the flowers are the tiny yellow central clusters, surrounded by a circle of red leaves. Dr. Poinsett of Charleston, S. C., introduced the poinsettia into this country from southern Mexico in 1835.

December 9. One would think it spring today except for the falling of leaves. I had to rake leaves off small plants again so they will not be smothered. More perennials were set out. I was glad the Oriental poppies and bleeding-hearts were marked with labels to keep us from planting over them.

An old friend, eighty-six years young, had lunch with us. He is starting a small nursery and was especially interested in named irises and roses. He wanted rose cuttings, bamboo shoots and ivy, which we gave him.

December 19. For the past three days we have had cold weather with ice. Conifers are attractive with their interesting cones and needles; deodar cedars have brown, rose-like burs. Our broad-leaved evergreens look healthy, too.

We made a white Christmas tree from a red-cedar (Juniperus). The tree was taken from a thick clump in the grove, and fluffed Lux was spread on it (two cupfuls of Lux in a cup of water).

This morning I cut evergreen twigs and berries from our shrubs, for wreaths and decorations. These garden gifts to the home were cut carefully to prevent injury to the shrubs. Branches dipped in starch and sprinkled while damp with artificial snow make interesting bouquets. To make wreaths, moss can be tied around wire coat hangers that have been rounded; if the greens do not have strong stems, they can be wired to toothpicks and pushed into the moss.

I received my first Christmas present! And wasn't I delighted to find the basket contained fat narcissus bulbs—Thalia, Dick Wellband and Cheerfulness. I found just the right place for them, and they were snug in the ground before night.

December 21. It is cold today, but at mid-day it was delightful to work outside in the sun. Leaves were removed from the rock garden, since they might cause plants to rot, and loam and sand were placed about the plants.

I was in another city for the night. The decorated homes and streets had a cheerful appearance. One large house viewed across a lake looked like a Christmas postcard. It was bright with electric candles and wreaths; in the glassed porch a golden lighted tree was seen, and suspended above the house was a golden moon and star.

December 25. It is here—the day of all the year when families gather and celebrate in happy fellowship! Many of my gifts were for the garden. We saw many kinds of Christmas trees when we ran into friends' homes to say "Merry Christmas," but the ones that appealed most to me were those the children had helped to trim.

December 28. The garden club again sponsored outdoor Christmas decorations. The colorful lights all over the city created an atmosphere of gaiety and gladness. I see in today's paper that the grand award for the most artistically decorated house of any size went to my nephew's Cape Cod type cottage. On either side of the front steps was a large electric candle. The two candles were made from tubes on which rugs had been rolled; the candlesticks were brake-drums from an old car, and the handles for them were pieces of watering hose. The candlesticks were painted white and the candles blue, wound around with a white calcimined garland; there were gold flame lights. On the door was a white basket containing shiny blue ornaments, a spray of whitened deodar cedar and its rose-like burs, and a few daisy-like flowers with petals of blue glass and small centers composed of a gold light.

Over the door was a lighted star within a white wreath. In windows stood graduated blue candle lights, and in the attic windows were single blue candle lights. These were made from holders for calendars, wired. A white tree with blue lights decorated the side porch. Inside was a small tree bright with colored lights. A nativity scene near the fireplace had a background of starry blue paper.

Through another window the dining table was glimpsed, with a red striped cloth; red striped candlesticks tied with red bows and holding white candles were placed toward each end. These were made with cane-shaped stick candy. In the middle of the table, around a cornucopia of beautifully arranged fruit, were small Santa Claus candles. There was a home-like festivity about it all.

December 31. Evergreens should have plenty of water now. We are thankful we have had rain. This morning there was heavy frost and ice, but I saw a few roses struggling to bloom. We will have no more roses in the garden for awhile. Some calendulas are flowering, and sweet alyssum does not look hurt. Many bulbs are coming up—Dutch irises, hyacinths and snowflakes. Soleil d'Or and paper-white narcissi are in bud.

Leucothoë is a desirable neighbor for mountain-laurel.
Its leaves and flower buds are purplish in the winter.

When cold days come it is good to know that scenes such as this one at Glen Saint Mary, Fla., will soon be repeated. Here the azaleas are outstanding, in a setting of moss-draped trees.

Chapter XII

Postscript

SUGGESTIONS FOR GARDEN CLUB PROGRAMS

> I do hold it in the Royal Ordering of Gardens, there
> ought to be gardens for all months in the year, in which
> severally, things of beauty may be then in season.
> —*Francis Bacon*

January Roll Call. Answer with the name of a local winter bird.
1. Construction of hotbeds and coldframes; their value.
2. Care of house plants; how to handle Christmas-gift plants.
3. Privacy in the garden; background, screening, hedges for winter color.
4. Pruning; when, how, why.
5. Trees for the landscape; proper planting and care.
6. Winter gardens of Florida.

Display terrariums; or arrangements of dried grasses, twigs, conifers, berries or flowers from the garden.

February Roll Call. Name of a seed catalog or garden magazine. Exhibit one.
1. Planning the garden; design, formal and informal.
2. Remaking an old garden; borders, edgings.
3. Walls, fences; garden furniture. Discussion: garden equipment; garden tools for women.
4. Something new; novelties for spring planting.
5. Talk on horticulture.
6. Alabama Azalea Trail.

Display basket of flowering shrubs or bulbs from the garden.

March Roll Call. A bulb that blooms in early spring. Exhibit new or unusual flower.
1. Soil and how to improve it; chemical reaction; plant foods; soil conservation.
2. Plants for sunny places, for shady places, for continuous bloom in the garden.

3. Let's have vegetables.
4. Garden pests; how to control insects and diseases.
5. How to make a lawn.
6. The century-old homes and gardens of Natchez, Miss.

Show of narcissus.

April Roll Call. Name and description of a tulip.
1. A garden of fragrance.
2. Vines for the garden.
3. Rock gardens, how to make; suitable plants.
4. Lily pools, how to construct; formal, naturalistic.
5. Talk on period gardens. Discussion: landscaping and planting communities.
6. Famous gardens of South Carolina.

Display specimen tulip or arrangement in which tulips are used for the living room.

May Roll Call. Name and description of an iris.
1. Garden pilgrimage or picnic.
2. Weeds and their control.
3. Wildflowers of woodland and field; native plants for gardens; preservation of wild life.
4. Annuals (general).
5. The old-fashioned garden.
6. Talk on flower arrangement; constructive criticism.
7. Garden week in Virginia; West Virginia's trees, fruits and agriculture.

Iris show; names of irises and their creators; or monochromatic arrangement of flowers to express gladness.

June Roll Call. Name and color of a rose.
1. Rose legends; care of roses.
2. Municipal rose gardens.
3. Lilies, old and new.
4. Summer mulch.
5. Outdoor life for the family; a livable garden.
6. Georgia peach festival; Georgia garden pilgrimage.

Display collection of roses, three or more different varieties; or arrangement of lilies for formal dinner table.

July Roll Call. A flower blooming at this time; or flower quotation.

1. Saving seed.
2. Care of the garden in summer.
3. Bird baths; proper use of garden accessories.
4. Watering and cultivating; nuisance plants.
5. Something old—an herb corner.
6. Gardens of Louisiana; horticulture in Oklahoma.

Display arrangement of vines and foliage for porch; or a tray arrangement of vegetables.

August Roll Call. Name of favorite annual; reason for choice.

1. What to do in the garden this vacation month.
2. Seed to plant in the frames for bloom next spring.
3. Perennials (general).
4. Harmonious color combinations.
5. Best vines for the garden (local); ground covers.
6. Historic gardens of North Carolina.

Display arrangement for entrance hall to express coolness.

September Roll Call. Name of an autumn-blooming flower.

1. A winter lawn.
2. Planning winter bouquets; drying grasses.
3. Propagation of plants.
4. Orchard fruits and berries for the small garden.
5. Planning next year's improvements; transplanting; junior garden club work; improvement of parks and playgrounds.
6. A view of gardens in Tennessee.

Show of dahlias; or low analogous arrangement suitable for breakfast room or bedside table.

October Roll Call. Name tree or shrub with brilliant fall foliage.

1. Bulb planting.
2. How to have bulbs blooming for Christmas.
3. Difference between true bulbs and bulbous plants.
4. Roadside beautification; preservation of natural beauty.
5. Low-growing trees and shrubs for year-round color.
6. Horticulture in Arkansas and lower Missouri.

Foliage arrangement for library.

November Roll Call. Name bulbs or seed to be planted now.

1. Tulip planting.
2. Fall-sown annual seed.
3. Advantages of fall planting.
4. Culture of succulents.
5. Putting the garden to bed.
6. Rose fields of Texas; annual Azalea Trail in Houston.

Chrysanthemum show; or fruit arrangement.

December Roll Call. Name of plant bearing berries now. Exhibit unusual berries.

1. Berry-bearing shrubs for the garden.
2. How to attract birds; feeding stations.
3. When to plant live Christmas trees; conservation of natural resources.
4. Forcing twigs indoors.
5. Talk on holiday decorations; legends of Christmas.
6. Consider gardens of "My Old Kentucky Home" and "My Maryland."

Christmas wreaths; or berry arrangement.

STATE FLOWERS AND BIRDS OF THE SOUTH

Virginia. Flowering dogwood (*Cornus florida*) was chosen for the state flower of Virginia in 1918. This is a native shrub or small tree growing from Massachusetts to Florida and Texas.

In 1912 Virginia passed a law protecting robins. They destroy numerous insects and are very fond of wild fruits. They have many call notes; the song is a cheerful warble.

Tennessee. The iris was selected as the Tennessee state flower in 1933.

The mockingbird was adopted as the state bird on April 19, 1933. This year-round southern songster is a welcome inhabitant of any garden.

North Carolina. The dogwood was adopted as the state flower of North Carolina by the General Assembly of 1941.

In 1943 the cardinal was declared to be the official state bird. Its varied song and rich plumage is familiar throughout the South.

242

In many eastern states wild dogwood transforms the
woods to a fairyland of beauty in early spring. Virginia
and North Carolina have chosen it as their state flower.

An avenue of hoary live oaks at The Oaks, an historic estate near Charleston, S. C.

Cardinals eat seeds, especially of weeds and grasses, as well as ants, crickets, grasshoppers and fruit; they prefer wild fruits.

South Carolina. The Legislature of South Carolina adopted the Carolina jessamine (*Gelsemium sempervirens*) as the state flower on February 1, 1924. This is a native climber with evergreen leaves growing from eastern Virginia to Florida and across the southern states to Texas. The flowers have a delightful fragrance in spring, especially pleasing at night.

By act of law the palmetto tree was designated the official state tree in 1939.

In 1948 the Carolina wren was adopted as the state bird of South Carolina. This bird's habitat is from Illinois and Connecticut to the Gulf. It may be heard every month. This gay songster lives mostly on caterpillars, grasshoppers, beetles and weevils.

Georgia. The cherokee rose (*Rosa lævigata*) was accepted by Georgia as its state flower in 1916. This rose has become naturalized in the southern states. It is a high climber bearing large single blooms in early summer, followed by attractive hips. It has prickly green branches and shiny leaves.

In 1928, school children selected the brown thrasher as Georgia's state bird. It winters in the South Atlantic and Gulf states and destroys insects and worms.

Florida. In 1909, the orange blossom was chosen as the state flower of Florida. These more or less thorny trees or shrubs are natives of the subtropics and tropics.

On April 23, 1923, the mockingbird was approved as the state bird.

Alabama. The goldenrod (Solidago) was approved as the state flower in 1927. In late summer and autumn this blooms along highways and in fields practically all over the United States. There are many species, some with white flowers.

The yellow hammer was adopted as the state bird of Alabama on September 6, 1927. It is also known as the golden-winged woodpecker or flicker. It is fond of wild fruits and spends much time hunting ants. The habitat is northern and middle United States and south from Florida to Texas.

Mississippi. In 1900, Mississippi selected *Magnolia grandiflora* as the state flower. This ornamental broadleaf evergreen tree is native from North Carolina to Texas and the upper part of Florida. The large, fragrant blossoms appear in late spring and off and on during the summer.

The mockingbird was selected as the state bird in 1920.

Louisiana. *Magnolia grandiflora* was adopted in 1900 as the flower for this state.

The eastern brown pelican was selected as the state bird. This is a southern and tropical bird wintering on the Gulf coast and along the South Atlantic coast to South Carolina. These pelicans have a greenish pouch and live mostly on small fish. The song is a mournful cry. The nests, in rushes or bogs, are often washed away by floods.

Arkansas. The apple blossom was adopted as the state flower in 1901. The pinkish white blooms are borne in showy clusters in spring as the tender leaves appear.

On March 5, 1929, the mockingbird was adopted as the state bird of Arkansas.

Texas. Bluebonnet or buffalo clover (*Lupinus subcarnosus*) was approved as the state flower of Texas in 1901. These natives of Texas have racemes of deep blue flowers dotted with white.

On March 20, 1919, Texas chose the pecan as the official state tree. It originally grew wild from Indiana south to Alabama and Texas.

The western mockingbird was selected as the state bird on January 31, 1927. It is found in the southwestern United States north to Oklahoma and California. Weed seeds and ground insects as well as wild fruit constitute its food.

Oklahoma. Mistletoe was adopted as the floral emblem of Oklahoma in 1893. This was the first state in the South to adopt a state flower. (New York was first in the United States, when school children chose the wild rose in 1891.) Mistletoe was so abundant in early days that the pioneers got a profit from shipping it east to sell. It is a parasite on deciduous trees. The short spikes of flowers are followed by round white berries used for Christmas decoration.

The redbud (Cercis) was chosen as the official state tree of Oklahoma in 1937. It is ornamental as a specimen or in shrub borders. The attractive flowers come in spring before the heart-shaped leaves. This native makes a beautiful sight in woodlands or in gardens.

244

The large white flower clusters of *Viburnum Opulus* are succeeded by red fruits. This fine shrub grows to 12 feet.

Whoever makes a garden. . . .
Works hand in hand with God.
—*Douglas Malloch*

Oklahoma selected the bobwhite as its state bird. The name bob-white comes from the whistle note of this well-known partridge, the loved game bird of the South. It nests on the ground and spends much time in thickets.

Lower Missouri. The hawthorn (Cratægus) was adopted in 1923 as the state flower of Missouri. This native shrub or small tree of the temperate regions of the United States has attractive flowers and fruits and is usually thorny.

The bluebird was adopted as the state bird on March 30, 1927. This "herald of spring" ranges throughout the United States east of the Rocky Mountains. The major part of its food is insects.

Kentucky. The goldenrod (Solidago) was approved as the state flower of Kentucky.

The cardinal or redbird was adopted as the state bird on February 26, 1926.

West Virginia. Rhododendron maximum was chosen as the flower of the state in 1902. The hardy rhododendron will grow north as far as Canada and south to Georgia. It displays its beautiful lavender, pink and white flowers in summer.

The tufted titmouse was selected as the bird of West Virginia. It inhabits the eastern part of the United States. It is a friendly bird nesting near the ground, sometimes in a hollow tree.

Maryland. Black-eyed susan (*Rudbeckia hirta*) was approved as Maryland's state flower in 1918. This is an annual or biennial, na-tive over a good part of the South, thriving even on dry ground.

The Baltimore oriole was chosen as the state bird. Its song is a clear warble and its call a mournful whistle. The main food is beetles, ants, caterpillars and grasshoppers.

It is gratifying to notice that the various states are paying more attention to the flowers, birds and trees chosen as their own. Even hotel and restaurant menu cards often picture them. In some states roadside plantings of the state flower are featured. Perhaps in years to come, as motorists drive through different states, they will be able to recognize each one by its plantings. This public awareness is due in great part to the work of garden clubs.

I cannot bring this book to a close without applauding the great garden club movement that is sweeping over our country. On city, county, state, regional and national levels, federations of garden clubs are participating in the development of horticulture, and each group is appreciative of the achievements of the others.

There are numerous phases of garden club work. Different clubs undertake projects that are of benefit to the public as a whole, as well as to their own members. Some of these activities include the establishment of garden centers to provide information for gardeners, the holding of flower shows, of flower show schools and garden pilgrimages. The planning and planting of parkways, roadside beautification, memorial trails and municipal gardens are phases of garden club work that are of immense civic importance. Preservation of wildlife, of trees and flowers, and the establishment of bird sanctuaries are further aims of many clubs.

With the garden clubs sponsoring junior clubs, we of the South are confident that the rich horticultural heritage we enjoy will be preserved for all time.